A
Complete
Guide to
Technical
Trading
Tactics

Founded in 1807, John Wiley & Sons is the oldest independent publishing company in the United States. With offices in North America, Europe, Australia, and Asia, Wiley is globally committed to developing and marketing print and electronic products and services for our customers' professional and personal knowledge and understanding.

The Wiley Trading series features books by traders who have survived the market's ever-changing temperament and have prospered—some by reinventing systems, others by getting back to basics. Whether a novice trader, professional, or somewhere in-between, these books will provide the advice and strategies needed to prosper today and well into the future.

For a list of available titles, visit our web site at www.WileyFinance.com.

A
Complete
Guide to
Technical
Trading
Tactics

How to Profit Using Pivot Points, Candlesticks & Other Indicators

JOHN L. PERSON

WILEY

John Wiley & Sons, Inc.

Published by John Wiley & Sons, Inc., Hoboken, New Jersey.
Published simultaneously in Canada.

For general information on our other products and services, or technical support, contact our Customer Care Department within the United States at 800-762-2974, outside the United States at 317-572-3993 or fax 317-572-4002.

Wiley also publishes its books in a variety of electronic formats. Some content that appears in print may not be available in electronic books.

For more information about Wiley products, visit our web site at www.wiley.com.

Library of Congress Cataloging-in-Publication Data

Person, John L.
    A complete guide to technical trading tactics : how to profit using pivot points, candlesticks & other indicators / John L. Person
        p. cm.
    "Published simultaneously in Canada."
    Includes bibliographical references and index.
    ISBN 0-471-58455-X (cloth)
    1. Stocks—Charts, diagrams, etc. 2. Investment analysis. 3. Futures.
4. Options (Finance) I. Title.

HG4638 .P47 2004
332.63′2042—dc22

                                                                2003026687

Printed in the United States of America

10 9 8 7 6 5 4 3 2 1

Contents

Preface   ix

Acknowledgments   xv

CHAPTER 1   **Introduction to Futures and Options: Understanding the Mechanics**   1

How the markets work, the elevator analogy, product for the times, important terminology such as margin, contract specifications, and leverage

CHAPTER 2   **Fundamentals: The Market Driver**   19

Supply and demand issues, economic growth and productivity effects, major economic reports and their in role in market prices

CHAPTER 3   **Technical Analysis: The Art of Charts**   33

Western-style bar charts and key reversals, point-and-figure charts that focus only on price, market profiling, price and time analysis

CHAPTER 4   **Candle Charts: Lighting the Path**   43

Enlightening charting technique and its colorfully named patterns—hammers, stars, spinning tops, dojis, hanging man, and others—powerful reversal patterns, reliable continuation patterns, key examples in the dollar and bonds

CHAPTER 5   Chart Analysis:
Volume, Open Interest, Price Patterns   67

Volume and open interest rules for traders, M tops and W bottoms, trend lines, measuring patterns, the head-and-shoulders, triangles, pennants and flags, diamonds, wedges, funnels, gaps, islands, rounded bottoms, oops signals, opening range breakouts

CHAPTER 6   Pivot Point Analysis:
A Powerful Weapon   93

The pivot point formula for target trading, calculating support and resistance levels, importance of multiple verification from several sources, the P3T trading technique, weekly and monthly charts and numbers, risk management techniques

CHAPTER 7   Day-Trading, Swing Trading:
Acting on Analysis   113

Trading to bounce off target numbers, calling tops and bottoms, weekly chart magnets, harami cross and other candle clues to market reversals, pivot points save the day, lining up the stars, the verify-verify-verify approach

CHAPTER 8   Technical Indicators:
Confirming Evidence   135

Moving averages and trends, simple rules with averages, tweaking and visualizing MACD, stochastics, false signals, Gann's key numbers, Fibonacci ratios and projections, time counts for cycles, Elliott wave and its clues

CHAPTER 9   Market Sentiment:
What Traders Are Thinking   161

Getting a market consensus from contrary opinion, *Commitments of Traders* reports, margin rate changes, *Market Vane Bullish Consensus* report, put-to-call ratios, volatility index (VIX), when the boat is tipping over, media effect

CHAPTER 10 Order Placement:
Executing the Plan   171

Importance of getting an order right, online platform concerns, impact of market conditions on orders, 14 top order entry selections you need to know, orders in after-hours trading, spreading concepts

CHAPTER 11 The Mental Game:
Inside the Trader **189**

Conquering fear, learning discipline, improving confidence, suggestions for success, I'll-think-about-it syndrome, the paper trader, fear and greed factors, becoming a specialist, setting up an investment diary, setting a positive mind frame,
dealing with adrenaline, establishing goals, positive affirmations, stress relief
techniques, rewarding success to build success

CHAPTER 12 The Tactical Trader:
Tips and Techniques That Work **203**

Pyramiding approaches, scale trading, stop reversals, breakouts, momentum trading, the Friday 10:30 a.m. rule, stop placement near a magnet, trading multiple
contracts

CHAPTER 13 Options:
A Primer **217**

What options are and how to use them with futures, simple puts and calls,
options premiums, the Greeks, comparison shopping, strangles and straddles,
eight top option spreads, delta neutral techniques

CHAPTER 14 Closing Bell:
My Top 10 List **235**

What the experts suggest, top 10 trading thoughts, measuring success

Glossary **241**

Bibliography **253**

Index **255**

Preface

The purpose of this book is to share some of the tips, techniques, and observations that have worked for me and other highly successful traders. After nearly 23 years as a registered broker in the futures and options field, I have come to know quite a few successful traders and have personally made many successful trades. I have also experienced my share of disasters and have known traders and investors who were doomed for permanent failure. Therefore, I am writing this book to help the new individual investor understand the mechanics of the markets and to serve as a refresher for the seasoned veteran trader.

Most of the trade examples demonstrated in this book were direct trade recommendations from either *The Bottom Line Financial and Futures Weekly Newsletter* or those that appeared in the daily Dow report provided through the Chicago Board of Trade web site and at www.nationalfutures .com. Rather than demonstrating just one methodology of trading tactics using pivot point analysis, I wanted to show through various techniques how you can implement these calculations with other methods and indicators. Much of what I have learned over the course of 23 years in the industry did come from hard work and, I must admit, being around the right people at the right time. I do not want you to abandon your knowledge of traditional technical analysis techniques. I would just like you to be open to integrating the numbers to help you confirm, validate, and identify entry and exit points when trading.

I also want to relay the message that mathematically calculated support and resistance numbers, or pivot points, work on different markets and should be derived from different time frames—not only from a daily basis, but also from a weekly and monthly time frame.

In addition, as most of the readers either know or will find out, trading is also a combination of strong emotional and personal characteristics. Through my experience and observations, I want to share and explain what works and what does not but, more important, to disclose why things go wrong when they do for those who failed. I believe it is important to take an inventory, so to speak, when things go right to capitalize on that experience by examining what you did so the results can be repeated. It is just as important to examine what went wrong so you can learn from the experience. By sharing with you the experiences and techniques that I and other professional traders have learned, the hope is that you will benefit and become a more profitable trader.

I firmly believe that traders from all different levels of experience will benefit from the information contained in this book, whether it is actually gaining a new understanding or a new technique or refreshing, reviewing, or reviving your memory about tactics, strategies, or trading techniques that an advanced trader may have forgotten.

My professional history may explain my qualifications for writing this book. I started in this business as a runner on the floor of the Chicago Mercantile Exchange in 1979. To illustrate a reference point in time, the Dow Jones Industrial Average was near the 900 level. The S&P 500 Index futures contract did not even exist back then. I became a registered commodity broker in 1982 and worked up through the ranks in the industry as I was studying economics at Loyola University. The head of the research department at the firm where I worked was George C. Lane. He, of course, is credited with developing the oscillator system known as stochastics. He was the first boss who tutored me in the art of technical analysis. Little did I know at that time that a true master of technical analysis was going to be responsible for helping to create the intrigue, financial rewards, and passion for the futures industry that I have had throughout all these years.

Granted, there were other individuals who had an influence on my career. Jack F., an old member of the Chicago Board of Trade, helped me understand the importance of moving averages and the aspect of long-term charts. Back in 1985 and 1986 in what I call the great bond market boom, he was instrumental in helping me understand how to ride a strong trending market. In 1986, I captured what I call a winning tidal wave bull market run that remains legendary to this day for those who were on board with me, as well as friends who invested and knew me well.

Another broker at a firm where I worked taught me this strange and unique method of plotting unconventional trend lines to predict price and time coordination. Harry A. was his name and this guy would tell you on a Monday that at 11:40 a.m. Wednesday the high in bonds would be $78^{12}/_{32}$. Come Wednesday at 11:45 a.m. or so, the high was $78^{11}/_{32}$, and I would watch the price take a disastrous plummet. His method, as I later found out, was based on Drummond geometry.

I had the privilege to work with a former chairman of the Chicago Board of Trade, Bill Mallers Sr., who was always looking for a new system. His thirst for achievement and passion for the markets amazed me. Another man in the office who worked for Bill Sr. was a fairly quiet, yet confident, guy. He always had a cigar stub in his mouth—never did smoke but just chewed on them. He sat near me and time after time would overhear my recommendations to clients, in particular my points of support and resistance. Almost on a daily basis he had the same target numbers, usually within a point or tick of mine. That is when we discovered we were doing the same thing. The amazing thing was he claimed to be a direct student of Charles Drummond.

I was also fortunate to have been introduced to another fascinating man, Dan Gramza, an instructor for several futures exchanges and firms worldwide. His understanding of the market and the relationship between time, price, and volume is incredible. His teaching also included a wonderful tutoring in candle charting. When I discovered that, he humbly mentioned that he knew Steve Nison and "helped" write some of Steve's first book. When I got home, I immediately searched for the book in the storage box and, sure enough, there it was in the acknowledgment section on page IV. Not only was Dan mentioned in one of the best books on the basics of candle charting, in my opinion, he helped write chapter 8 in Steve's book.

My experience has ranged from learning stochastics from the creator of the indicator, moving averages from a famous floor trader and options from my own experience, Drummond geometry from two different fascinating people at two different times in my career, pivot point analysis, and then candle charting techniques from what I would call a master.

In March 2003 I started hosting a radio program titled, *The Personal Investment Hour*. The format was to invite expert traders and analysts to share with listeners who they were and what they do to trade successfully. My guests have included John Murphy, Martin Pring, John Bollinger, Victor Niederhoffer, Gerald Appel, Linda Bradford Raschke, Larry Williams, and a fabulous roll call of other top experts. Most guests were thrilled to come on and share their story and methods. Some of the contents of those interviews are mentioned in this book as well. In fact, the interviews were recorded and archived on my web site, www.nationalfutures.com, where anyone can go to listen to them.

By writing this book, I can share with you how and what I do to produce the analysis that goes out every week in *The Bottom Line Financial and Futures Newsletter*. I believe my experience in the industry and the techniques that I have developed can be instrumental in helping you to become a better trader. I believe that you can successfully learn to better integrate the two elements of market analysis: time and price. The elements that I have focused on from the technical side are:

- Pivot points, a leading price predictor that is based on price points using different time frames.
- Cycle analysis, which deals with predicting market turning points based on time.
- Candle chart patterns, which are based on price relationships between the open, high, low, and close and past chart points such as old highs or lows.
- Fibonacci ratio corrections and extension studies, which are based on past price points.

Other studies such as volume are used to gauge the level of participation and to help uncover the strength or weakness of a market trend.

The last—and maybe the most—important aspect of trading that this book covers is evaluating the psychological makeup of traders and providing exercises that can help those who are having a rough period overcome their problems. Learning who you are and how you react to market conditions is a vital aspect of trading.

I hope that reading this book will help you have a better understanding of what it takes to trade and to broaden your horizons in investing in the futures and options market. More important, I want you to know how to learn to do it on your own. Industry experts agree that about 80 percent of the people who trade lose. With those odds against you, you need all the help you can get! Individual speculators need to know that it is a rewarding adventure as long as they can make it against the markets and their biggest competitor, every other trader. As a zero-sum game, for every loser there is a winner in futures trading. Or another way to think about it, perhaps, is that 20 traders are taking the money of 80 other traders.

If you are going to trade successfully, you need to understand that it requires hard work and, above all, to think of trading as a business. As you read this book, I hope you learn that you do not need to have an IQ of 160 or be a mathematician or possess superhuman skills to be successful. What you do need to have is a fascination for this business, patience, discipline, a trading plan, identification of what type of trader you are, risk capital, and the desire to improve your financial life.

Through the development of technology and the Internet, more information is accessible today for the individual speculator than ever before. I sincerely believe a knowledgeable and educated investor is a better trader.

So if you are trading or are getting ready to trade, try to work at continually learning what is available to you. Cutting-edge technology will continue to offer more powerful and helpful trading tools to individual traders. It is up to you to learn how to use them to your advantage. I hope that you will benefit from the tips and techniques that are mentioned in these pages and certainly hope that you can apply them successfully in your trading.

JOHN L. PERSON

Palm Beach, Florida
March 2004

Acknowledgments

Writing requires intense devotion and discipline; I now have a new sense of respect for anyone who has ever written any books or published material, especially on the subject of technical analysis. I have many people to thank—those who were indirectly responsible and influential in my education throughout the years and, of course, my family, especially my wife, Mary, who also tolerated my perseverance for finishing this book at the expense of ignoring her and asking too many questions when I had computer problems.

Mom, I know you wanted a lawyer in the family; instead you got a futures trader. My son, John Paul, who decided not to get in the investment business; instead, he followed the entrepreneurial spirit and opened his own chain of cell phone stores. There is still a chance to convert him back to the investment world: He likes my stock picks!

Special thanks to the Friday night "wanders" group, the best support group of friends one could ever have. Those I wish to mention directly: Lan Turner from Gecko Software, Stuart Unger, Barry Isaacson, Cheryl Fitzpatrick, Rory Obractin, and Jonathan W. Dean from FutureSource; Dan Gramza for inviting me to his class and taking my calls; Barbara Schmidt Bailey and Ted Doukas from the Chicago Board of Trade; and James Mooney, president of Infinity Brokerage Services.

The more analysts and authors I met, the more I found how truly fortunate I was in having Pamela van Giessen of John Wiley & Sons as my editorial director. Thank you, Pam! My special thanks go to Darrell Jobman, who was directly responsible for orchestrating and directing me through the whole process of this project and directly responsible for helping to get this material organized and published.

J. L. P.

A
Complete
Guide to
Technical
Trading
Tactics

CHAPTER 1

Introduction to Futures and Options

Understanding the Mechanics

Success is turning knowledge into positive action.

Thinking is easy, acting is difficult, and to put one's thoughts into action is the most difficult thing in the world.

—Johann Wolfgang von Goethe

G oethe could have been referring to paper trading versus the act of actually trading when he wrote the phrase above. Trading is exactly that: putting your thoughts or convictions about a price move into action by entering an order and placing money at risk.

Investing is a totally different ball game. This book is about trading. The purpose of trading is to turn over or buy and sell (sell and buy) to build cash in an account by capitalizing on changes in price. It is not about acquiring and holding assets or property.

Futures trading is becoming more attractive than ever before as investors transfer their knowledge and trading skills from the stock market boom of the late 1990s to more active markets where the idea of creating wealth is still alive. As the equity markets became consumed by the bear market mentality liquidation phase, investors with knowledge of technical analysis and computer skills flocked to open futures accounts to trade e-mini S&P 500 and e-mini Nasdaq 100 index futures.

Stock market firms and brokers have developed futures divisions, and day-trading education experts have crawled out of the woodwork to teach investors the art of day trading those products. Some of the numerous quality instructors come with a very high tuition cost; others are not so expensive.

Most likely, learning about trading at a reasonable price is why you are reading this book. However, reading this book alone will not guarantee that you will succeed in trading. You need to read this book, practice its principles, and continue your trading education, realizing that the biggest obstacle in trading is what is between your left and right ears. I believe the techniques in this book are excellent strategies, and I hope you will apply and benefit from them. Teaching someone to become a successful trader and letting them experience the power of financial rewards is a satisfying and rewarding pursuit.

As investors look for markets beyond stocks or mutual funds in which to put their money, they will find a whole new world out there with different products to trade, among them futures. You may be among those investors who are afraid of and concerned about trading futures because of what you heard about them in the past. There are good reasons for being nervous about treading into any new market. But consider the scandals that have plagued Wall Street in the post-bubble era and may continue for some time. As history shows, there have been countless scandals on Wall Street in the past, and there almost certainly will be more in the future. So-called traditional investing in stocks is not immune to risk and has its own set of problems.

The question is: Will confidence in America's corporate leadership return sooner rather than later? Stock ownership is at the highest level per capita in America's history. More investors and private traders participate in the markets than ever before. In addition to stocks and mutual funds, there are a host of stock-related derivative products—exchange-traded funds such as QQQs, options such as the OEX, and many, many others including a relatively new and spectacular market development called single stock futures. The price direction of equities and all of these derivative instruments boils down to what will happen to the underlying forces of earnings and growth.

Here is a brief story that may shed light on Americans' changing viewpoint about investing. I was giving a seminar on the futures markets to an investment club. One older gentleman said his money was safe in the bank, and he wouldn't give his money to the stock market again.

I asked, "Why do you feel that way?"

He responded, "They are all crooks!"

"Well, if you think like that, why are you at a futures seminar?" I asked.

"I always thought they were risky, but now I want to learn for myself," he replied.

"Futures trading is risky," I agreed, "but what gave you the impression not to open a futures account before?"

"My stock broker told me not to trade commodities, that I would lose my shirt," he said. "So I kept buying the stocks he recommended, and, instead, I lost my shirt with him."

Not a happy story, but the amazing development is that the gentleman is getting back on the horse after falling off, this time getting his own education and finding out for himself whether futures are for him.

This book is designed for people like him and for the more experienced technical trader as well. If you had a similar experience, then keep reading and studying and you will continue to increase your knowledge and competence. With that, you will gain confidence. The more knowledge and information you have about a subject, the better you will become in dealing with it. As we all know, knowledge is power.

Every investor should know that trading is like riding an elevator. You get on if you want to go up and then get out once you are where you want to be. If you want to go up but then realize that you are going down instead, bail out. Get off the elevator and get back on another ride going up. Risk management and turnover are the keys to successful trading.

TRADING MENTALITY

Most new investors are not familiar with trading the short side of the market. I have listened to many novices say that they have a hard time comprehending how to sell something they do not even own. I always tell them that even if they buy a futures contract to go long, they are not going to own anything (except in rare instances where they may take actual delivery of some physical commodities).

All futures traders are doing is speculating on the direction of prices on a given product during a given time period. If they are right, they get rewarded; if they are wrong, of course, they get penalized. Remember the elevator analogy. If a building has 100 floors and you are on the 50th floor, you can play a guessing game to see if the elevator goes up or down and by how many floors. You can take the ride, but you don't have to own the elevator to do so.

The principle of trading is a very simple concept although we, as humans, tend to make it quite complicated, especially those who have a hard time comprehending selling short. Trading is just a matter of interested parties coming together and speculating whether the price of a specific commodity is going to go up or down. It is that simple.

Let's say Bill believes the price of commodity XYZ is going up, so he buys. A second trader, Pete, believes the price is going down, so he sells short. One could win, one could lose. Or, believe it or not, both Bill and Pete can be right and make money during the same day with their opposite positions. Similarly, both could also lose within the same trading day doing the exact opposite trade at the same time. It happens all the time. Volatility is the reason. Get to know that term as well as *whipsaw, choppy, erratic market behavior,* and other terms used in connection with volatility.

The market's behavior reflects the emotional condition of those who are doing the trading. The market is the by-product of those who use it. Sometimes it seems like a jungle. It can be financially rewarding and exciting like discovering a wealth of mineral deposits in a hidden cavern behind thick brush. It can also be like enjoying the beauty and splendor of a sunset off the coast of Florida with the sun's light descending on the low clouds as palm trees sway in the breeze. But it can also provide some of the scariest and most financially dangerous adventures you will ever experience.

Trading will probably test your emotional strength and psyche. It will be the ultimate financial, emotional, and intellectual challenge you will ever encounter. Fear, doubt, complacency, greed, anxiety, excitement, false pride—all can interfere with rational and intellectual thoughts. It is those feelings that create the jungle, and you may need help to overcome that jungle of emotion. Conquer those feelings and you may find the holy grail of trading: a confident winning attitude.

Reading this book will give you the knowledge necessary to improve your life as a trader. You will be taught to take the emotion out of trading and to develop a method or trading plan. Remember, "Those who fail to plan, plan to fail." I have devoted a chapter to the mental aspect of trading (Chapter 11) because I believe about 80 percent of successful trading is based on emotional makeup. The way to increase your confidence and competence levels is through knowledge, and that comes from learning solutions to problems and then applying or executing what you learn.

HOLDING PENALTY

As you learn different trading styles, remember this key concept: Futures are a trading vehicle and not—I repeat, not—a buy-and-hold, long-term investment platform. Do not try to dictate or get married to an idea about the direction you think the market should go. This approach can lead to financial donations to other traders' wealth, to an increase in your knowledge about your brokerage firm's money wire transaction process, and, worse yet, to getting wiped out.

You need to work at this business. You need to manage and maintain your positions and monitor price action. Game plans need to be established, and you will need to be flexible and quick to act. Access and communication to stay in touch with the market is important when you are trading.

Futures trading should be used to make money on a price movement. It should not be a personal vendetta, trying to prove that you are right in your opinion of what the market should do. That outlook is why there are all kinds of clichés about taking profits. For instance, "A profit is a profit, no matter how small." That is a great line, but let's define "small profit." Coming to this business to risk thousands of dollars to make a hundred dollars or so isn't the way this trading environment should be used.

Another old saying describes someone who takes small profits and lets big losers ride: "Eating like a bird and crapping like an elephant." That is the essence of a habit you don't want. If this is a syndrome that you fall into, Chapter 11 offers exercises to help you work through it. If you catch yourself getting into that habit, stop trading. Try not to get used to taking small profits constantly and letting losses get large before taking them. You need to develop good discipline and strong emotional traits. Otherwise, fear of losing will hinder your performance.

Think about this: If trading were easy and such a sure thing, why would you have to sign all of those disclaimers about how dangerous it is when you fill out an account application at a brokerage firm?

So far I have mentioned buying, selling, winning, losing, and human emotions, and I have not yet covered a single aspect of technical analysis. This approach to the subject reflects my belief about what I consider the most important aspect of trading: your mental and emotional capacity.

GETTING TECHNICAL

Technical analysis is the study of a market's price data, which is created by the emotions of the participants. Price reflects the current or anticipated value of a market from a supply and demand perspective. Price is the true and absolute reflection of value, as perceived by the various market participants at a particular point in time.

There are a number of different forms of analysis. This book will go into further detail on most aspects of technical analysis, but my focus is on market reversals incorporating pivot point analysis with other methods to nail down time and price predictions.

All traders have access to four common denominators: open, high, low, and closing price. How you analyze, interpret, and act on the information available is what gives you a trading style that differentiates you from other traders. Successful traders interpret correctly and act swiftly. There are five business days in every week and usually four weeks in every month. One day within a month will usually mark a price high, another day will generally mark a low, and the market will close somewhere between those points. Those facts define the monthly range. The successful trader does not consistently make a habit of buying the high of the range or selling the low of the range.

But before jumping ahead of ourselves into subjects covered later in the book, we need to review what the futures markets are all about. Seasoned traders may be able to skip over the next sections, but those new to futures should read them carefully because they contain important concepts and terminology that make futures different from most other markets.

GETTING INTO FUTURES

For futures traders, the choice of products varies from the traditional to the exciting new trading vehicles now available. Everyone can relate to many of these markets that you use every day, from energy products such as crude oil or natural gas to agricultural markets such as meats, grains, and the so-called softs (coffee, sugar, cocoa). Prices are dictated by supply and demand functions that often are affected by weather.

In addition to supply/demand influences, futures markets may provide a safe-haven security function. Precious metals such as gold may start to increase in price as investors on a global scale believe it is necessary to hold on to hard assets instead of paper assets in times of political tension or because they fear potential inflation resulting from the massive liquidity pumped into the global economy from 2001 through 2003. Financial instruments such as Treasury notes and bonds and currencies are also popular trading vehicles.

In short, diversified products in all of these areas are available to futures traders and provide advantages in liquidity and leverage. Many of these markets also offer direct electronic access to traders. As long as there are products subject to supply/demand and price fluctuations that carry an element of risk, there will be a role for futures in the business world.

THE FUTURES INSTRUMENT

Many people, including traders, refer to commodities and futures as one and the same thing. To clarify that point first, the term *commodities* means an actual physical product such as corn, wheat, soybeans, cattle, gold, coffee, crude oil, cotton, and the like. The term *futures* refers to the instrument or the contract that is actually traded on these underlying products. Futures contracts have set standards for quantity, quality, financial requirements, and delivery points, if any (many futures contracts have cash-settlement provisions so there is no delivery).

As the years have passed, futures contracts have been developed for new "commodities" such as foreign currencies and a number of financial instruments including interest rate products such as Treasury bonds and notes, stock indexes such as the S&P 500 index and Dow Jones Industrial Average, and, most recently, an innovative derivative product called single stock futures.

Unlike equities, where stocks are quoted in dollars per share, different commodities have different contract values and different point values. The table of contract specifications for major U.S. futures markets (Table 1.1) lists the symbols and sizes of various futures contracts. For example, the contract size for corn is 5,000 bushels. If the value of one bushel is, say, $2.00, then the overall contract value is $10,000. The full-size S&P 500 index futures contract has a value of $250 times the index. If the index is at, say, 1,000, the value of the contract is $250,000, considerably larger than the value of the corn contract.

Exchanges require a good-faith deposit—usually called *margin*, although it does not have the same meaning as margin in stocks—to play the game. For most futures contracts, you usually need to put up only 3 percent to 10 percent of the total contract value to trade. On the one hand, corn may have an initial margin requirement of $500 to $600—about 5 percent of the contract's value—with a maintenance margin of $300. For that amount of money, you control 5,000 bushels of corn and can go long, speculating that prices will climb in the future, or sell short, speculating that the price will decline. The more volatile S&P contract, on the other hand, has a margin requirement closer to 7 percent or 8 percent or $18,000 to $20,000. The amount of money required to trade a contract may dictate what you trade if you have a small account.

It has been argued that physical commodity products will find a fair value or an absolute value when they reach certain lows based on historical price comparisons and will never go to zero due to laws of supply and demand (Economics 101). Unlike stocks, commodities do not declare bankruptcy or go out of business.

The reason futures will always have some value is because they do not exist solely for traders to bet on price movement. Producers and end users are also major participants in most futures markets as they use futures to reduce risk from adverse changes in price and to discover the current fair value for products they have to buy or sell to stay in business. Traders in this category are referred to as *commercials* or *hedgers*.

You probably are in a second group: the individual speculator trying to capitalize on price swings created by the up and down forces in the marketplace. You may be trading from your home as a business or on the trading floor or trading as a sideline.

A third category of futures traders includes the large speculators or fund managers who pool investors' money together. These are sometimes referred to collectively as the *commodity funds*.

One advantage of futures trading is that the government gives you an idea what each of these groups of traders is doing each week in the

TABLE 1.1   Major U.S. Futures Contract Specifications

Symbol[a]	Futures Contract	Contract Size	Contract Months[b]	Exchange[c]
Interest Rates				
ED	Eurodollar, 90-day	$1,000,000	H, M, U, Z	CME
TB	Treasury bills, 90-day	$1,000,000	H, M, U, Z	CME
FF	Fed funds, 30-day	$5,000,000	All months	CBOT
EM	Libor	$3,000,000	All months	CME
TU	Treasury notes, 2-year	$ 200,000	H, M, U, Z	CBOT
FV	Treasury notes, 5-year	$ 100,000	H, M, U, Z	CBOT
TY	Treasury notes, 10-year	$ 100,000	H, M, U, Z	CBOT
US	Treasury bonds, 30-year	$ 100,000	H, M, U, Z	CBOT
MB	Municipal bonds	$ 100,000	H, M, U, Z	CBOT
Indexes				
SP	S&P 500 Stock Index	$250 × index	H, M, U, Z	CME
ES	E-Mini S&P 500 Index	$ 50 × index	H, M, U, Z	CME
DJ	Dow Jones Industrial Avg.	$ 10 × index	H, M, U, Z	CBOT
YJ	Mini-sized Dow	$ 5 × index	H, M, U, Z	CBOT
YX	NYSE Composite Index	$500 × index	H, M, U, Z	NYBOT
MV	Mini-Value Line Index	$100 × index	H, M, U, Z	KCBOT
NK	Nikkei 225 Stock Avg.	$ 5 × average	H, M, U, Z	CME
ER	Euro-top 100 Stock Index	$100 × index	H, M, U, Z	NYMEX
FI	FT-SE 100 Stock Index	$ 50 × index	H, M, U, Z	CME
MD	S&P Mid-Cap 400 Index	$500 × index	H, M, U, Z	CME
CR	CRB Futures Index	$500 × index	F, G, J, M, Q, X	NYBOT
GI	Goldman Sachs Com. Index	$250 × index	All months	CME
Currencies				
AD	Australian dollar	100,000 AD	H, M, U, Z	CME
BP	British pound	62,500 BP	H, M, U, Z	CME
CD	Canadian dollar	100,000 CD	H, M, U, Z	CME
EC	Euro currency	125,000 Euros	H, M, U, Z	CME
FR	French franc	500,000 FF	H, M, U, Z	CME
JY	Japanese yen	12,500,000 JY	H, M, U, Z	CME
MP	Mexican peso	500,000 MP	H, M, U, Z	CME
SF	Swiss franc	125,000 SF	H, M, U, Z	CME
DX	U.S. Dollar Index	$100 × index	H, M, U, Z	NYBOT
Metals				
GC	Gold	100 troy oz.	All months	NYMEX
SI	Silver	5,000 troy oz.	All months	NYMEX
HG	Copper	25,000 lbs.	All months	NYMEX
PL	Platinum	50 troy oz.	All months	NYMEX
PA	Palladium	100 troy oz.	All months	NYMEX
AL	Aluminum	44,000 lb.	All months	NYMEX
YG	Gold	33.2 troy oz.	All months	CBOT
YI	Silver	1,000 troy oz.	All months	CBOT

TABLE 1.1 Continued

Symbol[a]	Futures Contract	Contract Size	Contract Months[b]	Exchange[c]
Energy				
CL	Crude oil	1,000 bbl.	All months	NYMEX
HO	Heating oil	42,000 gal.	All months	NYMEX
HU	Unleaded gasoline	42,000 gal.	All months	NYMEX
NG	Natural gas	10,000 MBTU	All months	NYMEX
Grains				
C	Corn	5,000 bu.	H, K, N, U, Z	CBOT
W	Wheat, soft winter	5,000 bu.	H, K, N, U, Z	CBOT
S	Soybeans	5,000 bu.	F, H, K, N, Q, U, X	CBOT
BO	Soybean oil	60,000 lb.	F, H, K, N, Q, U, V, Z	CBOT
SM	Soybean meal	100 tons	F, H, K, N, Q, U, V, Z	CBOT
O	Oats	5,000 bu.	H, K, N, U, Z	CBOT
KW	Wheat, hard red winter	5,000 bu.	H, K, N, U, Z	KCBOT
MW	Wheat, spring	5,000 bu.	H, K, N, U, Z	MGE
Meats				
LC	Live cattle	40,000 lb.	G, J, M, Q, V, Z	CME
FC	Feeder cattle	50,000 lb.	F, H, J, K, Q, U, V, X	CME
LH	Lean hogs	40,000 lb.	G, J, M, N, Q, V, Z	CME
PB	Frozen pork bellies	40,000 lb.	G, H, K, N, Q	CME
Foods, Other				
KC	Coffee "C"	37,500 lb.	H, K, N, U, Z	NYBOT
SB	Sugar #11 (world)	112,000 lb.	F, H, K, N, V	NYBOT
CO	Cocoa	10 metric tons	H, K, N, U, Z	NYBOT
CT	Cotton	50,000 lb.	All months	NYBOT
OJ	Frozen orange juice	15,000 lb.	F, H, K, N, U, X	NYBOT
LB	Lumber, random length	110,000 bd. ft.	F, H, K, N, U, X	CME

[a]Exchange symbols; data vendors may use other symbols.

[b]Contract months:

F = January	N = July
G = February	Q = August
H = March	U = September
J = April	V = October
K = May	X = November
M = June	Z = December

[c]Exchange abbreviations:

CBOT	= Chicago Board of Trade
CME	= Chicago Mercantile Exchange
KCBOT	= Kansas City Board of Trade
MGE	= Minneapolis Grain Exchange
NYBOT	= New York Board of Trade
NYMEX	= New York Mercantile Exchange

Commodity Futures Trading Commission's *Commitments of Traders* report. I cover this subject in more detail later in the book, but the report is sort of like getting the inside scoop on who is doing what—like a delayed report on legalized insider trading.

EXCHANGE FUNCTION

Exchanges provide the contracts and the facility (trading pit or computer) where buyers and sellers can come together to trade, all monitored carefully by the exchange under the oversight of federal regulators to preserve the integrity of the market. Futures exchanges make a major point of providing a level playing field for all participants and ensuring that the integrity and financial soundness of the marketplace remains intact. After all, if you have a winning trade and want to take your profits, you need to trust that the money you earned and deserve will be available. The futures industry is built on the principle of integrity.

A few years ago the Chicago Board of Trade celebrated its 150th anniversary. Originally established as a centralized marketplace for grain trading, it has become known for its financial products and is one of the highest volume exchanges in the world. The Chicago Mercantile Exchange, also mostly known today for its financial products, and the New York futures exchanges also trace their roots to the 19th century. So futures markets have been around for a long time and will continue to exist in the future.

Just as the Chicago Mercantile Exchange moved from trading eggs and butter to products such as currencies, the Eurodollar, and stock indexes, exchanges are constantly evolving to meet the changing needs of consumers and producers, adding new and exciting trading vehicles to the futures industry. For example, milk producers saw a need to hedge their risk against often-volatile price movement in the cash market as values move from an extreme low to an extreme high. The Chicago Mercantile Exchange recognized the dairy industry's needs and created a marketplace for participants to hedge their production or purchase needs. Major corporations such as Kraft Foods can now use futures to hedge against losses in the cash market.

DIGGING INTO FUTURES

Futures have a number of features that require more attention, beginning with the concept of margin. As previously mentioned, margin in futures is really a security deposit or performance bond.

Typically, only a small fraction of the contract value (usually 3–10 percent) is required as a security deposit. With such a small deposit, it takes only a small price move to produce a big percentage return, providing the power of leverage for which futures are known.

Exchanges set the minimum performance bond requirements for each contract and can change those requirements without notice, depending on market conditions. Brokerage firms may increase the amount of money required beyond what the exchange has set if additional protection is deemed necessary. Sometimes this is done if volatility or price swings are larger than normal and the firm believes clients are at more risk than usual. For example, if the Federal Reserve makes a sudden interest rate adjustment, the market may panic, causing wild price moves. These volatile price fluctuations may be the basis for a decision that the amount of money required to trade should go up (or down) significantly at a moment's notice.

Although brokerage firms can require more than a minimum performance bond, they cannot lower the amount below the minimum requirements that the exchanges have set. Most trading firms post their margin requirements on their web sites. For exact updates, you can always contact the exchanges for quick access to current information.

The current system used in the industry is known as SPAN margining— Standard Portfolio Analysis of Risk System, developed by the Chicago Mercantile Exchange in 1988. Basically, it is a computer-generated calculation that takes into account a trader's total position to help determine the risk associated with that position. This position could include strictly futures or could involve an intricate options and futures strategy.

Margin and leverage give futures an advantage over other investment instruments, but it is also a two-edge sword. During an adverse price move against your position, the concept of leverage can turn into a bad situation as losses can grow exponentially. Overleveraged positions and undercapitalized investors do get blown out, that is, positions and accounts can be liquidated with large losses and sometimes can leave large debits. However, traders do have control over leverage. By simply adding funds to the account to match the full value of the contracts you are trading, you can set up a situation where you no longer have investment leverage.

Within the system of margin, you should be familiar with two terms: initial margin and maintenance margin. *Initial margin* is the amount of money you must have in your account to establish a futures position. If the market moves against your position and the amount in your account drops below the *maintenance margin*, you will get a *margin call* and must replenish your account to the initial margin level immediately to maintain your position.

We can illustrate the margin system using coffee futures. With coffee futures trading around 60–65 cents a pound in 2003, the New York Board of

Trade's initial margin requirement was about $1,700 and the maintenance margin was $1,200. Based on a contract of 37,500 pounds and a price of 60 cents a pound, the total contract value was $22,500, putting the initial margin at about 7.5 percent of the contract's value. If the price of coffee futures goes up just 2 cents a pound, you have a gain of $750 or a return of about 44 percent on your initial margin money. However, if the price of coffee drops 2 cents a pound—not an unusual occurrence—you have a loss of $750 or 44 percent.

Some traders think they are required to have $1,700 plus $1,200 or a total of $2,900 in their account to trade one coffee futures position. This is not so. The rules of margin are that you need at least $1,700 in your account to enter a coffee position. If your account balance drops below $1,200 at any time, as it would with a 2-cent price decline, then you may receive a request to send in more money to get your account balance back to the original $1,700 level.

When a margin call is generated, it is advisable to discuss the situation with your broker/trading advisor. From a regulatory standpoint, margin calls must be discussed with the client and met as soon as possible. Generally, clients are given a reasonable time to meet a margin call, depending on the amount of money involved and the nature of the situation. Brokerage firms have the right and the obligation to ensure the financial integrity of the marketplace and, therefore, may liquidate your positions to ensure that your account is restored to the proper margin requirements. Thus, it is important to stay in tune with the markets and in touch with your broker when you are holding positions.

There are two other ways to meet a margin call: (1) You may liquidate the position at a loss or (2) the market may make a reversal, trading back in your favor and taking you off margin call status.

The open trade equity in your account is credited or debited each day as the settlement price fluctuates. This futures industry practice is called *marked to market*. Traders often do not regard a setback as a loss until they are out of the market, and they are only looking at a so-called paper profit until they close out a winning position. It is a good idea to have excess capital in your account beyond what is required. I recommend having at least 50 percent more than the initial margin requirement for each position you plan to take as a longer-term trade. For day traders, maintenance margin is sufficient.

Futures contracts often involve large quantities of product with a fraction of the total contract value needed as a good-faith deposit. Not many people have $200,000 in cash to purchase a home, so they apply for a mortgage and put 3 percent to maybe 20 percent down. But buying a home and trading futures aren't the same because of the leverage factor, and that is why options have become extremely popular since the early 1990s.

Investors who buy options have a right, but not an obligation, to fulfill the terms of an options contract at a specific strike price. They can buy calls to take advantage of price increases or buy puts to take advantage of price decreases. The risk in buying options is limited to the initial premium paid to acquire the option plus the commission and transaction fees associated with the transaction; that means no margin calls in the event of a short-term adverse price move. Simply stated, option buyers can enjoy staying power and a predetermined risk level.

However, buying options is limited to a certain time period, and if the market does not move enough in your direction in that prescribed period of time, your entire premium or investment will be lost.

Chapter 13 is devoted to a comprehensive description of trading in options and the logical approach for understanding the terms and uses of different strategies.

CONTRACT SPECIFICATIONS

In addition to the margin/security deposit difference, futures contracts have several other features that make them different from equities, as Table 1.1 indicates. Futures come in different contract sizes and expire in specific months. Equities all are priced on a uniform per-share basis, and they do not expire (although a company may go out of business, which could cause your investment to "expire"). Stocks may also have splits and reverse splits, and some even pay dividends.

With equities, you can maintain a long-term position indefinitely. With futures, you can also have a long-term position, but that will require that you roll over from one contract to the next, liquidating your holding in an expiring contract and establishing a new position in a contract month that is further away.

Novice traders and even traders coming off an exchange floor to trade from a computer need to realize that different futures markets trade in different contract months, at different times of the day, and at different exchanges. In stocks, you have one symbol for Intel (INTC) or IBM (IBM) or every other individual stock. In futures, a June contract for Japanese yen is not the same as a September Japanese yen contract, for example, and they have different symbols.

First, you need to know the symbol for the market you want to trade— CL for crude oil, for example. Most quote vendors use the same symbols as they are pretty much a universal language in the futures industry. However, some vendors use the symbol CC instead of CO for cocoa or SU instead of SB for sugar. The mini-sized Dow contract may be YJ, YM, ZJ, or some other symbol specific to a data service or brokerage firm. Most applications have a menu of symbols so you can look up the quotes or charts you want.

Second, you need to know the symbols for each month. This can be somewhat confusing, especially to newcomers. The list of symbols for each contract month is shown at the bottom of Table 1.1. Notice that March is the only month that even contains the month's symbol, H, as a letter in the name of the contract month. The trickiness in properly identifying a futures contract is one reason new traders find futures trading more complicated than equity trading.

It can lead to a hazardous situation when you are rolling out of a contract that has been trading for a while and switching to a new one. For example, if you have been trading a June contract and have to shift to the September contract as the June contract expires, you may still be in the habit of using June. When placing orders, a slip in identifying a contract can create problems and cost you money. Placing an order for a June contract when you really mean to trade the September contract can easily happen in futures trading if you get careless. There is a window of time when the June contract will still be trading but not actively as most of the trading activity shifts into the next month. For commodities, that time period is between the first notice day and the last trading day for a contract. Orders will still be accepted for the expiring month in that time frame, and it will be up to you to cover your error if your order gets you into the wrong contract month. (Note: The trading tactics section in Chapter 12 provides a technique that some big traders and floor professionals use as first notice day approaches. It may benefit you to be aware of the first notice day trick.)

Third, you may need to know the exchange where the contract you want is traded. Although a number of futures markets are traded on only one exchange, some are traded at several exchanges. For example, if you want to trade hard red winter wheat, you have to specify the wheat contract traded at the Kansas City Board of Trade, not the wheat contracts traded in Chicago or Minneapolis.

Fourth, you may need to be specific about the time of day you want to trade or the size of the contract you want to trade. Table 1.1 does not show all the symbols differentiating between the day session's regular trading hours and the electronic or after-hours night sessions. Nor are the symbols given for most of the mini-sized electronic products traded at the Chicago Mercantile Exchange and the Chicago Board of Trade.

ELECTRONIC ERA

More than 70 percent of all futures markets now trade around the clock, including agricultural markets that once were traded only in the pits of an exchange during a relatively short daily session. Orders can be placed electronically on most companies' online trading platforms, although many firms do not accept open orders and contingency orders for some markets. Chapter 10 explains the order process and contingency orders. It is also advisable to check with your trading firm regularly regarding any changes in trading hours and to see which orders are acceptable.

The electronic product that started it all for the futures industry came from the Chicago Mercantile Exchange, as you might expect, when it developed Globex and launched trading in the e-mini S&P 500 and Nasdaq 100 index futures contracts. These contracts have been particularly attractive to former investors in the stock market and are now among the most actively traded futures contracts.

The Chicago Board of Trade launched a mini-sized contract based on the Dow Jones Industrial Average in April 2002, and its popularity accelerated in 2003, reaching a daily volume of more than 60,000 contracts a year later. The contract has several key features that make it an attractive trading vehicle:

- A 100 percent electronic market with 24-hour access.
- Lower margin than other stock index futures in dollars and as a percentage of contract value ($2,700 versus $3,563 for the e-mini S&P in the middle of 2003).
- Simpler calculating and tracking components as the Dow only has 30 underlying stocks to monitor.
- For those with blue-chip stock portfolios, easier hedging by being able to go short the Dow as easily as going long. Dow futures correlate closely with the underlying Dow Jones Industrial Average.
- More spreading opportunities because the mini-sized Dow can be traded against individual single stock futures, Diamonds or S&P 500, Nasdaq 100, or other index futures.
- Smaller minimum price fluctuations. Each point or tick in the mini-sized Dow is $5. Each point in the e-mini S&P is $50, with the minimum tick size a quarter of a point or $12.50. The two contracts trade in about a 10-to-1 relationship—a 10-point move in the e-mini S&P and a 100-point move in the mini-sized Dow are each worth $500. A move of that size would equate to an 18.52 percent gain for the mini-sized Dow versus a 14 percent gain for the e-mini S&P, using the margin amounts previously mentioned.

Perhaps the biggest attraction of the mini-sized Dow is that it is based on the best-known U.S. stock market barometer, which is more than a century old and recognized around the world. When you ask how the stock market did today, most people think of the Dow.

INVESTMENT REVOLUTION?

Next to the electronically traded stock index contracts, probably the most exciting new futures market area is single stock futures (SSF). SSFs were launched on two new U.S. exchanges on November 8, 2002, after a two-decade moratorium on that type of contract. They had been trading on foreign exchanges with moderate success for some time but had been banned in the United States by an agreement that allowed trading to begin in stock index futures in 1982. The realization that the United States might lose out on market share to foreign competitors in a potential major new market was high on the list of factors that prompted politicians and regulators at the Securities and Exchange Commission and Commodity Futures Trading Commission to finally resolve jurisdictional issues to allow trading in SSFs.

SSFs are an innovative product and could change the way the world invests on Wall Street in the future. Investors who have limited their investments to the stock market especially may benefit from this new market. Imagine having the leverage to trade 100 shares of a popular stock for only a 20 percent margin requirement and not having to pay a stock firm the broker loan rate to sell a stock short (if they can loan it to you at all). Assume, for example, that Microsoft is priced at $25 per share. The futures contract size is 100 shares so the contract value is $2,500. With an initial margin requirement of 20 percent of the value of the contract, you have to put up only $500 to either buy or sell Microsoft futures instead of $1,250 it would take to buy 100 shares of Microsoft shares at the minimum margin rate in the stock market.

With SSFs you can open a futures trading account, buy a cash Treasury bill, and trade a broad range of markets beyond SSFs while earning interest instead of paying interest. The best part is being able to go long or short without prejudice and having access to the market by trading from your computer at home or work. These developments may not make broker-dealers happy but are good news for individual traders.

BULL MARKET FOR FUTURES

These stock-related trading vehicles reinforce my optimism about the popularity of futures trading, not only in the United States but also around the globe as people attempt to increase their wealth and raise their standard of living. I believe the explosive growth in futures has come out of the dismal losses many investors suffered during the great bear market in equities since the peak in 2000.

Investors are now becoming more educated and open to other opportunities rather than limiting themselves to recommendations from their stockbroker or investment advisor. The story earlier in this chapter about the gentleman who never traded futures because his stockbroker said he would lose his shirt is a testimonial to the fact that more and more investors— most likely, people just like you—want to learn more.

Here is another example. I gave a seminar presentation in August 2002 to the Chicago chapter of the Cornerstone Investors Group, speaking to about 70 people. I asked how many folks in the audience were trading futures. I believe about three people raised their hands, and I think two were clients of mine.

The president of the group, Mark Anderson, invited me back in April 2003, reminding me that I said to his group in 2002, "If the balance of you are not trading futures, then you will be sooner or later." Just eight months after that 2002 seminar, I asked the same question at the April seminar, which had about 85 people. First, the investment club membership had grown and, second, it seemed like almost everyone raised their hands. I was shocked!

What happened here? Well, this investor group had started to learn and discovered the benefits of trading futures and how to apply technical analysis to the markets. They were taking control of their own financial destiny.

A whole lot of people are now interested in the futures markets and not just from the town of Schaumburg, Illinois, or in Tampa Bay, Florida, where the Cornerstone group was founded. The reach of traders wanting to learn this form of derivative trading stretches to Ireland, England, Europe, Asia, Australia—worldwide. I hope this book helps to keep you focused and financially prepared for the years ahead and helps you with the process of continually learning the ebb and flow of the markets.

CHAPTER 2

Fundamentals

The Market Driver

*Everyone needs constant education and training.
The more you keep yourself informed, the better
honed your instincts and decision-making
capabilities.*

—Linda Conway

The term *fundamental analysis* refers to the study of tangible information about a market such as supply and demand statistics and expectations about what these numbers might be. Markets are a two-way street: Supply and demand are key factors in determining price, and price often is a factor in supply and demand.

Supply and demand comes from the perceived value that is placed on a stock, commodity, or any derivative product. In its simplest definition, *supply* is the amount of a given stock, product, or commodity that is available to the market, either in excess or limited at a given price depending on the number of sellers. Price establishes a resistance level when the supply of a particular product or stock is adequately provided.

Demand, the amount of buying or lack of buying, plays an integral role in establishing how high or low prices can go and is generated by buyers. Demand establishes a support level for prices.

Numerous events directly affect the outcome of both supply and demand, but some are more critical than others. For example, for agriculture products from grains to livestock, weather is a crucial element in determining supply. In the event of a drought, grain production could be in short supply and livestock could suffer weight loss or be forced to market in large numbers if it appears scarce feed may become too expensive. In harsh

19

winters, grain movement could be slowed and livestock could perish, resulting in supply disruptions that could cause prices to go higher in a steady or rising demand environment.

THE FED FACTOR

In the financial arena, when the Federal Reserve lowers short-term interest rates, economic activity theoretically accelerates due to an increase in commerce as a direct result of the cost of doing business becoming less expensive. However, events do not always unfold as theory suggests.

The Federal Reserve began an aggressive campaign to lower interest rates to kick start the U.S. economy in 2001. It cut short-term rates 13 times, 11 of those cuts amounting to 4.75 percentage points coming during 2001, a difficult period for the U.S. economy. Then in November 2002 the Fed cut rates another 50 basis points in what it called a "preventive" action against possible economic weakness as the United States was preparing to attack Iraq to combat global terrorism and oust Saddam Hussein and his weapons of mass destruction. The invasion was a quick one—I think the UN Security Council meeting debates took longer than the actual military operation.

However, U.S. economic growth still did not accelerate as expected, so on May 6, 2003, the Fed slashed rates for the 13th time. That 25-point cut dropped the Fed funds rate to 1 percent, and Federal Reserve Chairman Alan Greenspan even mentioned combating potential deflation as a reason for making this move!

The whole investment world did an about-face. Most people thought the Fed was getting closer to actually raising interest rates rather than lowering them, and there was speculation that the Fed would take other unconventional means such as buying back 10-year and 30-year bonds to lower rates for longer-term maturities. Mortgage rates fell to the lowest level in nearly 50 years. The market's focus shifted to watching the Producer Price Index, the Consumer Price Index, and employment plus any other reports that would hint at a stronger manufacturing sector as well as any that would indicate a decrease in the jobless rate.

These were some unconventional responses to some unconventional moves, but the key point is that it is important to grasp the significance of the underlying economic fundamentals and the implications they might have for any market you are trading.

Interest rates control the cost of money. Those who can foretell what money will cost to lend or borrow have the upper hand in the investment community. Rates dictate many other factors, especially because they are one of the variables in calculations to determine fair-market values from stock index futures to the broker loan rates for stock traders. It isn't just mortgage companies that have to guard against changes in interest rates, but a broad range of businesses have to consider interest rate levels in their plans.

REPORTS, REPORTS

One of the advantages of trading futures is that the government releases dozens of reports every week, and the media provides additional material that offers insights into what might lie ahead for market prices. Determining the direction of the economy from reading economic reports is vital for understanding the potential for the direction of interest rates as well as gauging the health of the various sectors of the economy.

For example, government reports such as those on employment may reveal what the potential for future household disposable income is and give analysts and economists an idea of how much spending could occur based on the number of Americans working. News articles give you the ability to follow and understand the political scene, both on international and domestic levels. If Congress passes a bill to donate more wheat than expected, then this action may have a more bullish impact on the price of wheat futures. Or if Congress passes laws to change the tax rate on capital gains, you might be able to speculate on what the stock market or other financial markets may do.

If the European Central Bank announces a lower than expected interest rate adjustment, it is likely to affect the value of the euro and, inversely, the U.S. dollar. If values of these currencies shift abruptly and to a severe degree, then, of course, products that are imported and exported would be priced differently and, ultimately, could cause a ripple effect on costs and prices of goods and services in the United States and overseas.

One reason you want to be educated and up-to-date on developments in the economy is because they usually dictate how different financial products and futures prices will perform. The stock market likes to see healthy economic growth because that usually equates to better or substantially larger corporate profits. The bond market prefers a slower, more sustainable growth rate that will not lead to inflationary pressures. By watching and tracking economic data and getting insights from analysts and economists, investors will be better able to keep in tune with the markets and their investments.

In fact, you should be aware of what could happen before most reports are released. That is why news services often give the schedule for current events and special reports. Publications such as *Barron's*, *Investors Business Daily*, or the *Wall Street Journal* will often give you a consensus of analysts' opinions on what to expect and show you what you need to know to stay in tune with the markets. Most futures brokerage firms also provide special calendars that include the dates and times that most major economic and agricultural reports are released.

Trading is not an easy venture, and one helpful bit of advice I would emphasize is that you should always be aware of the day's current events and scheduled reports if you are in the markets. Not knowing what day or time a report is released could be hazardous to your financial health. Knowing about a major report before it is released is often useful because you have a chance to eliminate a surprise from an adverse market move. Even if you are not a fundamental trader, you should, at the very least, be aware of the main fundamental factors that might affect the markets you are trading and the impact reports and events may have on the market.

WHAT TO WATCH, WHAT IT MEANS

Here are some of the economic terms, events, and reports that U.S. traders should know and watch, including a brief explanation of why they are important to investors. If you did not pay attention in your economics classes, this section will bring you up to speed.

Federal Open Market Committee (FOMC) Meetings and Policy Announcements   The FOMC consists of seven governors of the Federal Reserve Board and five Federal Reserve Bank presidents. The FOMC meets eight times a year—roughly every six weeks—to determine the near-term direction of monetary policy. Whether there is a change in rates or not, the FOMC announces its decision immediately after FOMC meetings.

A few accompanying statements the Fed may make after announcing any adjustments in interest rates may have as much influence on markets as a change or no change in rates themselves. For example, the FOMC may take a "neutral" stance on the outlook for the economy. Or it may point to prospects for growth or suggest the potential for economic weakness or inflationary pressures. The FOMC actions or comments can have a powerful impact on markets.

Treasury Bonds, Bills, and Notes   The U.S. government issues several different kinds of bonds through the Bureau of the Public Debt, an agency of the U.S. Department of the Treasury. Treasury debt securities are classified according to their maturities:

- Treasury bills have maturities of 1 year or less.
- Treasury notes have maturities of 2 to 10 years.
- Treasury bonds have maturities of more than 10 years.

Treasury bonds, bills, and notes are all issued in face values of $1,000, though there are different purchase minimums for each type of security.

Interest Rates, Financial Markets and Bonds   U.S. Treasury bonds, by virtually any definition, are simply a loan. The U.S. government borrows the funds it needs to operate, including financing the federal deficit. Ultimately, taxpayers will have to pay back the loan.

When a bond is issued, the price you pay is known as its *face value*. Once you buy it, the government promises to pay you back on a specific day known as the *maturity date*. It issues that instrument at a predetermined rate of interest, called the *coupon*. For instance, if you buy a bond with a $1,000 face value, a 6 percent coupon, and a 10-year maturity, you would collect interest payments totaling $60 in each of those 10 years. When the decade is up, you get back your $1,000.

If you buy a U.S. Treasury bond and hold it until maturity, you will know exactly how much you're going to get back. That's why bonds are also known as *fixed-income* investments—they guarantee you a continuous set income backed by the U.S. government. What confuses most investors in bonds is the concept of yield and price. Simply stated, when yield goes up, price goes down, and vice versa.

Government Reports

Beige Book   A combination of economic conditions from each of the 12 Federal Reserve regional districts, the *Beige Book* is aptly named because of the color of its cover (really). This report is usually released two weeks before the monetary policy meetings of the FOMC. The information on economic conditions is then used by the FOMC to set interest rate policy. If the *Beige Book* portrays an overheating economy or inflationary pressures, the Fed may be more inclined to raise interest rates to moderate the economic pace. Conversely, if the *Beige Book* portrays economic difficulties or recession conditions, the Fed may see a need to lower interest rates to stimulate activity.

Gross Domestic Product (GDP)   GDP is the broadest measure of aggregate economic activity and accounts for almost every sector of the economy. Analysts use this figure to track the economy's overall performance because it usually indicates how strong or weak the economy is and helps to predict the potential profit margin for companies. It also helps analysts determine whether economic growth is accelerating or slowing down. The stock market likes to see healthy economic growth because that translates to higher corporate profits and higher share values.

International Trade and Current Account Figures   These numbers measure the difference between imports and exports of both goods and services. Changes in the level of imports and exports are an important tool for gauging economic trends, both domestically and overseas. These reports can have a profound effect on the value of the dollar. That value, in turn, can help or hurt multinational corporations whose profits overseas can diminish when they convert their funds back to the United States, especially if the U.S. dollar is overvalued. Another valuable aspect of such reports is that imports can help to indicate U.S. demand for foreign goods, and exports may show demand for U.S. goods in overseas countries.

Index of Leading Economic Indicators (LEI)   This report is a composite index of 10 economic indicators that typically lead overall economic activity. The LEI index helps to predict the health of the economy and may be an early clue about the prospects for recession or economic expansion.

Consumer Price Index (CPI)   The CPI measures the average price level of goods and services purchased by consumers and is the most widely followed indicator of inflation in the United States. Monthly changes represent the inflation rate that is quoted widely and influences a number of markets.

Inflation is a general increase in the price of goods and services. The relationship between inflation and interest rates is the key to understanding how data such as the CPI influence the markets. Higher energy prices, manufacturing cost increases, medical costs, imbalances in global supply and demand of raw materials, and prices of food products all weigh on this report. For example, if gas prices at the pump escalate and the cost to fill up your car rises from, say, $30 a week to $50 or even $60 a week, you will have less spending money for other items. It may not affect you immediately, but a longer duration of higher prices will hit your pocketbook.

Even weather can be a factor for short-term changes in food prices. What would be the cost of tomatoes at the grocery store after a damaging freeze in California or in Georgia? Maybe $3 or $4 per pound? Any grocery shopper can probably recall when such price spikes occurred. The restaurants that serve salads lose revenue as well as the farmer whose crop is destroyed.

These factors all play a part in the CPI number. The core rate is the inflation number that excludes the volatile food and energy components. Economists track these numbers; you should, too.

Producer Price Index (PPI)   Formerly known as the Wholesale Price Index, the PPI is a measure of the average prices for a fixed basket of capital and consumer goods paid by producers. The PPI measures price changes in the manufacturing sector. The inflation rate may depend on a general increase in the prices of goods and services.

Institute of Supply Management (ISM) Index   Formerly known as the National Association of Purchasing Managers (NAPM) survey, the ISM report provides a composite diffusion index of national manufacturing conditions. Readings above 50 percent indicate an expanding factory sector, readings below 50 percent, a contracting sector. The ISM Index helps economists and analysts get a detailed look at the manufacturing sector of the economy, a major source of economic strength that can have a bearing on the nation's employment situation, a key to economic health.

Durable Goods Orders   This report (Manufacturers' Shipments, Inventories, and Orders) reflects new orders placed with domestic manufacturers for immediate and future delivery of factory-made products. Orders for durable goods show how busy factories will be in the months to come as manufacturers work to fill those orders. The data not only provide insight into demand for things like washers, dryers, and cars but also take the temperature of the strength of the economy going forward.

Industrial Production and Capacity Utilization   These rates measure the physical output of the nation's factories, mines, and utilities and reflect the usage level of available resources. Because the manufacturing sector accounts for an estimated one-quarter of the economy, these reports can sometimes have a big impact on stock and financial market movement. The capacity utilization rate provides an estimate of how much factory capacity is in use. If the utilization rate gets too high (above 85 percent), it can lead to inflationary pressures.

Factory Orders   The dollar level of new orders for manufacturing durable and nondurable goods shows the potential for factories to increase or decrease activity based on the amount of orders they receive. This report provides insight into the demand for not only hard goods such as refrigerators and cars, but also nondurable items such as cigarettes and apparel.

Business Inventories   Fed Chairman Alan Greenspan is said to be among those who watch the report of business inventories, so you should become familiar with it as well. This report shows the dollar amount of inventories held by manufacturers, wholesalers, and retailers. The level of inventories in relation to sales is an important indicator for the future direction of factory production.

Consumer Confidence   If there is one area that has been watched most carefully in recent years, it is consumer sentiment. Several surveys or polls gauge consumer attitudes. Among the best known are those conducted by The Conference Board and the University of Michigan. These surveys reveal what consumers think about present conditions as well as what their expectations are for future economic conditions.

The level of consumer confidence is generally assumed to be directly related to the strength or weakness for consumer spending, which accounts for two-thirds of the U.S. economy. Generally speaking, the more confident consumers are about their own personal finances, the more likely they are to spend. If they have money in the bank and feel confident that their job is secure, buying an extra gadget or splurging on a night out usually won't be any trouble. In contrast, if times are tough, then the purse strings get pulled in.

These indications from one month to the next give analysts an idea of the potential for shifts in future spending habits that can help or hurt developments in the economy from durable goods sales to home or car purchases.

Employment Situation   The key to consumer confidence often depends on the status of jobs. The monthly unemployment rate measures the number of unemployed as a percentage of the nation's workforce. Non-farm-payroll employment tallies the number of paid employees working part-time and or full-time in the nation's business and government sectors.

Several important components are included in this report, one being the average hourly workweek that reflects the number of hours worked in the nonfarm sector. Another component is average hourly earnings, which shows the hourly rate employees are receiving.

There are two portions of this report, one a weekly report released every Thursday morning and the other the more influential monthly figures that are usually released on the first Friday of every month.

Employment Cost Index (ECI)   The ECI provides a measure of total employee compensation costs, including wages and salaries as well as benefits. It is the broadest measure of labor costs and helps analysts determine trends in the cost that employers have from paying employees. This measure can give economists a clue as to whether inflation is perking up from a cost of business standpoint. If a company needs to pay more to hire qualified workers, then the cost of doing business increases and profit margins are reduced. Companies usually have to raise their prices to consumers as their costs increase. That is when the inflation theme starts to play out.

Productivity and Costs   *Productivity* measures the growth of labor efficiency in producing the economy's goods and services. *Unit labor costs* reflect the labor costs of producing each unit of output. Both are followed as indicators of future inflationary trends. Productivity growth is critical because it allows for higher wages and faster economic growth without inflationary consequences.

Personal Income and Spending   *Personal income* is the estimated dollar amount of income received by Americans. *Personal spending* is the estimated dollar amount that consumers use for purchases of durable and nondurable goods and services. This economic number is important because if consumers are spending more than they make, the spending will stop eventually, thus causing a downturn in the economy. Another aspect to consider is that consumers who save may be investing in the markets, and that activity can increase the value of stock prices. In addition, it can also add liquidity to the banking system if the money goes to savings or money market accounts.

Retail Sales   Retail sales numbers measure the total sales at stores that sell durable and nondurable goods. These figures can reveal the spending habits of consumers, and the trend of those spending sprees, more often than not, can influence analysts' expectations for future developments in the economy.

Housing Starts   This report measures the number of residential units that are about to be constructed, a backbone of the American economy. When you purchase a new home, you are giving a boost to not only the raw material suppliers, builders, and their industries, but also to the producers of durable goods items such as refrigerators, washers, dryers, furniture, lawn care products, and many other items related to making a home. This is known as a ripple effect throughout the economy. Think of all the jobs produced from construction to factory and transportation and even communication and technology that go into the building, financing, and furnishing a new home.

   The economic impact is substantial, especially when there are a hundred thousand or more homes built in a month around the country. At the very least, the data from housing starts can help project the price direction for the sector of stocks involving home builders, mortgage bankers, and appliance companies. Lumber and copper futures prices used to be dramatically affected by the housing starts figure. However, since the development of prefab and new construction materials, especially fiber optics and plastics (PVC, polyvinyl chloride, used for plumbing rather than copper), these products are now less sensitive to building industry trends.

New Home Sales   Like housing starts, the level of new home sales (committed sales) indicates housing market trends. This information provides another gauge for not only the demand for housing but also economic momentum. People have to be feeling pretty comfortable and confident in their own financial position to buy a home. Furthermore, as previously mentioned, this narrow piece of data has a powerful multiplier effect throughout the economy and, therefore, across markets where you may have your investments.

Existing Home Sales   Existing home sales (the number of previously constructed homes with a closed sale during the month, also known as *home resales*) are a larger share of the market than new home sales and provide another indication of housing market trends. This statistic also provides clues to the demand for housing and for economic momentum based on the ripple effect.

Mortgage Bankers Association Purchase Applications Index   This weekly index of purchase applications at mortgage lenders is a good leading indicator for single family home sales and housing construction and is another gauge of housing demand and the resulting economic momentum.

Construction Spending   This report goes beyond housing to show analysts the amount of new construction activity on residential and nonresidential building jobs. Commodities such as lumber are sensitive to housing industry trends. In addition, business owners usually will put money into the construction of a new facility or factory if they feel confident that business is good enough to validate an expansion.

Consumer Credit   One of the American consumers' pastimes is to say "Charge it" to purchase goods and services on their credit cards. Overall changes in consumer credit can indicate the condition of individual consumer finances. On the one hand, economic activity is stimulated when consumers borrow within their means to buy cars and other major purchases. On the other hand, if consumers pile up too much debt relative to their income levels, they may have to stop spending on new goods and services just to pay off old debts. That stoppage could put a big dent in future economic growth.

The demand for credit can also have a direct effect on interest rates. If the demand to borrow money exceeds the supply of willing lenders, interest rates rise. If credit demand falls and many willing lenders are fighting for customers, they may offer lower interest rates to attract business.

Other Reports and Information

The government isn't the only source of information vital to the markets, of course. Private research reports, company reports, and even anecdotal evidence gleaned from the news or from your neighborhood may provide clues about the future of the economy and market prices.

For example, you may be able to take the temperature of the economy by watching travel reports. Are people going on vacations? Are they taking two weeks or just three days? Staying close to home or going to exotic places? Listening to your friends talking about their vacations and watching airline traffic statistics may give you clues about travel that may be a good guide for what's happening to the economy that, in turn, may have a bearing on what you are trading. In good times people tend to spend bigger money on a vacation, where the number one activity is shopping, according to *Travel* magazine. Lots of consumer spending says a lot about the vibrancy of the economy and supports higher stock market prices. If you trade energy, more travel means airline fuel consumption goes up, and that may trigger an increase in energy prices.

Statistics and reports from a number of private sources can back up or refute your observations. Reports from weather services may keep you ahead of the crowd on crop developments or prospects for heating oil. The National Oilseed Processors Association releases reports about the soybean "crush" that can help you analyze the outlook for not only soybeans but the feed component for livestock markets as well. The American Petroleum Institute releases weekly statistics on energy production and stocks. There are many other similar sources of information, not to mention the dozens of specialty newsletters providing information, insights, and advice on every market.

Then, of course, there are the earnings reports and other information released by thousands of public companies that drive the prices of individual stocks. Because there are many more equity traders in the investment world than there are futures traders, you may be more familiar with these reports. If the equity markets generate normal or even subnormal returns based on a historical standard as some forecast for the next few years, then the appetite for making money may attract individual investors to move into futures products because of the leverage available in futures and options. And many futures traders will have to become more familiar with what affects the prices of stocks as new demands and needs for products that combine features of stocks and futures are introduced.

Futures and options activity will continue to expand and change as both types of traders come to markets such as the popular e-mini S&P 500 index futures, which went from a daily volume of around 300,000 contracts in February 2002 to as many as 1,000,000 contracts a day within a matter of months. Those numbers offer proof that stock investors are flooding into the futures markets. The debut of single stock futures in November 2002 gave individual investors the unique opportunity to trade individual stocks with the features and benefits of the futures markets and will send futures volume in stocks-related markets even higher.

More participation from a wider variety of players may create more volatility, making it more important than ever to know what to look for in reports and how they may affect price behavior. When looking at company numbers, it is vital to decipher what the actual financial strength of the company is and to listen to what guidance is being given for that company's future. If a company president or CEO states that earnings were good based on spending cuts rather than revenue growth and, in addition, indicates that future sales may be slow, then that information would not bode well for that stock's price. Further, it might suggest that all companies in that sector might be susceptible to a slow period or economic contraction.

Therefore, it is relevant to discuss earnings and other aspects of analyzing stock prices such as supply and demand and their perceived valuations in addition to general economic numbers. The common and most popular gauge of stock value is the price/earnings ratio (P/E). The calculation is simple: Just divide the stock price by the earnings. A stock priced at $60 and earning $6 per share has a P/E ratio of 10. There are several other means of analyzing a stock's value: changes in sales figures, announced increases in dividend payouts, amount of debt, new contracts that will generate more revenue, takeover situations, stock buy-back plans, and so on.

The leader or largest capitalized company in a sector or industry group may set the tone for that sector and help drive prices in either direction. So it is important for stock index futures traders to follow the developments of key stocks or sectors. Listening to the earnings reports or conference calls may give you facts rather than brokers' opinions on what was said and provides another form of fundamental analysis.

STAYING WITH THE INFORMATION FLOW

I have just described only a few of the more popular economic reports and indicators released every day. As you can see, there is definitely enough information released to create fuel for the fire that causes volatility in the markets, emphasizing the importance of staying on top of the daily calendar of events, especially when you have positions that may be affected by these reports. Awareness of what is going on around you can help you become a successful trader.

Market participants change, money flow changes, the world political scene changes, the market's focus changes. The reports mentioned and their significance will probably evolve over time just as they have in the past. For example, the old NAPM survey is now the ISM Index. And you may remember when money supply M-1 and M-2 figures were a big deal (1984) that everyone in the market had to follow.

The times do change, and entrepreneurs and swift students of the markets will rise to the occasion to understand what information will help give them an edge in an effort to beat the street. This business attracts the savviest and smartest people in the world. Some are extremely well schooled, and others are naturally gifted with good market sense and, well, sometimes with just plain luck. You need to be aware that those people are the ones you are up against as a market participant. If this is going to be your business, at least knowing what the other team players follow may help you in your own research.

Of course, even the biggest and smartest players lose sometimes. The markets do not discriminate. They like to take money away from the large commodity trading advisor who has an Ivy League degree and a Phi Beta Kappa plaque on the office wall as well as from the small speculator. As markets change and fundamental shifts in business cycles occur, you need to adjust so you can grasp where the market's focus is and find the reports and information that will keep you in tune with the fundamentals of the market.

CHAPTER 3

Technical Analysis

The Art of Charts

*The greatest ignorance is to reject something you
know nothing about.*

—Anonymous

ormulating a trading plan should include the initial entry position,
the risk management loss objective, and the targeted profit objective—in other words, everything about the trade from start to finish.
The type of analysis you do should lead to a means to determine those three
components of a trade before you ever get into it. For many traders, analyzing price data on a chart—technical analysis—is the solution. The emphasis here is how to understand and apply technical tools without the
syndrome of analysis paralysis—that is, when too many studies are done,
dominating the trader's time and leading to inaction. It's true that no one
ever lost money by not trading, but if you are a trader or trying to trade, decisions must be made.

How you proceed with your analysis may depend on your brain. An interesting concept of how the brains of individuals function, whether they
are male or female, comes from research that shows that the left and the
right sides of the brain interpret and process data differently. Determining
which side of your brain is the dominant side may help you understand the
form of market analysis that you might like to use.

The left side of the brain is the logical, methodical reasoning, and rational thinking half. It is the side of the brain that facilitates dealings with
the factual sciences and mathematics. A person who is left-brain dominant
may relate to and place more emphasis and confidence in support and

resistance levels derived from mathematical formulas such as pivot points and Fibonacci and technical indicators as well as cold, hard supply/demand reports or statistical data.

The right side of the brain, according to researchers and doctors, is the artistic dominating side. If the right side of your brain dominates your thinking as a technical chart analyst, then you have a strong tendency to re-member and recall chart patterns. You may put more confidence in repeti-tive chart pattern techniques and the ensuing theories of measurement techniques and methodologies behind these formations. For this kind of thinker, learning traditional chart patterns and Japanese candlestick forma-tions may evolve to become a reasonable method to interpret and process data to act on trading decisions.

Chart reading has fascinated traders for hundreds of years, even though it has never been totally accepted by academics and other market purists. Using charts to analyze markets and price movement is certainly not an exact science but, rather, a working form of art that sometimes depends more on what the eye sees than on a conclusive fact. I believe it is absolutely essen-tial that you develop at least the basic skills in the art of charting price moves if you want to become an astute trader, even if you are more comfortable trading based on fundamentals and facts.

There are three main popular charting techniques: bar charts, point-and-figure charts, and candlestick charts. Another technique of charting or watching price patterns and the behavior of the market is market profiling. The importance of any type of charting is to help understand where market prices have been and, based on past historical reactions, to predict where prices may go in the future.

Determining the trend or direction of prices is one of the main objectives of chart analysis. Pattern recognition leading up to a chart setup is another purpose of chart work. The more times you identify the characteristics of a pattern and the frequency it repeats itself, the more likely you will get the experience and confidence you need to follow the next similar pattern with a trading decision. The outcome from doing your work on the charts should be profits resulting from making the trade. If the pattern fails to produce the desired results, then you should be able to determine when to cut and run from the trade to avert a financial disaster.

This chapter covers the basics of bar charts, point-and-figure charting, and market profiling. Chapter 4 focuses on a more visual method of charting, candlesticks, and Chapter 5 provides a more extensive explanation of chart patterns that apply to several types of charts. You'll also find suggestions in this chapter on where to access data and where to obtain further educa-tional material and books so you can enhance your trading knowledge in areas that appeal to you.

BAR CHARTS

Bar charts are the standard means of chart analysis and probably the most widely used charting form and technique.

The concept of a bar chart is simple. On a graph the horizontal axis represents time, and the vertical axis represents price levels. Within that graph, a single bar or vertical line will represent the range or the high and low points that prices reached during a given time period. A small hash line or horizontal mark on the left side of the bar identifies the opening price; another hash mark or horizontal line on the right side of the bar indicates the closing price for that time period (Figure 3.1). The time represented by the vertical bar could be 1 minute, 5 minutes, 60 minutes, a day, a week, a month, or even a year.

The relationship between the current time frame's range and the previous time frame's open, high, low, and close is significant. Here are four classifications of bars that have more significance to analysts:

1. One of the more popular, well-known bars is a *key reversal*. The bearish key reversal (Figure 3.2) makes a higher high than the previous time frame and usually closes below the prior time frame's close and the general trend direction. This occurrence is frequently accompanied by unusually strong volume and indicates the trend is reversing. An S&P 500 index chart shows a good example (Figure 3.3). The exact opposite occurs for a bullish key reversal in a downtrending market—lower low than the previous time frame and then a close above the prior time frame's close.

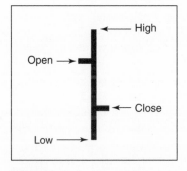

FIGURE 3.1   The basic bar.

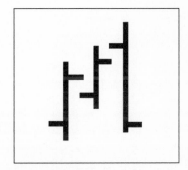

FIGURE 3.2   Key reversal.

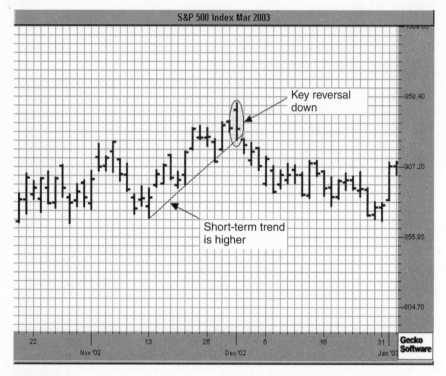

FIGURE 3.3   Shifting into reverse. (*Source:* Gecko Software, Inc. Reprinted with permission.)

2. The *outside bar* (Figure 3.4) occurs when the current range takes out the previous time frame's high and low, but the close is consistent with the current trend. It usually signals the continuation of the market's direction.

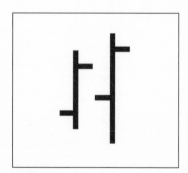

FIGURE 3.4   Outside bar.

3. The *settlement price reversal bar* (Figure 3.5) occurs when the bar moves in the same direction as the previous time frame's bar—a higher high and higher low for an uptrending market—but closes lower than the previous time frame's settlement price.

4. The *inside bar* is exactly what it sounds like (Figure 3.6). The current bar's high and low are within the previous time frame's high and low—that is, the whole current range is within the previous bar's range. The close is not considered important by most chartists. What is important is how the market behaves in the next time frame. A breakout either way of the inside bar range gives a buy or sell signal, based on the theory that there is a continued price move in the direction of the breakout.

Figure 3.7 displays all four of the preceding bar examples and shows the ensuing price results.

Of course, one bar usually does not make a chart pattern. However, training your eyes to quickly spot a bar that may lead to identifying a pattern or formation is what learning chart analysis is all about. Once you see a formation and study a repetitive result time after time, your confidence level will increase and, thus, you may be able to pull the trigger quicker to execute a trade faster.

The analysis of the chart is the same whether each bar represents a minute, 5 minutes, 12 minutes, 30 minutes, an hour, day, week, or month. The time frame you choose depends on how close you want to be to the market and how many trading opportunities you would like to see.

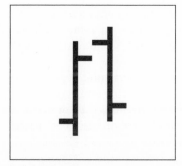

FIGURE 3.5   Settlement price reversal.

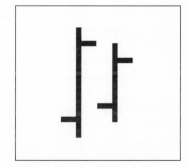

FIGURE 3.6   Inside bar.

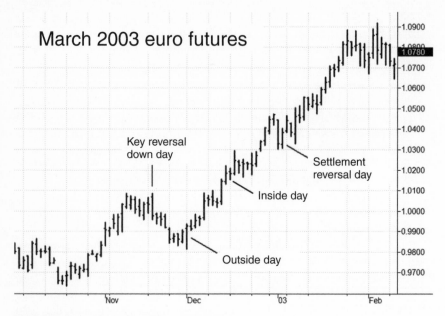

FIGURE 3.7   Multiple one-bar signals.

POINT-AND-FIGURE CHARTS

The point-and-figure method of charting has a long history. Author and well-known technician John Murphy estimates the development of point-and-figure charts goes back to sometime in the 1880s or 1890s, but they have not been popular with futures traders in recent years.

Point-and-figure charts have one unique difference from other charts: Time is not a concern; only price action is. The vertical axis represents price, the same as a bar chart. Instead of bars for a time period on the horizontal axis, however, the columns on a point-and-figure chart alternate between Xs for upward price movement and Os for downward price movement, changing from one character to the other when a specified amount of price movement occurs.

Each box on a point-and-figure chart represents a price unit. If prices are moving up, an X is placed in a box as each new higher price unit is achieved. When prices turn lower by a set number of boxes (price units), a new column of Os begins to the right of the column of Xs, and Os continue to be added to the bottom of that column as each new lower box (price unit) is reached.

A price reversal equal to one box size may result in the formation of a new column. A method of smoothing out fluctuations is to only record price reversals that exceed a set number of boxes. The number of boxes is called the *reversal amount*, and a new column will not be started until price has retraced by that amount. Standard plots would usually be stated as something like 10 by 3, that is, 10 points per box with a three-box (30 points) reversal amount. Thus, a new column of Xs or Os would not begin unless the market reversed by 30 points.

When you update a point-and-figure chart, you're only concerned with high and low prices. The closing price is unimportant. You remain in the current column as long as the price action continues in the same direction. If you are making a column of Xs and the high for the period moves up at least one more box, then add an X to the column. Of course, if the high is more than one box higher, then fill in all of the boxes to match that high price. As long as the market continues to make higher highs, continue filling Xs in the current column and ignore the lows during the period you are plotting.

If the market does not make a higher high and the low for the session is not three boxes lower than the highest X (assuming that is your reversal amount), then there is no update for the chart for that period. In a quiet market, you may not make a mark on a point-and-figure chart for an extended period of time, whereas you add a bar to a bar chart for every time period, even when there is minimal price movement.

For more volatile markets such as the stock indexes or bonds, I would suggest 8 by 3 as parameters, as Figure 3.8, the September 2003 bond futures

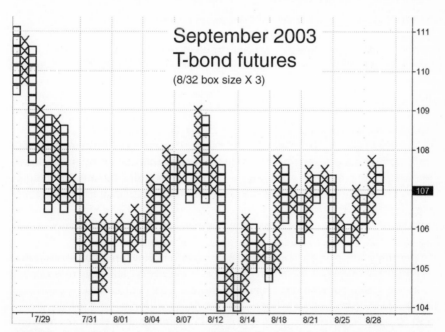

FIGURE 3.8   Point-and-figure chart. (*Source:* eSignal. Reprinted with permission.)

chart, illustrates. Increasing the reversal number will effectively make the point-and-figure chart less sensitive; decreasing the reversal number will make it more sensitive to recording price moves.

The important fact to remember is that the price action on a point-and-figure chart may occur over the course of a day, a week, a month, or a year. The time period is irrelevant for the point-and-figure chartist. I have seen some floor traders use the point-and-figure method for intraday charts, penciling Xs and Os on the backs of trading cards and on graph paper. For them, these charts make it easy to see trend lines and breakout points because the focus is on specific price points.

For a beginning chartist, I would strongly consider starting with bar charts. Point-and-figure charting needs tweaking or optimizing to determine the right box size and reversal amounts for each market and for the time frame and sensitivity that you might want to fit your own trading style. For those who enjoy a challenge of learning a different charting method, *Point & Figure Charting* by Thomas J. Dorsey discusses this type of charting in more detail.

MARKET PROFILING

Market profiling is a relatively new (1984) and highly sophisticated method of plotting market action and is a truly unique way of organizing and collecting market-generated time, price, and volume information. This method converts the data into recognizable structures based on the bell curve and helps traders decipher and identify where and how buyers and sellers enter the market.

Market profiling effectively organizes price and time information so that traders can see which price levels the market accepts or which price areas the market rejects. Using sophisticated software, market profiling outlines the market's assessment of true value, volume analysis by price level and market participant type, and a long-term overview of the balance and imbalance of buying and selling pressure and its application to long-term and short-term trading strategies.

The Chicago Board of Trade holds copyrights to the data in the Liquidity Data Bank™ (LDB), which is the basis of its marketprofile℠ software. Using the marketprofile program, time brackets are typically assigned to each 15-minute period of trading and then cataloged. (The time bracket period was changed from the original 30 minutes to 15 minutes on January 2, 1990.) For example, the "y" bracket may start at 7 a.m. and go to 7:14:59 a.m. A small "y" is placed at each price increment where a trade occurs during the first 15 minutes of trading and identifies the opening range. The

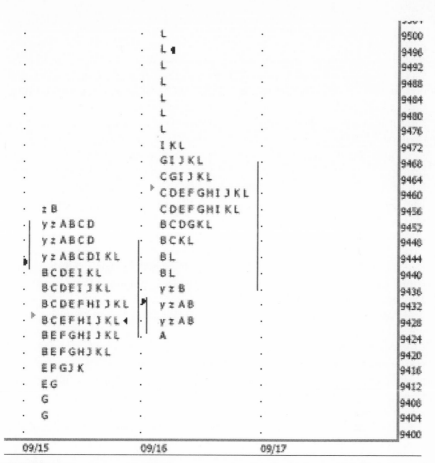

FIGURE 3.9 A mini-sized Dow contract chart using marketprofile[SM] with 30-minute time brackets. (*Source:* eSignal. Reprinted with permission.)

next time bracket is "z," from 7:15 a.m. to 7:29:59 a.m., followed by "A" for 7:30 a.m. to 7:44:59 a.m., "B" for 7:45 a.m. to 7:59:59 a.m., and so on. Figure 3.9 shows two marketprofile days for mini-sized Dow futures, but using the 30-minute time brackets. As trading action unfolds, you can see where the concentration of prices is taking place and what happens when the market approaches a higher or lower price plateau.

Retail traders have paid little attention to this technique, but some exchange members and institutional desk traders use this method to develop a better understanding of market behavior and to find value and trading opportunities. It combines the keys of market analysis—volume and price in a given period—and analyzes acceptance or rejection of a given price level as validated by volume.

While I am on the subject, one reason day traders like intraday charting periods such as 5, 10, or 15 minutes is because they divide the regular trading session equally into the same time periods that make up the marketprofile time brackets on the floor. Even 60-minute charts are just the sum of four complete 15-minute time brackets. You can use 12, 20, 29, or some other odd number of minutes, but if the professional traders are not doing that, then it probably is not a wise decision for you to create some new time division.

The Chicago Board of Trade offers educational materials on market-profile. The Chicago Mercantile Exchange (CME) also has classes on market profiling as well as on candlesticks and other technical analysis areas. Dan Gramza is one of the instructors. If you ever have the opportunity to take a course on trading taught by Gramza, I strongly recommend that you take it. With all the get-rich-quick, hyped-up fluff being marketed by so-called experts these days, it is hard to find a class that can impress a 20-year veteran like myself—you know the expression, "It's hard to teach old dogs new tricks." However, Gramza is more than qualified in market knowledge, and his demeanor and method of teaching are superb.

For a current schedule of classes and the names of instructors, go to www.cme.com and click on "education." In addition to the CME education department, which uses a classroom equipped with unbelievable state-of-the-art equipment and individual computer workstations for each student, some data vendors offer marketprofile as a premium service. CQG (www.cqg.com) and eSignal (www.esignal.com) are among those companies.

CHAPTER 4

Candle Charts

Lighting the Path

War is such that the supreme consideration is speed.

—Sun-tzu, *The Art of Warfare*

M any believe that trading is financial warfare. It is either kill or be killed; the winner is the one who will reap the spoils of war— namely, financial gain. The futures arena, after all, comprises a zero-sum game.

It has been stated that, when there is blood in the water, there may be sharks. In the business of trading, there are many great white sharks lurking in the water. The competition is fierce because this industry attracts the sharpest minds, highly educated individuals, and men and women of varying degrees of moral scruples.

In this business speed sometimes is the supreme consideration when it comes to order execution, not only for entering positions but even for exiting the market. Candle charting, in my opinion, can help speed the analytical process and uncover the psychological or emotional makeup of the market and can give you an edge in seeing the next directional move the market may make.

Japanese candle charts have been receiving increasing notoriety since Steve Nison wrote his first book on the subject in 1991, bringing the concept to the attention of many traders in the West for the first time. I have had the pleasure of working with Steve in a Webinar for the Chicago Board of Trade (CBOT) when we did a presentation combining pivot points (discussed in Chapter 6) and candle charting techniques to help identify market reversals in the CBOT mini-sized Dow futures contract.

I also had Steve on my radio show to help shed light on how he first learned about this advanced and unique method of charting. He explained that a broker in his office at Merrill Lynch had been receiving a chart book from Japan, and he became extremely curious about the formations that the candles made. He took it from there, going to Japan to learn more about charting and devoting many hours to studying this form of technical analysis.

Candle charting originated in Japan centuries ago. It is a method of looking at data differently than what had been developed in western cultures. The advantage of using candle charts in place of bar charts is that you can use the same techniques and analysis as you do on bar charts, and you can enhance that analysis with the diverse and unique signals that candles generate with their more sophisticated, graphic style that allows a quick visual analysis of price action. More and more analysts have turned to candles, so you should at least become aware of what this three-dimensional approach to charting is all about.

ANY MARKET, ANY TIME FRAME

Like a bar chart, each time period produces a price bar called a *candle*. Each candle has a different characteristic that represents the difference or distance between the high, low, open, and close. Candle charting techniques can be used on data from whatever time period you choose—minutes, hours, days, weeks, or months. It lends itself to pattern recognition, trend lines, support and resistance, channel lines, and all the other typical technical analysis features.

Candle analysis usually is not limited to a single candle but is based on several bars forming a pattern and on the location of that candle or pattern within overall market action. First, however, you have to learn how to read one candle.

The key feature of the candle is the *body*, the difference between the open and close prices. Using the conventional way of displaying candles, a dark body indicates that the closing price was below the opening price (Figure 4.1), and a white or hollow body indicates that the closing price was higher than the opening price (Figure 4.2). (Note: Some software vendors use the color red instead of black to designate candles that have a close lower than the open and the color green instead of white or hollow candles that have a close higher than the open. Many software programs allow you to adjust these colors and styles yourself. Check with your software provider.)

A single candle does not tell you if the close is higher or lower than the previous time period, indicating only whether the close is higher or lower than the open for each candle. The emphasis on the body is based on the belief that the most important price action for the period takes place between

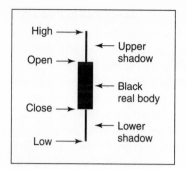

FIGURE 4.1 Close below open.

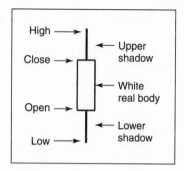

FIGURE 4.2 Close above open.

the open and close while the price action outside the body, the upper and lower *shadows*, is less important.

CANDLE PATTERNS

Individual candles and formations have some very interesting and descriptive names. The *hammer* (Figure 4.3) indicates a reversal or a bottom is near after a downtrend. When a similar candle formation appears after an uptrend, the name transforms into *hanging man* and indicates a top is near. Three main characteristics are needed to hammer in a bottom:

1. The real body is at the upper end of the trading range. The color (white or black) is not important.
2. The lower part, or the shadow, should be at least twice the length of the real body.
3. The body should have little or no upper shadow and look like a shaved-head candle.

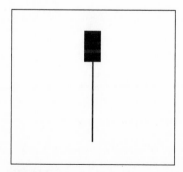

FIGURE 4.3 Hammer.

The *star* (Figure 4.4) appears at the top of an uptrend and can signal a reversal. Again, the color does not matter, but the body should be at the lower end of the trading range with a long upper shadow. The significance here is that it shows the market opened near the low of the day, then had an explosive rally that failed, and closed back down near the low of the day. Usually there is little or no lower shadow, looking like a shaved bottom.

When this pattern is at the bottom of a downtrend, it is called an *inverted hammer*. The color (white or black) is not important. This is not a tremendously reliable candle as a bottom indicator on its own. Usually a white candle opening above the inverted hammer's body in the next trading session can verify the potential buy signal.

Spinning tops (Figure 4.5) have small real bodies usually with small upper and lower shadows. These formations indicate a tug-of-war occurring between buyers and sellers

The *doji* (Figure 4.6) has nearly the same opening and closing price. This candle typically indicates a change of direction. Doji are more powerful as an indicator of a market top, especially after a long white or hollow candle, meaning the market closed above the open during the previous period. Doji signify indecision and uncertainty. They can also indicate bottoms, but more signals are needed to confirm a bottom than just using a doji. There are several types of doji: the *gravestone* (Figure 4.7), *dragonfly* (Figure 4.8), and *rickshaw* (Figure 4.9).

An *evening star* (Figure 4.10) is a three-candle formation that signals a major top. The first candle normally has a tall white or hollow real body. The second candle has a small real body (white or black) that gaps higher and can be a star candle. A doji can also be in the middle; that is considered even more bearish. The third candle has a black body, and the important point here is that it should close well into the first candle's real body.

FIGURE 4.4   Star.

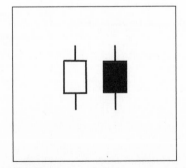

FIGURE 4.5   Spinning tops.

FIGURE 4.6   Doji.

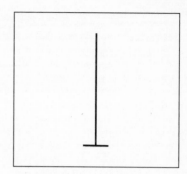

FIGURE 4.7   Gravestone.

FIGURE 4.8   Dragonfly.

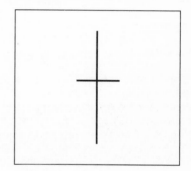

FIGURE 4.9   Rickshaw.

Another example of this type of pattern is the *abandon baby*. It is extremely rare and is a very potent top or bottom signal. Figure 4.11 illustrates the similarities to the evening doji star.

Similar to the evening star, the *morning star* (Figure 4.12) is a major bottom reversal pattern that is a three-candle formation. The first candle has a long black real body. The second candle has a small real body that gaps

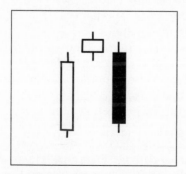

FIGURE 4.10   Evening star.

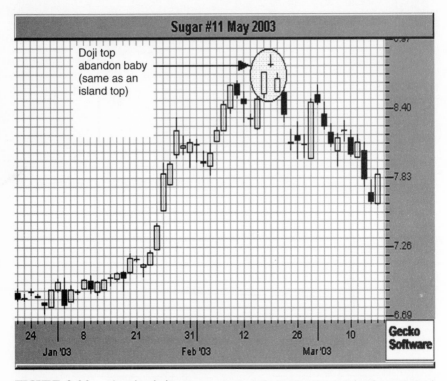

FIGURE 4.11   Abandon baby. (*Source:* Gecko Software, Inc. Reprinted with permission.)

lower than the first candle's body. The third candle's body sometimes gaps higher than the second candle's body, but this does not happen often. It is important that the third candle be a white candle and close well above the midpoint of the first candle's real body.

The *shooting star* (Figure 4.13) is a two-candle pattern. The second candle gaps higher than the prior candle's real body, which is usually a white or hollow candle in an uptrending market. However, the color of the star, or second, candle is not important. This pattern signals that the longs are failing to maintain the upward momentum.

The *bearish engulfing pattern* (Figure 4.14) has a distinct look. The black candle's real body (close lower than the open) completely covers the real body of the previous white or hollow candle (close higher than open). It is important to note that the open is higher than the first candle's real body, and the close is below the lowest portion of the first candle's body. The bearish engulfing pattern occurs during an uptrend and signifies that the momentum may be shifting from the bulls to the bears.

The *bullish engulfing pattern* (Figure 4.15) reverses everything you just read about the bearish engulfing pattern. The real body of a white candle

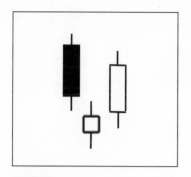

FIGURE 4.12   Morning star.

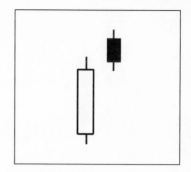

FIGURE 4.13   Shooting star.

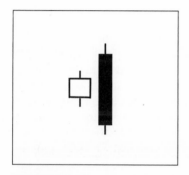

FIGURE 4.14   Bearish
engulfing pattern.

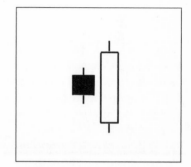

FIGURE 4.15   Bullish
engulfing pattern.

completely covers the previous black candle's real body. It is also relevant to note that the opening is lower than the first candle's real body, and the close is above the high end of the first candle's body. The bullish engulfing pattern appears during a downtrend, signifying that the momentum may be shifting from the bears to the bulls.

The *dark cloud cover* (Figure 4.16) is another bearish reversal signal that usually appears after an uptrend. The first white candle is followed by a black candle. The important features are that the dark candle should open higher than the white candle's high and should close well below the midpoint of the white candle's real body.

The *piercing pattern* (Figure 4.17) can be considered the opposite of the dark cloud cover. The piercing pattern is a bottom-reversing, two-candle pattern. It requires the first candle to be a long dark candle, and the second candle must gap open lower than the first candle's body (lower than the previous bar's close). The other important characteristic is that it closes well above the midpoint of the long, dark first candle.

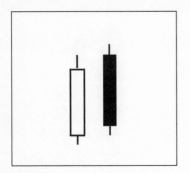

FIGURE 4.16   Dark cloud cover.

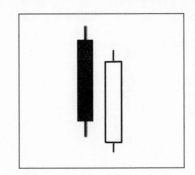

FIGURE 4.17   Piercing pattern.

The *harami* (Figure 4.18) has a small real body that is entirely within the prior candle's body. This is known as a reversal pattern or a warning of a trend change, especially at market tops. It is not important what the colors of the bodies are, but I notice that the more reliable signals are generated when the colors are opposite. If the second candle looks like a doji instead of a spinning top, this would be considered a harami cross. Those are rare and are more powerful sell signals at market tops.

With a *bearish harami cross* (Figure 4.19), a long white candle signifies the market closed above the open with little or no shadows at both ends, followed in the next time period by a doji in the middle of the real white body. Especially after a long advance, this tells me that buyers are changing their minds and the market is changing hands from bulls to bears or sellers are entering the market. If this formation occurred on high volume or at an important pivot point target near the high, a short position would be warranted or,

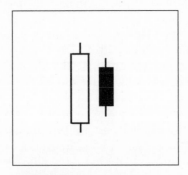

FIGURE 4.18   Harami.

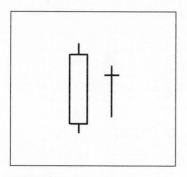

FIGURE 4.19   Bearish
harami cross.

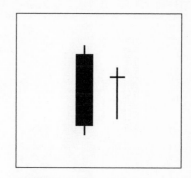

FIGURE 4.20   Bullish harami
cross.

at the least, further examination of a potential shorting opportunity should be explored.

A *bullish harami cross* (Figure 4.20) occurs in a downtrending market, and the exact opposite of a bearish harami would be true. The first candle is usually a long dark candle signifying the market closed below the open with little or no real shadows at both ends, followed in the next trading session by a doji within the real dark body.

The *three crows* (Figure 4.21) pattern has three long or relatively longer than normal candles that close on or near their lows. This pattern can signify a potential top when the market is at a high, especially after a long extended trend.

The *three white or advancing soldiers* (Figure 4.22) generally demonstrates a sign of continuing strength, especially in the beginning stages of an uptrend as prices start to advance from a bottom.

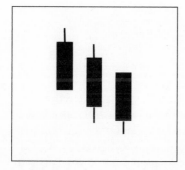

FIGURE 4.21   Three crows.

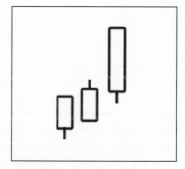

FIGURE 4.22   Three white
soldiers.

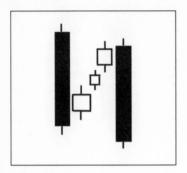

FIGURE 4.23   Bearish falling three.

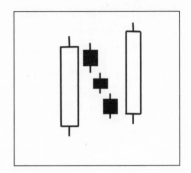

FIGURE 4.24   Bullish rising three.

The *bearish falling three method* (Figure 4.23) is a bearish continuation pattern often associated with a bear flag formation on a bar chart. The pattern starts with a long dark or black candle followed by three white candles that close higher than the open. The three little candles usually remain within the range of the first black candle, including both the real body and shadows. Some argue that this pattern works with just two candles in the middle, but the actual textbook classification is three white candles. The last portion of this formation is a long dark candle that closes below the first black candle's close. This continuation pattern indicates prices will continue lower.

The *bullish rising three method* (Figure 4.24) is a bullish continuation pattern with the same characteristics as the bearish falling three method but with just the opposite types of candles. During the beginning stages of an advancing price trend, an unusually long white candle is followed by three smaller dark or black candles that stay within the range of the first long white candle. The last candle is a powerful advancing white candle that should open above the previous session's close and should close above the first long white candle's close as well. This is like a bull flag formation on western bar charts and often indicates still higher prices to come.

READING CANDLE CHARTS

Now it's time to look at the charts to see these candle patterns in action. Figure 4.25 provides an excellent opportunity to examine several topping and bottoming formations in Treasury bond futures. The first one highlighted is a shooting star formation, indicating that a top in the bond market was developing. As a general guideline, market tops take more time to develop than market bottoms. To illustrate this point, note the retest of the high that forms a secondary bearish pattern, a bearish engulfing candle.

FIGURE 4.25 Candle tops and bottoms. (*Source:* FutureSource. Reprinted with permission.)

Let's focus on the meaning of this candle. The challenge of the bulls' resolve to move the price higher is defeated by sellers when the price cannot successfully reach and surpass a new high. The significance of the secondary pattern is that it reinforces the first bearish pattern and graphically illustrates the market's rejection of an attempt to reach a higher price. It shows that buyers were liquidating longs not only when near the close of the previous day but also below the open of the previous day. That clearly shows sellers wanted to exit the door in a hurry.

With that signal, you can develop a trading plan to sell short in whatever form of trading vehicle that may be—selling futures, buying puts, taking a reverse position in an opposite-like trading market such as a long stock position, and the like. You might decide, for example, to sell below the low of the bearish engulfing candle. In this example, I would want to place a stop above the high of the shooting star candle and then trail the stop lower according to your comfort level. (Stop placement techniques are covered in more detail later in Chapter 12.)

The reverse of a shooting star formation is the hammer, which sets the bottom for the market. As the shooting star indicated a top, the hammer is a reliable bottom reversal candle. Look at the normal ranges for the majority of the candles in the downtrend, and you will not see a candle with a similar range and that long a lower shadow. The uniqueness of the hammer candle after a long downdraft is the first clue that a bottom is in place. The same type of price action occurred as with the shooting start but in reverse: Sellers were drying up, and buyers took over as market participants accepted the low in price.

You may also hear terms for such conditions as a *blow-off top* or *exhaustion* momentum patterns. These labels indicate that the price move or trend has run its course and is ready for a reversal.

Figure 4.26 provides a valuable lesson for the importance of multiple engulfing candles or more time periods that were consumed by one so-called benchmark candle—in this case, we'll call it a *pillar of strength*. In this significant and powerful reversal formation, notice that it takes only one candle to reverse the price action from the three previous periods. The long

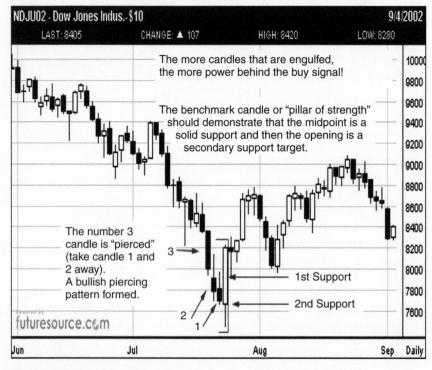

FIGURE 4.26   Pillar of strength. (*Source:* FutureSource. Reprinted with permission.)

white candle engulfed the preceding number 1 and number 2 candles and then penetrated and closed at the midpoint of candle number 3. This occurrence makes a valuable point: The more candles that are engulfed, the more power behind the signal.

With a benchmark, cornerstone, or pillar of strength candle (the reverse would be a *pillar of weakness* for a bearish engulfing pattern), the midpoint of the candle is a target for the first support level. The opening should always be considered the second level of support or the last bastion for a bullish defense line. Note on the chart how the first support point held the corrective pullback during the first few days in August as the price came back down to retest that midpoint and then shot back up to continue the advance.

Figure 4.27 shows another example of a pillar of strength bullish engulfing pattern on the cocoa futures chart. Notice the market retests the low (point A) several sessions later as a hammer candle forms. The shadow is about twice the measurement of the real body. The candle preceding the

FIGURE 4.27   Consuming candles. (*Source:* FutureSource. Reprinted with permission.)

hammer is a doji. That alone is a warning signal that a potential change in direction is coming.

Look at how the pattern develops: doji, hammer, hammer, dark spinning top, dark candle (lower close than open), and then the pillar of strength. That single benchmark candle consumed the real bodies of four previous candles. What a setup! The double bottom or, in essence, a triple bottom indicated the bottoming pattern was finalized with the benchmark candle. That area of congestion where smaller real bodies were consumed was the final blow for the bears. Remember, the benchmark candle should provide the first support level at about the middle of the range of its real body. In this case, a retest of that level never happened.

Let's look at shooting stars as reliable top reversal candles. On the example silver futures chart shown as Figure 4.28, I identified a shooting star followed by a potential doji in January 2002 (last two candles on right side) after about a seven-week run to the upside. This market was due for a correction. I had made a sell recommendation in a weekly newsletter, *The Bottom Line Financial and Futures Report*. That formation indicated that a

FIGURE 4.28   Shooting star top in silver. (*Source:* FutureSource. Reprinted with permission.)

tug-of-war was going on between the bulls and the bears, and that a top had formed based on those combined candles. More important, I had a second-opinion indicator using pivot point analysis (discussed in detail in Chapter 6).

Look at the after picture (Figure 4.29). It shows a powerful selling wave took command of the price in silver after this topping pattern occurred.

The weekly U.S. Dollar Index futures chart (Figure 4.30) illustrates that candle chart patterns work not only on daily charts but for other time periods as well. This chart is a great example of a market that had multiple trading signals. Look at the shooting star formation that exposed the turning point for the market during the first week in July. The next candle was a hanging man that certainly warned that the trend was changing. The aftermath was a complete market reversal that resulted in a 950-point decline within 2½ months.

Look at the bearish harami that formed at the end of January. The market had made a long advance over nearly four months, and a long white candle formed (meaning the market closed above the open and there were little or no shadows). The next candle was a doji where the market had a wide

FIGURE 4.29   The market flamed out. (*Source:* FutureSource. Reprinted with permission.)

FIGURE 4.30   Candles signal changing trends. (*Source:* FutureSource. Reprinted with permission.)

range but closed at or near the open. Another observation is that the market was forming a major double top with the June high.

A plan of attack might be to sell short a position and place an initial stop as a close-only order above the January high. The reason I would have used that as my risk target is that if the market retested that high, I would not want to be stopped out and then have to watch the market price fall off from the high. I would want to be out only if a new all-time high close above that level signaled the market's acceptance of a new high price and would probably advance to newer highs.

Eight to ten new records is one candle formation that I have not used often but does warrant mentioning. According to Japanese candle charting practices, when the market price either advances or declines by making eight to ten new highs or lows, it can signal that the advance or decline should subside. Such an occurrence could warrant establishing a position. In a bearish market, for example, when the eighth or ninth new low occurs and a bullish candle such as a hammer or a doji appears within one or two days, then a bottom potentially could be formed. I would construe that as a buy signal and put a stop close-only order below the lowest low. If the market truly is ready to turn around, it should not close below the established low at that time. The opposite is true for bullish or advancing markets.

Look at the weekly U.S. Dollar Index chart again (Figure 4.30). If you count how many higher highs were made after the low in September 2001, you will see that nine record highs occurred prior to a bearish harami cross in early 2002. The ninth high was actually made by a doji. This confirmation by a different technique should have helped to initiate a response such as developing a short trading strategy. In addition to just selling a futures position, a trader is now armed with a good indication that the market may fall and may decide instead to buy put options, sell calls, or form some other bearish option strategy.

Now examine Figure 4.31 for the after picture. Remember, this is a weekly chart so this move did not just happen overnight. Also, note that another eight to ten new records situation developed again on the downtrend in the first half of 2002. This chart demonstrates that candle patterns do work on different time frames.

FIGURE 4.31 Broken records. (*Source:* FutureSource. Reprinted with permission.)

A casual investor who may want to pick trades more carefully should be aware of the eight to ten new records high or low technique. When analyzing markets and trading for profits, the more studies that can strengthen your conviction or give you more confidence to do the trade and or stay with a position, the better.

The bearish harami cross is a short seller's most powerful weapon. The U.S. Dollar Index chart (Figure 4.31) provides a dynamic example of this trading signal. The fact is that the longer the time period, the longer the trade signal may work.

Looking at a shorter time frame, a bearish harami on a 15-minute chart for the Dow Jones Industrial Average futures contract (Figure 4.32) warned that a short-term uptrend might be coming to an end. The long white candle is followed by a doji, which forms the two-candle harami cross pattern. The next candle is another doji, which appears to be the straw that breaks the bulls' backs as they toss in the towel.

The bearish harami cross is confirmed by yet another formation, a bearish engulfing pattern. Notice that the long dark candle engulfs the preceding white candle plus the prior two dojis and even closes below the open, close,

FIGURE 4.32 Crossing sign. (*Source:* FutureSource. Reprinted with permission.)

and low for all three of those time frames. That bearish engulfing pattern—or "tower of weakness" as I call it—was the sell signal that indicated you should head for the hills if you were long or to sell and then place stops above the high of that move. At the very least, identifying this sequence of patterns may have kept you from staying long or, worse yet, buying the high of that move.

CANDLES PLUS

Various candle patterns alone provide excellent trading signals for any time frame. In addition, however, you should be using other technical studies such as stochastics and moving averages or perhaps moving average convergence/divergence (MACD) as well as pivot point analysis to help give you the confidence you need to execute a trade. Once you have the knowledge that you need to identify what the formation means as market conditions change, you will understand when and why to enter a trade or to bail out of a position.

To further highlight my point about using different time frames and techniques, let's look at three charts for Japanese yen futures. First, let me make a few observations about the foreign exchange market, the largest financial market in the world with a daily turnover of more than $1.5 trillion. Forex markets have no physical location and no central exchange, operating through an electronic network of banks, corporations, and individuals trading one currency against another.

Forex trading has increased tremendously since the late 1990s as more individual traders have become aware of currency fluctuations and the advantages of cash forex trading over trading in currency futures. In addition to 24-hour trading, most forex firms do not charge commissions or exchange fees but pick up profits from their bid/ask spreads. Most forex dealers offer free real-time quotes, charts, and online order entry platforms all on one screen and provide demo accounts to practice trading with free real-time quotes. One such company, Proedgefx.com, handles substantial volume and offers some of the tightest spreads in the industry.

Technical traders are attracted to the forex market because candlestick charting and almost all forms of technical analysis work with this incredibly liquid market, because substantial leverage is available, and because trends can persist for many months or even years due to the influence of government policies and political pressures. As participants, hedge funds and large financial institutions also tend to exert their influence to keep currency values in line. Many U.S. forex firms are now registered with and regulated by the Commodity Futures Trading Commission and National Futures Association.

The chart examples used here, however, show the yen futures contract traded at the Chicago Mercantile Exchange, the finest exchange in the world for currency trading for a position trader or someone who wants to trade options on currencies. The first is a monthly chart (Figure 4.33) of the Japanese yen from late 1996 through February 2002. What does this chart reveal to you? Some might conclude that the lows in 1998 could be retested and that the market has more room to go lower. However, I saw an area where the 2002 market was testing the lows of the moving averages in 1998, not the actual lows. Go back in time and think what was happening in 1998—the Asian financial crisis, Long-Term Capital Management hedge fund collapse, the Fed lowered interest rates, and Japanese Central Bank intervention was helping to prop up the yen.

The second chart (Figure 4.34) is a daily chart of the March yen contract that indicates a potential bottom forming in February 2002. A potential bullish piercing pattern and the inability of the market to show any follow-through weakness near a substantial low pretty well gave a clue that a benchmark low was being established.

FIGURE 4.33   Monthly yen: What does it say? (*Source:* FutureSource. Reprinted with permission.)

FIGURE 4.34   Daily yen: Go long? (*Source:* FutureSource. Reprinted with permission.)

One more aspect about deciding on the future price direction of this market was that the overall pessimism of analysts, traders, and the media was high. *Bullish Consensus* and the Commodity Futures Trading Commission's *Commitments of Traders* report revealed that large and small speculators were mostly short this market and that commercial traders were long. (These reports are discussed in detail in Chapter 9.)

Here's a summary of how a decision was made to go long or to buy call options:

- The investment community was extremely bearish.
- The monthly long-term chart showed the current market price was digging into the area where the moving average lows (not price lows) had occurred in 1998.
- The daily chart was demonstrating that prices were supported near the 7450 level.
- On a fundamental note, the Japanese Central Bank was intervening to support the yen's value, adding a strong buying force to the market mix.

Now you have a market that has made a significant decline back down to an area where governments step in to provide price protection and the speculating community was bearish after the fact. The daily candle charts were signaling to me that the downmove was subsiding. The third chart (Figure 4.35) shows what had happened on the June yen chart and why it helps not to get too "bearish in the hole." The fact that the charts from different time frames helped me conclude that a buying opportunity might exist was also the correct call.

The move that occurred between the 7450 and 7950 levels resulted in a short, sharp 500-point rally. Notice that it took this market nearly another month to begin moving, but move it did! Of course, you might say, "Well, that was too long to wait around to make money." Fine. The important point is that you can see that selling short would have been a bad decision with prices near the 7450 area. This type of charting analysis may not have gotten you to buy the low and stay with the position, but I do believe that by checking different time periods you would not have sold short either, risking a lot of money.

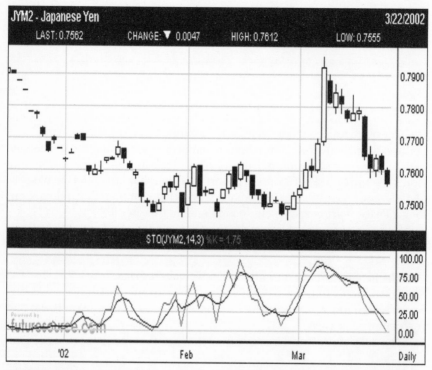

FIGURE 4.35   Daily yen: getting the reward. (*Source:* FutureSource. Reprinted with permission.)

The weekly bond chart (Figure 4.36) provides another example of multiple candle patterns that come together to confirm price direction and give you confidence to act to stay on the right side of the market. The morning doji star that formed in March signaled that a major bottom was in place and gave a clear buy signal. Then the continuation pattern of a rising three method provided a clue that the trend was going to continue. Acting like the western bull flag formation, this pattern projected prices would reach the 108 level. As you can see from the chart, that price objective was attained, plus another 5 points.

One other point about different time frames: If it takes, for example, three time frames for a pattern to develop, it usually takes at least three or more time frames for the results—in this case, the price advance—to develop.

These aren't the only candle chart patterns and signals. However, if you would like more information on the complexities of this technique and want to continue your studies in this field, I can refer you to several books on this

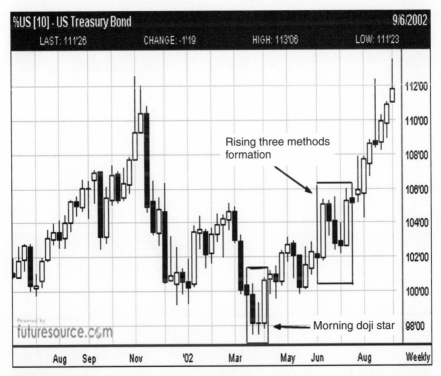

FIGURE 4.36   Multiple buy patterns in bonds. (*Source:* FutureSource. Reprinted with permission.)

subject. Start with *Japanese Candlestick Charting Techniques* by Steve Nison. Then study his other book, *Beyond Candlesticks,* or his recent video course. Libraries often have copies of these books, or you can go to a bookstore or to www.candlecharts.com to buy a copy for your personal library.

Also, as mentioned in Chapter 3, if you ever have the opportunity to take a trading course taught by Dan Gramza, I strongly recommend that you consider taking it.

One final point: Like other techniques, candle chart analysis is not an exact science. It is always necessary to validate signals and chart patterns manually, even when you have expert software designed to identify various patterns for you. I still believe the best way to get a feel for the market and to watch for certain identifiable patterns is by looking at the chart and incorporating other techniques such as moving averages and other forms of technical analysis for confirmation of a tradable setup. Looking at a chart with the pivot point numbers in front of you allows a more three-dimensional look into daily, weekly, or monthly price projections that could be of immeasurable value to your trading.

CHAPTER 5

Chart Analysis

*Volume, Open Interest,
Price Patterns*

*Choose a job you love, and you will never have to
work a day in your life.*

—Confucius

Now we are getting to the real meat and potatoes of technical analysis. This chapter explains and illustrates the importance of various chart patterns and analysis typically associated with bar charting but applicable to other types of analysis as well.

We look first at volume and open interest, two items included on many data services but which, for the most part, seem to be ignored by a lot of individual traders with whom I have talked. These are important tools so let's review the basics.

VOLUME

Volume is simply the number of trades executed during a specified period—one trader buys and one trader sells and the volume is one. The volume figure usually released by the exchange is a total for all of the contract months of a given market. For example, if the e-mini S&P trades the March, June, September, and December contract months, the volume represents the total of all the trades, long and short combined, for all the months.

Most technical analysts believe that volume is an indicator of the strength of a market trend. Because it is also a relative measure of the dominant behavior of the market, analysts regard volume as an important aspect of analysis, particularly when trading stocks. Futures exchanges do not release volume figures for a regular session until the next day for many contracts. As a result, futures traders have had to adapt by using other methods to detect market strength such as pivot point analysis, moving average studies, Bollinger bands, or simply chart pattern recognition skills. When the volume numbers are released by the exchanges, they can be used to verify the trend or price action from a daily charting perspective.

John Bollinger, one of my radio show guests, contends that "volume is everything," especially when combined with a trading tool such as Bollinger bands, which he developed, or Larry Williams's accumulation/distribution indicator. In fact, Bollinger, who has a Chartered Market Technician designation from the Market Technicians Association and has been an analyst for FNN and CNBC, calls volume "the crux of analysis." He also suggests that one of the best things a new trader can do to learn about the markets is to take a course in human psychology at a local community college. Bollinger has a wealth of technical knowledge, so his opinion is widely respected.

Volume is important because it is a measurement of the market's acceptance or rejection of price at a specific level and time. There are several guidelines for using volume analysis on price charts. The first one is that if a market is increasing in price and volume is increasing, the market is considered to be in a bullish mode and can support further price increases. The exact opposite is true for a declining market. However, if a substantial daily market price increase or decrease occurs after a long steady uptrend or downtrend and has an unusually high volume period, it is considered to be a blow-off top or bottom and can signal a market turning point or trend reversal.

OPEN INTEREST

Open interest reveals the total number of positions that are still open and outstanding, that is, they have not been closed by an offsetting trade or delivered upon. Remember, futures trading is a zero-sum game so that for every long there is a short and for every short there is a long—a buyer for every seller and a seller for every buyer. The open interest figure represents the longs or shorts but not the total of both.

Consider it like a money flow indicator. The general guideline for open interest is that when prices rise and open interest increases, this activity suggests that more new longs have entered the market and more new money is flowing into the market, reflecting why the price increased. Of course, the exact opposite is true in a declining market.

PUTTING THE DATA TOGETHER

The value of open interest figures comes from combining them with both price movement and data from volume to evaluate the condition of the market. If there is a price increase on strong volume and open interest increases, then this is a signal that there is more buying interest that could mean a continued trend advance. If prices increase but volume stays relatively flat or declines and open interest declines, then this reflects a weakening market condition. This is considered to be a bearish situation because the combination of rising prices and declining open interest indicates that shorts are covering by buying back their positions rather than new longs entering the market. That activity would give a trader a clue that there is a potential trend reversal coming.

It is important to understand the concept of matching price and trading activity. If you are watching a continuing long-term trend in a futures contract, whether the direction is up or down, and prices start to fluctuate with wider than normal daily swings or ranges—that is, extremely volatile movements—combined with unusually strong volume and a decline in open interest, you may be in a climaxing market condition and seeing a clue for a potential major trend reversal coming. Figure 5.1 shows an example that marked the end of a bull market in bond futures.

It appears that bond traders who were short threw in the towel by buying to cover their positions and that the longs took profits by selling out of their positions. All of this activity would explain the higher than normal volume. When the longs liquidated their positions, this was reflected by a decline in open interest.

As for the wild price advance, shorts were bailing out of the market almost in a panic state of mind, and longs were not willing to sell too cheap, explaining the upward price behavior. These three characteristics are needed to complete a climaxing top or bottom. Most volume and open interest followers watch for this setup as a major sell signal. This condition is exactly what happened to the bonds, producing a truly remarkable textbook sell signal.

These concepts of volume and open interest can help any trader understand the underlying market condition and the current trend. With that information, you may decide to buy dips instead of selling intraday rallies.

The fact that the exchanges do not publish open interest data for many markets until the following day at about noon is a problem for analysts. Estimated volume figures are available after the markets close but not the actual numbers. Most financial papers report the information the day after that. So it is important to know where to get the information faster than by reading it in the newspaper. If you want to learn to become an avid disciple of

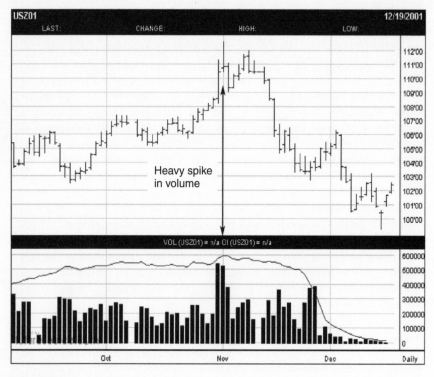

FIGURE 5.1   Spiking a bond bull. (*Source:* FutureSource. Reprinted with permission.)

charting and want information on volume and open interest sooner, you can go the exchange web sites.

CHART PATTERNS

Chart pattern recognition, without a doubt, provides a true sense of price forecasting, but it works significantly better in hindsight than it does in anticipating a price pattern for the future. You can watch for many patterns or formations on a typical bar chart, formations that have certain predictable qualities as you try to forecast a future price move. But chart analysis is like being an artist trying to paint a picture that some other artist started, illustrating why technical analysis is considered to be an art form rather than a work of science.

At the very least, chart pattern recognition is a subjective method open to different interpretations by different individuals. Every trader has to do his or her own homework. I might see a head-and-shoulders top pattern; you might be anticipating a long-term double bottom. Who is going to be right, only the markets will tell.

Good brokers may point out to their customers some opportunities that exist in the market, but really good brokers will insist that customers do their own homework and look at a chart themselves. The problem is that some customers don't know how or even what to look at! This book is intended to help those people.

The real essence of trading is to buy near levels of support and to sell near levels of resistance. The task of the analyst is to find out what is support and what is resistance. The job of a trader is to capture the market's reaction off those levels and profit from it.

This chapter shows you what I believe are the more reliable and popular chart patterns and how they can be effective in identifying support and resistance levels. More important is which ones generate reliable buy and sell signals. It was once told to me that the most reliable signal is the one that doesn't work. At the time I thought that didn't make sense until I understood why there are no guarantees in this business. Remembering that nothing is 100 percent reliable in technical analysis or in trading, let's look at some chart formations, and you can test for yourself what you see.

M Tops, W Bottoms, or 1-2-3 Patterns

One of the more reliable chart patterns is a *W bottom*, also known as a *double bottom*, with a higher right-side breakout. You want to be sensitive to this chart pattern because it has a higher frequency of occurring, but you want to make a note: Not all W bottoms break out to the upside or have the same type of reaction off the bottom.

The cocoa chart provided as Figure 5.2 illustrates how this pattern forms. Price makes a low after a downtrend (point 1), then rallies to make a reactionary high (point 2). Then the price falls back again to retest the low but does not go as low as the previous low (point 3), followed by another price rally that goes beyond the first reactionary high, generating a buy signal. In this case, the W or 1-2-3 formation was confirmed once the market closed above the November 1 high (point 2).

The inverse of this pattern is dubbed an *M top* or *1-2-3 swing top formation*. The market hits a high, sets back to an interim low, rallies but does not exceed the earlier high, and falls back below the interim low, the point at which a sell signal is generated.

Head-and-Shoulders Tops or Bottoms

The *head-and-shoulders top* or *inverted head-and-shoulders bottom* can be used not only to indicate price direction but also as a measuring or

FIGURE 5.2   W reversal. (*Source:* FutureSource. Reprinted with permission.)

projecting indicator (Figure 5.3). Head-and-shoulder tops or bottoms are considered to be a strong indicator of major trend reversals, depending on how the market reacts at the neckline of the pattern.

Four components are involved. Looking at the topping version of the pattern, first, the left shoulder is formed as prices rally and then fall back. Second, the market rallies again and a higher high occurs, forming the head. Third, prices slip back, reaching a low that about matches the previous low; rally to about the same height as the left shoulder high; then sink back again to the earlier lows, forming the right shoulder. The fourth element is the so-called neckline, a trend line along the bottoms of the two lows. If prices drop below the neckline, the reversing action of the head-and-shoulders topping pattern is completed, and prices are expected to continue to move lower after what is usually a tug-of-war in the vicinity of the neckline.

The symmetry or distance is important in the head-and-shoulders pattern. The distance from the left shoulder to the head should be about the same as the distance from the head to the right shoulder. The levels of the shoulder highs should be about the same as should the levels of the lows

FIGURE 5.3   Head-and-shoulders measurement. (*Source:* FutureSource. Reprinted with permission.)

that form the neckline. Next, if you measure the distance from the shoulder highs (some analysts use the top of the head) to the neckline and subtract that distance from the neckline, the result is the next price target level.

You can use the same type of process with an inverted head-and-shoulders bottom to project where the next higher price target should be.

Gap Analysis

The definition of a *gap* for a technical analyst is an area on a chart that is left blank when the market trades from one period to another above or below the previous time period's high or low price range. Gaps do occur frequently in illiquid markets and, thus, have no importance to you. However, when gaps occur in liquid markets and on high volume, those are the gaps on which you want to focus.

Gaps have several classifications and meanings. First, there are the *common gaps,* which are usually insignificant and are filled by prices retreating into the gap sometime down the road as they retest that price area. Previous levels left from gaps are considered targets of support when they are below the current market price or targets of resistance when they are above the current market price. The theory is that it took considerable energy to jump from one point to the next to create the gap in the first place. Returning back to that level is considered completing unfinished business.

The next type of gap often comes in a series of three (Figure 5.4). The *breakaway gap*, as its name implies, signals a break from the previous price direction and the beginning of a new direction. It usually occurs at an area of congestion near a top or bottom. The second gap in this series is the *midpoint* or *measuring gap*. That terminology again is probably self-explanatory as it signals that the move is about half over—that is, you can measure the distance from the first gap to the second and use that distance to get an idea where the market is headed. The third gap in this series is the *exhaustion gap*, which signals that market participants are tired and capitulating. It usually indicates that a directional trend is completed and a turning point is coming.

To illustrate a point about the validity of multiple verification techniques, not only were the three gaps on the sugar chart (Figure 5.4) present and ob-

FIGURE 5.4   Three gaps down. (*Source:* FutureSource. Reprinted with permission.)

vious but the distance of the gaps was essential in determining the bottom as well. In addition, the monthly pivot point support number was 6.09. The actual low was 6.11! But we'll get to pivot point analysis in Chapter 6. The soybean chart (Figure 5.5) also identifies a three-gap series clearly, in this case, in an uptrend. Identifying the three gaps may not have convinced you to enter a long position in soybeans, but I believe that if you identified them, it would have at least prevented you from going long at the top.

The last classification of gaps and the most powerful of all gap formations is the *island pattern* that occurs at a top or bottom. In an island top, the market gaps up from a previous bar, trades at the higher level for a bar or maybe a few bars, and then leaves a gap below the previous bar's range as prices collapse into a downtrend. It is a combination of an exhaustion gap on the upside and a breakaway on the downside and leaves a block of price action isolated by a void. The more popular islands stay within a three-bar period, but some technicians believe that price action over several days and even weeks can still form the island pattern.

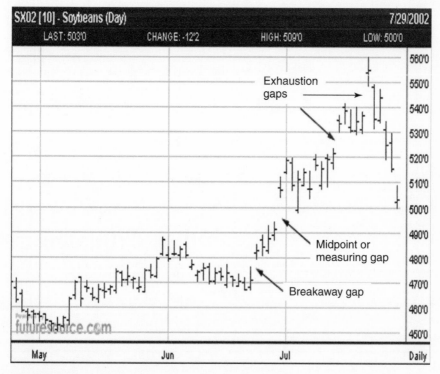

FIGURE 5.5 Three gaps up. (*Source:* FutureSource. Reprinted with permission.)

Islands generate a very strong signal and should not be ignored, as suggested by the island bottom on the sugar futures chart shown as Figure 5.6.

Trend Line Analysis

Trend lines are the simplest, most basic means of market analysis but get at the essence of what analysis and trading are all about. Identifying whether the market is moving up, down, or sideways and being able to profit from that information is the goal of every trader.

To draw a simple trend line, all you do is connect the dots, so to speak. For an uptrend, you just draw a line from one low on the chart to the next major low. The simple definition of an uptrend is a series of higher lows and higher highs.

Trend line analysis can be applied several ways in making a trading decision. Some traders use trend line breaks to enter a position. Others use the trend line as support in an uptrend, entering a long position when the price is near the extended support line. Others note that when prices get

FIGURE 5.6   Stranded on an island. (*Source:* FutureSource. Reprinted with permission.)

too far away from a trend line, they are likely to revert back to the trend line. For example, in late May silver futures prices moved way off the trend line formed during April and early May (Figure 5.7). When the market blasted up to the $5.17 high in early June (also a nice example of an evening star formation, by the way), notice how prices came back to the extended trend line.

Trading using trend line analysis is relatively simple but, like any other type of analysis, is not foolproof. Even if you have defined exactly where a trend line for an uptrend will intersect with prices on the chart, prices may not quite reach that point, leaving your order unfilled, or they may break through a support line and just keep going down, leaving you with a loss.

Again, a reminder: Technical analysis is not an exact science. Consider the trend line as only a guide to the direction of market prices.

One situation that deserves some discussion is the test of broken support. When long-term support lines are broken, traders usually talk about a breakout occurring. The momentum of the market causes prices to drop dramatically, and the price decline often is exaggerated. What can happen to

FIGURE 5.7   Sticking to the trend. (*Source:* FutureSource. Reprinted with permission.)

traders if they chase the market after the move has occurred is that when they sell short, they usually get filled at the low of that move.

If you study charts and trend lines, you will see that, in most cases, the market will try to retest the area from which it fell. In other words, once the support line is broken, the market will try to revisit that area, and the old support now becomes a new resistance level. The gold chart provided as Figure 5.8 shows how prices broke the uptrend line, only to come back to test it three days later. If you had been chasing the market, you might be short from the $310 to the $315 area instead of waiting for that retest near $325. Look at the results shown in Figure 5.9. A double top forms with a bearish dark candle signal, and the price fails from the retest of the support/resistance line.

Trend line analysis is a necessary foundation tool to help identify other chart patterns that develop from significant support and resistance price levels. It is subjective. What I see on the charts could be completely different from what you see. But that is one facet of what makes markets. The mar-

FIGURE 5.8   Test and retesting the trend line. (*Source:* FutureSource. Reprinted with permission.)

FIGURE 5.9   Tumble from a retest zone. (*Source:* FutureSource. Reprinted with permission.)

ket will judge who is right and who is wrong. The technical analyst just wants to follow the trend and profit from it. It is very important that you learn these charting techniques for yourself.

Trend Channels

Trend channels are self-explanatory—the market bounces between two parallel trend lines defined by the highs and lows that form the support and resistance boundaries. The trick is to successfully identify the support or resistance lines early in the channel's development. Once they are established, traders can go long or buy near the support line or sell short or liquidate longs near resistance lines. The element of risk is that the market breaks out from this channel or band.

Chartists can trade another method using these so-called bands: Buy once the market breaks out above the resistance line and sell when the market breaks below the support line. Keep in mind that once the market breaks out above or below its trading range, it generally will try to retest the original trend, as Figure 5.9, the weekly gold chart, and Figure 5.10, the S&P 500 hourly chart, illustrate.

Points A and B identify the uptrend on the S&P chart. Notice how the market danced or bounced off the trend line from point C to point D, a great example of the axiom, "What was once support is now resistance."

Triangle Chart Patterns

Charts display a number of triangle patterns, which usually reflect some type of congestion area or indecision about prices. There are three main types of triangles: symmetrical, ascending, and descending (Figure 5.11).

The *symmetrical triangle* is also known as a *pennant* or a *coiling formation* as the pattern forms from a series of highs that are lower than the preceding high and a series of lows that are higher than the preceding low. Triangles form as the market consolidates while market participants are deciding whether to commit to a position or add to positions already established. This so-called timeout period usually involves a decline in volatility.

FIGURE 5.10 Trending channels. (*Source:* FutureSource. Reprinted with permission.)

FIGURE 5.11   Multiple triangles. (*Source:* FutureSource. Reprinted with permission.)

Ascending triangles indicate an upward bias, with a flat top and a series of higher lows. Generally, the bottom slope of the triangle coincides with the trend or a trend to be. The example on the soybean chart (Figure 5.11), coming after an island gap and a gap higher, indicates a very strong upside reaction could occur, which, in fact, did happen. In this case, the market was too impatient to fill in the entire triangle with price action between the flat top resistance line and the upward sloping support line to complete the price action to form the apex of the triangle.

Similarly, the *descending triangle* indicates a downward bias—a flat bottom support off which prices bounce for a time and a series of lower highs that come together into an apex. It also flows with the direction of the trend or the trend to be.

As a rule, triangles are used as continuation patterns and serve as a measuring guide for the extent of a move. The length of time it takes the triangle or congestion area to form is regarded as the distance a market will move once it breaks out of the triangle pattern. The more powerful breakouts seem to occur when the triangle does not entirely complete the coiling process to the apex or tip of the triangle—the market appears to be impatient to advance or continue the move, as with the ascending triangle on the soybean chart (Figure 5.11).

If you buy the upside breakout of a symmetrical triangle in an uptrending market, then you should place a stop below the first low point that establishes the bottom support line. The reverse is true when you sell a downside breakout in a downtrend.

Here is a cautionary note: Triangles, just like other techniques, are not a completely reliable trading pattern. They do have false breakouts, and traders need to be aware that the longer the triangle takes to form, the less power the breakout usually has behind it. Generally speaking, based on a daily chart time frame, triangles can take 6 to 10 trading days or up to 2 weeks to develop, occasionally even longer. They can develop on intraday charts such as 15-minute and even 60-minute charts, and they can show up on weekly charts.

Monthly charts occasionally show triangles, but considering the length of time and rolling out of expired contracts in commodity markets, triangles are not so prevalent in my research. Due to the difference of seasonal price pressures on most commodities—harvest supply pressures for agriculture products, for example—pricing of deferred contracts makes triangles on monthly charts ineffective, in my opinion.

Wedge Patterns

Wedge patterns are simply longer extensions of the triangle. These patterns often form in the direction of the trend, meaning a rising wedge would form in an uptrend. The difference between a wedge and the triangle, in addition to taking longer to form, is that the market trades so that prices do not form a pattern anywhere close to the apex of the wedge.

The Eurodollar chart shown as Figure 5.12 illustrates a long-term price wedge. The trend is up, and notice how the pattern forms with increasing lows above support and decreasing highs below resistance. The distance of the wedge opening added to the point of the breakout, which occurs in mid-April, is the extension or measuring distance you can use to determine a price objective. This measurement is not an absolute rule of wedges as they can vary in length and size. If a chart pattern appears to be an elongated triangle but looks more like a flattened angle, then it is considered a wedge formation.

Diamond Formations

Diamonds provide another measuring technique that is reliable, but they are a rare occurrence. Most times they are considered a topping pattern, sort of like a head-and-shoulders top. They rarely show up as bottom patterns, but

FIGURE 5.12 Wedge measurement. (*Source:* FutureSource. Reprinted with permission.)

they can and do act as continuation patterns. When acting as a continuation pattern, you should consider them as a bull flag except the formation takes the shape of a diamond (Figure 5.13). The distance from the base of the move in March to the height of the diamond was the measurement you could have used to project the distance from the point of the breakout or the end point of the diamond to derive a price objective.

Flag Formations

Flags are much more common than the diamond or some other formations. Flags can be seen on five-minute to weekly charts and on rising or declining trends. In a rising market, the base of the flag is the starting point for a substantial price advance (or decline in the case of a bear flag formation). It is then followed by erratic and choppy downward price action that lasts for several time periods—a consolidation period or a timeout while the market sorts out buying and selling pressure. The flag usually forms a smaller countertrend that serves as a correction or a pause in a price trend before prices usually continue on in the direction from which they entered the

FIGURE 5.13   Diamond measurement. (*Source:* FutureSource. Reprinted with permission.)

flag formation. A flag on a daily chart can take as little as three to five days or as long as five weeks to form as the soybean chart provided as Figure 5.14 confirms. Of course, on an intraday chart whatever time period you are using would require at least three to five bars to form.

As a measuring technique, analysts take the distance from the bottom of the flagpole to the top of the pole. Then take that distance and extend it up (or down for a bear trend) from the bottom of the flag to get an idea how far prices will move (some add the flagpole distance to the breakout point to arrive at a price objective). Another old-time adage is that the flag flies at half-mast—that is, it is at the halfway point of an extended move—so you can expect prices to advance above the flag (in a bull trend) by the same distance as they moved up below the flag.

Pennants

Pennants are in the same category as a flag formation except that the shape of the consolidation area more closely resembles a triangle although it is

FIGURE 5.14 Displaying the flag. (*Source:* FutureSource. Reprinted with permission.)

slightly more condensed than the triangle. It is another portrayal of a pause in the trend and is usually a continuation pattern.

Funnel Formations

Funnel formations are also known as *foghorns* in view of the market's expanding tops and bottoms. They do not happen often and represent extremely choppy or volatile scenarios. They usually form in a series of three waves of higher highs and lower lows. Just when you believe the market has broken support, a rally occurs and makes higher highs. You would rather trade later than getting in at the early stage of this formation.

Figure 5.15, a soybean chart, captures a great example of an expanding top pattern. I numbered the highs and lows in the sequence that they occurred rather than try to identify waves to help illustrate the characteristics of the funnel top. Point 1 establishes the first high as it breaks out and closes higher than the currently established high back in January. Point 2 is the secondary high of the move. Point 3 is the first reactionary low from Point

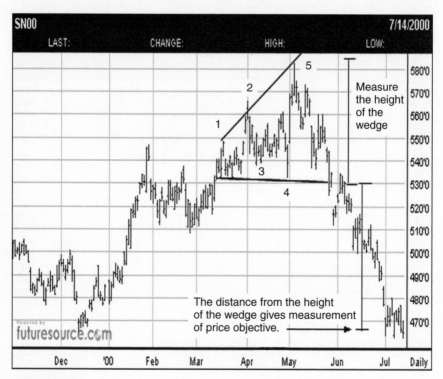

FIGURE 5.15 Expanding top means volatility. (*Source:* FutureSource. Reprinted with permission.)

2. Notice that the market makes a lower low at Point 4 and then Point 5 is a higher high than Point 2.

This pattern certainly can whipsaw a trader. Once you became convinced that support was broken at Point 4, new highs popped up. Then, just as you thought the move could continue higher as Point 5 took out Point 2, the market came tumbling down. Remember, volatility often marks tops and bottoms. This formation is another way of confirming that, when the market's trend does finally change, it usually is not a small price reversal, as the chart illustrates. These are the types of patterns that may give a trader the confidence to ride a trend a while longer.

Rounding Bottoms and Tops

Rounding bottom and top patterns clearly involve a longer-term trend reversal process. A market feature I heard about long ago applies here: Markets will try to scare you out or bore you out of a position. With the rounding bottom on the gold chart shown as Figure 5.16, you can see that you

FIGURE 5.16 Rounding bottom: How boring! (*Source:* Gecko Software, Inc. Reprinted with permission.)

could easily succumb to boredom during the gradual semicircular bottoming action.

The rounding bottom pattern can also be classified, to some degree, as an inverted head-and-shoulders formation and is also termed a *saucer bottom*. The battle between bulls and bears or buyers and sellers develops over a period of time to form this established basing action. The magnitude of the strength and reliability that this bottom pattern carries with it depends on the severity of the prior trend from which it developed. In other words, after a long and continuous downtrend, the shift or change in trend captured by a rising bottom can be a powerful reversal.

On Figure 5.16, for example, an extensive long-term decline brought prices down below $270 before the tide began to turn and prices finally advanced toward $390, nearly a 50 percent price appreciation. The long-term bottoming phase might certainly have distracted an investor from carrying a long position off the bottom, which occurred in February–March 2001. The majority of the rally did not even begin to take place until well over a year later when prices began to edge above the lip of the saucer in 2002.

The situation illustrated in Figure 5.16 is a great example of how a market can bore you out of a position. Investors can sometimes take the attitude that it will never move or it is in a trading range or, best of all, a better opportunity exists elsewhere. In this example, once the market finally breaks out, several bullish patterns develop including a symmetrical triangle to support a conclusion that higher prices were still to come. To summarize, rounding bottoms or tops require time to develop, and traders have to demonstrate patience during these basing periods as they can turn into reliable trend reversal patterns.

Opening Patterns

Many other chart patterns have been identified over the years, some complicated and some simple, and it would be impossible to cover the nuances of all these patterns. However, let me mention a couple of short-term patterns based on the opening prices of the regular trading session (although stock index futures trade almost around the clock, the open is considered to be the period when trading begins at the New York Stock Exchange, 8:30 a.m. Central time). These two patterns meet two of my criteria: simplicity and effectiveness.

Oops Signal   The first is the oops trade associated with Larry Williams, creator and developer of many trading concepts and author of a number of trading books, who solidified his reputation as a trading legend by taking a $10,000 account to more than $1 million in a highly publicized trading contest. The oops signal is based on trader psychology and gets its name from a simple conclusion, "Oops, we made a mistake."

When I interviewed Larry on my radio show, he explained that when a broker would report to a client that the client was stopped out of a position, the broker would say, "Oops, we lost." Sometimes the broker would say, "Let's go the other way." Then as the market turned around again, the client would hear those famous words, "Oops, we lost again."

The oops signal is a gap trading method that fades the direction of the gap. When a market opens lower than the previous day's low, a trader should place a buy stop a few ticks above the previous day's low, as Figure 5.17 illustrates. When a market opens higher than the previous day's high, a trader should place a sell stop a few ticks below the previous day's high, as shown in Figure 5.18.

Markets sometimes gap open in one direction as traders react to an economic report, a news event, or some other surprise factor. The outcome of that gap is based on the opinions that are formed by the masses as traders chase the market. Then as prices accelerate in one direction, human psychology and rationale begin to kick in. Traders come to their senses and re-

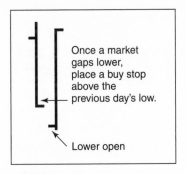

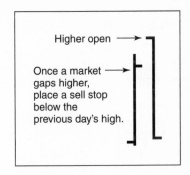

FIGURE 5.17 Oops buy signal.

FIGURE 5.18 Oops sell signal.

alize that the market's price may possibly have overreacted to the initial news or event that created the gap in the first place.

The oops signal capitalizes on this fake-out situation. What makes the signal work is that, as traders return to a rational state and reevaluate the impact of the event on market values, prices are susceptible to a reversal that can move values back in the opposite direction of the gap. These reactions tend to work better in countertrend conditions—for example, taking a sell oops signal in an uptrend.

The oops signal is like a key reversal described in Chapter 3. The market gaps higher on bullish news but fails to maintain momentum and reverses lower. If traders get suckered into a long position based on the bullish news and then see the market head lower and below the previous day's close, they are likely to conclude, "Oops," scramble out of the long position, and maybe even sell short, compounding the force to drive prices lower.

Using a stop order to enter a position in the opposite direction of the gap reduces the risk of a true sentiment change in the market based on supply or demand conditions. If the event produced a true change in market value, the opening gap might be a breakaway gap condition described earlier in this chapter. A stop order would prevent you from getting in front of this freight train that may be the start of a big move.

Figure 5.19, the mini-sized Dow futures contract, illustrates two classic oops signals. The first one shows a higher open in an uptrend, so a countertrend sell stop was placed a few ticks below the prior day's high. This trade would have been a very nice position trade for approximately 400 points if the stops were managed effectively. The second oops signal occurred in a short-term downtrend, so a buy stop was placed above the prior day's low for another countertrend trade. If you were to hold this position more than one day without proper stop or risk management, a nice short-term trade could have resulted in a loss.

FIGURE 5.19   Profitable oops signals on mini-sized Dow futures. (*Source:* FutureSource. Reprinted with permission.)

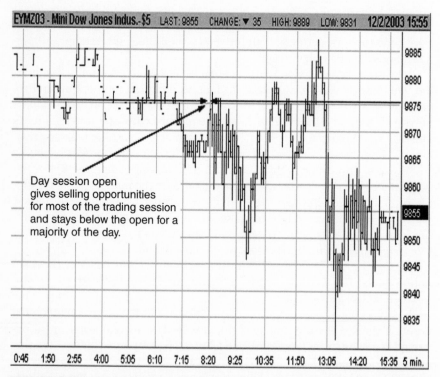

FIGURE 5.20   Opening range breakout pattern. (*Source:* FutureSource. Reprinted with permission.)

Opening Range Breakout   A second pattern based on the open is the opening range breakout method described by Larry Pesavento, another master technician and trader. The opening price will be near the high or low of the day 67 percent of the time, according to Larry. Usually it is within 10 percent of the exact high or low. This is valuable information for a day trader, who wants to be a buyer when prices are above the opening range and a seller when prices are below the opening range.

Figure 5.20 reveals how this concept works on a 5-minute chart of the mini-sized Dow futures contract for December 2, 2003. Note that the market did trade for the majority of the day below the day's opening range, which was near the high of the day. Figure 5.21 is a daily chart of the same contract so you can gauge the scope of the daily range and see prior historic values. More important as it relates to this concept, look at how many times the open is, in fact, near the actual high or low for the day.

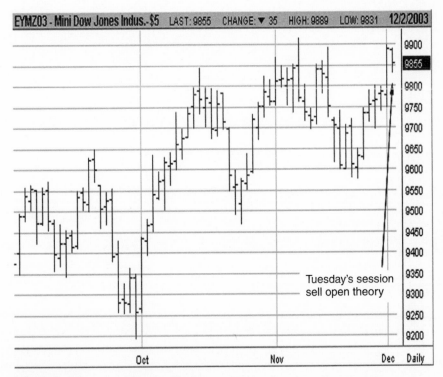

FIGURE 5.21   Opening price relative to the day's high or low. (*Source: FutureSource. Reprinted with permission.*)

Of course, as with anything related to charts and markets, nothing is perfect about trading signals based on these opening patterns, which almost require that you be a day trader to use them. All markets form patterns, and many of these patterns repeat themselves consistently. But they may not materialize often, and even when you recognize them, there is no guarantee they will develop like the textbook examples.

CHAPTER 6

Pivot Point Analysis

A Powerful Weapon

Man's mind, once stretched by a new idea, never regains its original dimension.

—Oliver Wendell Holmes

Pivot point analysis is a famous technique that is used as a price forecasting method by day traders and floor traders alike. I know it is very popular among professionals—I am one of them who uses it in my studies and market analysis.

Numerous advisory services, brokerage firms, and independent traders use one form of it or another. *Support/resistance, price range forecasting, pin-pointing tops and bottoms,* and *target trading* are some of the other terms that are used to refer to numbers derived by pivot points. For most traders on the floors of the exchanges, pivot point numbers are considered to be common knowledge from the old school of trading. The influx of electronic off-floor day traders has really started to expand, and with that expansion comes the need for traders to educate themselves about various types of analysis.

Pivot point analysis is a leading indicator rather than a lagging indicator like most of today's popular technical indicators that are based on past price action. It gives a trader the early advanced target levels that, in many cases, turn out to be the actual high or low and sometimes even both for a given trading session, as chart examples in Chapters 7, 8, and 9 will show.

Most novice individual investors and even brokers are not familiar with pivot point analysis. Many inexperienced investors may have a hard time incorporating this technique into their trading toolbox due to the time that it takes to calculate the numbers. But make no mistake about it. Professionals look at this analysis and so should you.

MY START WITH PIVOT POINTS

Before going any further, let me explain how I became interested in pivot point numbers. I picked up on the method back in 1985 as a colleague was showing me how to day-trade the Swiss franc and the deutsche mark. It worked fairly well in those days so I incorporated it into my analysis of the market for which I really had a passion, bonds.

After using them for some time as a crutch, I was losing interest as a day trader. Then I experimented with using this concept for a longer time period, a week. Wow, what a discovery!

Then I came to the conclusion that I would try to use them on a monthly basis because, after all, I was a follower of daily, weekly, and monthly charts. In fact, the Chicago Board of Trade used to give out a monthly bond chart, and a friend from the floor and I would get together for homework sessions. We would do longer-term chart studies using moving averages. I figured, why not look at the monthly price target, too? Wow again! I discovered that I could look at a potential price range target in the future based on price action in the past. The longer the time frames, the more power these points seemed to have.

I also discovered the power and leverage of options as they were introduced to the futures market with the first options market being, you guessed it, bonds. I hit a grand-slam home run that lasted through most of 1986. You see, I was bullish and the era of Reaganomics was happening! Interest rates were declining from 14 percent and bond prices were exploding (bonds have an inverted relationship between yield and price). That was a great time. I made a lot of money, and I made other people a lot of money, too.

I somewhat retired after that and went to Miami and invested in a charter boat business, purchasing an interest in a 42-foot Morgan 416 sailboat. The problem is that I never chartered it because I was the one who always took it out. So the business was never a business. Have you heard the old expression that a boat owner's two best days are the day he buys a boat and the day he sells it? I have to disagree although it is true that boats are a money pit and that whenever you buy anything that has "marine" in front of a necessary item to make the vessel run, the price of that part moves exponentially higher in cost.

The long and short of it is that I got rid of the boat, got married (I am still happily married to the same woman), and went back into the futures business. It took time for me to find the groove and to get back into the markets, mainly because not only did the markets change but so did the U.S. and global economies as well. The Persian Gulf war had taken place, the former Soviet Union was coming apart, East and West Germany were reuniting and, as you know, 24-hour trading was emerging. Markets were now open constantly. New markets were being launched or evolving around the globe, too—the CAC, the DAX, the MATIF, and many other foreign stock, futures, and options exchanges.

I got back in business at First American Discount Corp. with Bill Mallers Sr., a former chairman of the Chicago Board of Trade. He introduced me to this secret technique he was developing for a trading program. As it turned out, a portion of this top-secret method was, not surprisingly, pivot point analysis. The kicker is that traders are still using this analysis today, and I incorporate it on a daily, weekly, and monthly basis. That background is what this chapter is all about. I want to demonstrate that the pivot point analysis formula works on different markets and on different time frames.

PIVOT POINT FORMULA

The *pivot point number* is the sum of the high, low, and close divided by three. This is the basis for the other pivot point analysis calculations. Here is the common mathematical formula for pivot point analysis where P = pivot point, C = close, H = high, and L = low:

$$P = \frac{H + L + C}{3}$$

To get the first resistance level ($R1$), take the pivot point number times two and then subtract the low:

$$R1 = (P \times 2) - L$$

To find the second resistance area ($R2$), add the high to the pivot point number and then subtract the low:

$$R2 = (P + H) - L$$

For the first support level ($S1$), take the pivot point number times two and then subtract the high:

$$S1 = (P \times 2) - H$$

For the second support area ($S2$), subtract the high from the pivot point number and then add the low:

$$S2 = (P - H) + L$$

Some people have experimented with different variations to account for the entire time period's price action. For example, one variation adds the open to the high, low, and close and then divides by four to derive the pivot point value. I do not use this variation as it is an additional variable to input, and the importance for the pivot point is in the weight the close has in relationship to the high and low or the range.

One trader asked me how to change the numbers to take into consideration those markets that trade 20 or 24 hours a day around the clock and then experience tremendous gaps on the next day's regular session open. An approach that we discussed was to use the open of the next day instead of the close from the prior day to calculate the pivot point. Then the support and resistance formulas would apply for the balance of the calculations.

However, I have several issues with this method. For one, you have no time to prepare for your trading day because you need to wait until the open. More important, I apply the prior night's session high or low that would include the day session range, whichever figure is greater, and then use the day session's close. For example, the time period for e-mini S&Ps begins at 3:45 p.m. (Central time), and the close is the following day at 3:15 p.m. I use the high and low during that entire session for the day's range. I apply the same concept to other markets, including the mini-sized Dow, bonds, currencies, and metals.

BEHIND THE ANALYSIS

Whatever formula you use to get the pivot point number that is the basis of this analysis, you can see that it involves several steps and is somewhat detailed. Here is my interpretation for the rationale behind the calculations. Consider the pivot point as the average of the previous session's trading range combined with the closing price. The numbers of support and resistance that are calculated indicate the potential ranges for the next time frame, based on the past weight of the market's strength or weakness derived from calculating the high, low, and distance from the close of those points. Pivot point analysis is also used to identify breakout points from the support and resistance numbers.

The previous session's trading range could be based on an hour, a day, a week, or a month. Most trading software includes these numbers on a daily basis so that you do not have the tedious chore of doing it the old-fashion way—by hand using a calculator. (The really old-fashion way doesn't use even a calculator). Don't make your job harder; try the easy way using a computer program like the one I developed so that I can calculate the numbers on a daily, weekly, and monthly time period relatively quickly and for most markets (available to clients by fax or e-mail, or by viewing on line).

I do the daily numbers at the end of the day to help me identify the next day's potential range or support and resistance points. It gives me a head start on my analysis so I am prepared for the next day's work. It helps me plan my trades. Similarly, the weekly numbers are done at the end of every week, and the same goes for the monthly numbers.

Because most technical analysis is derived from mathematical calculations, the common denominators that are used are the high, low, close, and open. These figures are used for plotting most common charts, for example. More notable techniques such as moving averages, relative strength index, stochastics, and Fibonacci numbers are all calculated using mathematics based on those price points of interest. These prices are also what the newspapers publish.

As technical analysts, we are trying to use past price behavior to help us get an indication of future price direction. This approach sounds absurd because no one can predict the future, right? Well, I am not trying to predict the future. I just want an idea of where prices can go in a given time period, based on where they have been. After all, isn't that similar to the concept of drawing trend lines?

VERIFY, VERIFY, VERIFY

We have all heard the slogan about how to be successful investing in real estate: LOCATION, LOCATION, LOCATION. (Is that another symbolic reference that involves the Fibonacci number three?) In the trading business a similar important rule is what I call the rule of multiple verification: VERIFY, VERIFY, VERIFY. More than likely, I picked up this belief by reading a book back in 1981 or 1982 by Arthur Sklarew, *Techniques of a Professional Commodity Chart Analyst*. In writing about the rule of multiple techniques (page 3), he states:

> *Technicians know very well that price chart analysis is not an exact science. No single chart technique yet discovered is infallible. Despite this lack of perfection, price chart analysis can very often give reliable forecasts of trend direction . . . Confirmation is therefore an essential component of every valid chart signal. In addition to comparing price charts of different contract months and time scales, it has been my experience that the accuracy of any technical price forecast can be improved greatly by the application of a principle that I call the "Rule of Multiple Techniques."*
>
> *The Rule of Multiple Techniques requires that the chart technician not rely solely on one single technical signal or indicator but look for confirmation from other technical indicators. The more technical*

indicators that confirm each other, the better the chance of an accurate forecast. The logic behind this rule is that, if individual time-proven techniques tend to be right most of the time, a combination of several such techniques that confirm each other will tend to be right even more frequently.

I do not believe Sklarew talked about pivot point analysis as a means of technical analysis nor was he aware at the time he wrote that book of the art of candle charting. I believe that had he been, those ideas more than likely would have been in his book.

Verify, verify, verify. (Remember that slogan because it has to do with the development of my method of analysis described later.) What it really means to me is this: Before deciding to invest or make a trade, if I understand the underlying fundamentals, I would want to look at a chart to confirm the trend, and then I would look at varying technical indicators to help confirm my beliefs. By incorporating different techniques such as pivot point analysis, I have figures that help speed up my analytical process. With these numbers I can draw lines on my charts indicating support and resistance levels to see if they help clear the visual picture.

Let's do the math calculation on the monthly pivot point support number for sugar that was mentioned in the previous chapter. If you recall, I said the target support number was 6.09. The range for the previous month (September) for the March 2002 sugar futures contract was a high of 7.80 cents a pound and a low of 6.40 cents with the close at 6.63 cents. Working the formula, you have 20.83 as the total of your prices divided by 3 for a pivot point number of 6.943. Multiply the pivot point number by 2 (13.886) and subtract the high, and you should show 6.09 (rounded off) as the Support 1 number for the month of October. The sugar chart shown as Figure 6.1 shows the actual low was 6.11 cents, which occurred eight business days into the month of October—two ticks from the projected pivot point support number! In addition, that low of 6.11 was reached in two days, forming a double bottom.

I was already armed with the knowledge from the chart that a three-gap formation had formed, signaling the downmove was nearly over, especially after the third gap, the exhaustion gap, was identified. Knowledge of the monthly pivot number combined with gap analysis provided a strong, highly probable buy signal. The results speak for themselves.

The pivot point analysis method used to target the exact low is not an exact science, and you have to allow for a margin of error in using these numbers. If anything, it can give you confidence to enter a position and implement a sound trading plan. At the very least, you should not have gotten caught up in selling short at that level. If you had identified a buying oppor-

FIGURE 6.1 Sugar on target. (*Source:* FutureSource. Reprinted with permission.)

tunity based on the signals on the sugar chart, the biggest dilemma would have been to decide where to get out and how long to hold the position.

Study the price action in February on the live cattle futures chart provided as Figure 6.2. Cattle had approximately a 300-point range during February. So what method would have helped give you a clue to sell near 76.00? Let's apply the pivot point formula on the monthly data, using February's high (76.52), low (73.62), and close (74.20). Once you work the calculations, you will see that the price projections were 77.68 for Resistance 2 and 75.94 for Resistance 1. The actual high was 76.05 made on the ninth trading day of the month! Combine the monthly target resistance figures with candle charting techniques, which identified a potential variation of a dark cloud cover pattern on the seventh trading day of the month, and you are armed with a powerful combination. You could have developed a trading plan to sell short at R1 75.90 (rounded down) and used appropriate stops. If you had done the monthly numbers and said to yourself, "I'll take a look at that market if it gets near my price projections," you may have acted on a short position and profited nicely.

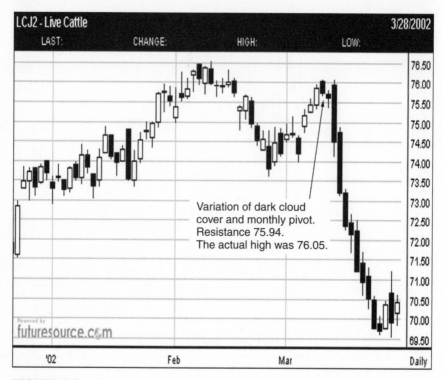

FIGURE 6.2   Getting short in cattle. (*Source:* FutureSource. Reprinted with permission.)

Let's look at it another way. If you just had the pivot point numbers alone and thought the market was going higher, checking the figures first might have saved you from buying the high. You may not have necessarily gone short, but I believe you would not have gone long either. You should be starting to see the value in using pivot point numbers.

As for the support numbers, the calculations put S1 at 73.04 and S2 at 71.88. Granted, the market moved below 70.00, but the S2 number would have given you a great target to shoot for if you wanted to cover a short position or wanted to look at the market for other clues to initiate a position. As you can tell, not many other signals were available, other than the record eight to ten candle pattern, to warn that the trend was concluding.

If professional traders—mainly floor traders—are looking at these numbers, why wouldn't you want to look at them as well? Anything that can help you make better decisions for determining a game plan that integrates a better level of risk and a potential profit objective can't be bad. Remember, you won't know where you are going if you don't know where you have been.

That is what this method helps you to do—navigate future price moves based on the previous time frame's data.

FINDING EQUILIBRIUM

Keep in mind the reasoning behind the numbers. At any given time, there is an equilibrium point around which trading activity occurs. For day traders in active markets such as stock index futures or financial instruments, this equilibrium point serves as the pivot or focal point for floor traders, the professional locals who trade positions around that point during the day. When prices move away from the pivot number up or down, there are zones of support and resistance that can be derived from the prior trading period's range. This range around the focal point then sets an established value in the market. Violation of these price bands or trade zones leads to changes in valuation and the potential entry of new players into the market.

Trading for the day will usually remain between the first support and resistance levels as these professional floor traders make their markets. If either of these first levels are penetrated, off-floor traders and other traders may be attracted into the market. This increased activity can give the market the momentum it needs to break out into a new range or to move to the next target zone.

These breakout points usually reverse their roles and serve as test points once a breakout occurs. For example, the prior resistance becomes the new support or the prior support now becomes the new resistance. The range of trading has expanded, and if a second support or resistance level is broken, then the potential for further momentum develops as longer-term traders and new traders may be attracted.

The price parameters used by floor traders and other industry analysts can be calculated with the preceding formulas. Knowledge of these levels can help you set your own targets or at least give you insight as to what the pros on the floor are using. This knowledge is especially useful when there is hardly any outside influence on the market from fundamental changes such as news events, economic data, or reports.

As long as no significant news events have taken place between the close and the next trading session's open, locals tend to move the market and trade between themselves and the "paper" or orders from brokerage firm customers. These price swings generally will only move between the pivot point and the first band of support and resistance.

If prices move to the first or even second resistance calculation and if you have confirmation from an additional technical indicator such as MACD or stochastics, the confirmation creates a higher confidence level to act on a sell signal. Combine those signals with a familiar candle chart pattern such as a dark cloud cover or a bearish engulfing pattern or bearish harami cross and you have a powerful sell signal. Because pivot points are developing a large following among off-floor traders as well as locals, they should be in your arsenal of technical trading weapons.

The difference between successful traders and not-so-successful traders is what they do with the price data they all have, how fast they process the data, and then how they apply or execute that knowledge. Pivot points can give you the edge as fast as you calculate the data. A computer can facilitate your analysis, but the best trading system I know is still the individual trader who has a proper education and a proper method for observing, interpreting, and evaluating a particular trade setup. A great trading system is not the computer or software program, but the individual who can make calculated decisions based on the data, an analytical process that pivot point analysis can speed up.

PIVOT POINTS IN ACTION

The easiest way to help show how pivot point analysis works is with a few examples. First is a 60-minute candle chart showing S&P 500 index futures for August 20–21, 2002, shown as Figure 6.3. Using the pivot point formula, you can calculate the target numbers for August 21 from the trading session data on August 20. The candles inside the box show the trading range and price swings from that day when the high was 949.5, the low was 931.50, and the close was 939.8. Calculating the numbers gives you a pivot point of 940, producing targets of 958 for R2, 949 for R1, 922 for S2, and 931 for S1.

If you did your homework or downloaded the analysis from the National Futures research advisory web site after the close on August 20, then you would know what I call the key target numbers: R1 of 949 and S1 of 931. Examining the chart, a nice trade sell setup evolved after the secondary failure of 949. Even if you didn't sell short, I believe you would not have gone long at that level either. The better setup, however, came as a buy signal from the positive reactionary bounce off the 931 key support (S1) number as a bullish harami formed. A nice day-trade could have been made with a stop placed under the established low of 931.

Again, if you did not want to go long, then the S1 support level would absolutely have saved you from getting caught up in a bear trap by selling what turned out to be the exact low of the day. The day's price action swung between the initial high at 949.7 and the fall to 931 before rallying back up through 949 to the 952 area, dropping back to the 937 level and then blasting off to new highs by the close. Figure 6.3 helps to illustrate the theory that markets will establish a range and trade within that range in any given period of time and shows the power of the pivot point method.

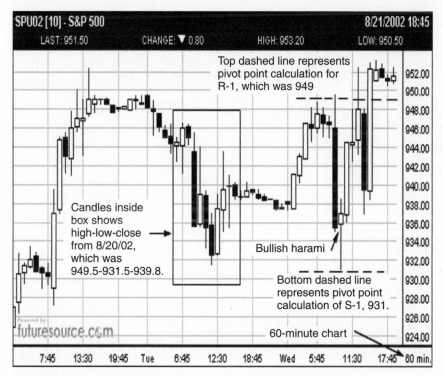

FIGURE 6.3 S&P pivoting off points. (*Source:* FutureSource. Reprinted with permission.)

One other coincidence that should be pointed out is that on August 20, the high was 949.5 and the low was 931.5, almost the same as the calculations for R1 and S1 and the actual highs and lows for the next day, showing the tendency for prices to remain in a range. Also, note that the market traded at the pivot point resistance level several times. I've noticed markets bounce off support or resistance target levels two, three, and even four times. As a general rule, I usually will only take a trade based off the first test of the S1 or R1 pivot number. The reason, as an old saying goes, is that if you go to the well one too many times, then the well will run dry on you. By the time a trader gets used to or identifies a particular pattern, the pattern can change, resulting in a loss.

P3T SIGNALS

Now let me introduce you to what I call the trading method for P3T signals—Person's Pivot Point Trade signal. P3T combines techniques of pivot point analysis, candle charting, and technical indicators such as stochastics to help confirm trade setups or turning points to capture and profit from a price move.

Following are some examples of different markets and different time frames to help illustrate the powerful signals that develop using this combination.

On a daily chart for silver (Figure 6.4), I identified that the market had formed a shooting star followed by a potential doji after about a seven-week runup. This pattern indicated that the market was due for a correction. That formation indicated a tug-of-war between the bulls and the bears and that a top had formed, based on those combined candles.

I had a second-opinion indicator using pivot point analysis on a monthly time frame to determine the potential price range or support and resistance point for the next month. Most traders who are familiar with pivot point analysis associate it with day-trading and do calculations only on a daily basis, but this example shows you why daily, weekly, and monthly calculations can be extremely successful and offer a more powerful method of analyzing price objectives.

FIGURE 6.4 Setup in silver. (*Source:* FutureSource. Reprinted with permission.)

The high for March silver in December was $4.635, the low was $4.125, and the close was $4.58. The pivot point calculations made $4.7737 (rounded off to $4.775) the first resistance and $4.2637 the first support. The exact high was $4.775!

Now look at the after picture shown in Figure 6.5, which shows a powerful selling wave that took command of the price in silver following the bearish candle pattern. Not only did the pivot point calculation numbers alert me to the potential high almost two weeks in advance, but the candle pattern also confirmed it.

The January slide took prices close to the $4.2637 pivot point calculation for the S1 support target. The actual low in January was $4.205—not exact but darn close. Combining pivot point analysis with candle charting techniques and then including a Western market indicator such as the stochastic oscillator may give you better trading signals and verification so you can have more confidence in your own trading abilities.

Figure 6.6, the weekly chart for U.S. Dollar Index futures, with exponential moving averages for three time periods added, provides another great before-after example, illustrating that candle chart patterns and pivot

FIGURE 6.5   Afterglow in silver. (*Source:* FutureSource. Reprinted with permission.)

FIGURE 6.6   P3T trade in U.S. dollar. (*Source:* FutureSource. Reprinted with permission.)

point analysis work together with other indicators not only on daily charts but for other time periods as well. Look at the shooting star formation that exposed the turning point for the market during the first week in July. The next candle was a hanging man, which certainly warned that the trend was changing. The result was a complete market reversal that resulted in a 950-point decline within $2\frac{1}{2}$ months.

After another rally that recovered most of the gains following the mid-September low, look at the bearish harami that formed at the end of January. The characteristics were that the market had had a long advance (nearly four months), and a long white candle had formed (meaning the market closed above the open and there were little or no shadows). The next candle was a doji where the market had a wide range but closed at or quite close to the open. Another observation is that the market was forming a major double top from the prior high.

A plan of attack would be to sell short and place the initial stop as a stop close only order above the January high. The reason I would have selected that as my risk target was, if the market retests the high, I would not want to be stopped out and then have to watch the market price fail off the high. I would want to be out only if prices made a new all-time high close above that level, which would signal the market's acceptance of a new higher price plateau and would probably spark an advance to newer highs.

But it gets better. The week of the long white candle (January 25, 2002) has a high of 120.30, a low of 118.02, and a close of 120.18. By using the pivot point calculations, the key target resistance (R1) is 120.98. Combining that target number with the bearish harami cross gave a powerful one-two punch of confidence to sell short. As you can see, the high that next week (February 1, 2002) was 120.88 as the doji candle formed.

Yes, I know it was not exactly on the number, but again it was close enough. With confirmation from the candle pattern and the prior high back in July 2001, this classified as a picture-perfect P3T sell signal!

Take a look in Figure 6.7 at what happened to the U.S. Dollar Index after the bearish signals at the double top. In addition to those signals, the

FIGURE 6.7   U.S. dollar follows the script. (*Source:* FutureSource. Reprinted with permission.)

three exponential moving averages (4-, 9-, and 18-week periods) made a
dead crossover in April (when the short-term moving averages cross below
the longer-term moving averages, a sell signal is indicated). The dollar's
value continued the trend lower for many months.

Now let's confirm the amazing discovery that pivot point analysis might
combine with candle chart patterns to offer traders a powerful and consistent method for verifying trade signals. Figure 6.8, the 60-minute chart of
crude oil futures, was printed out on August 1, 2002. Based on price action
from the previous week (July 26, 2002, high of $27.75, low of $25.95, and
close of $26.54), the R1 price target for the week was $27.54.

By doing your homework on Friday or by downloading the numbers
from the National Futures advisory service web site, you would have been
armed with the potential price range for that week. It would have alerted
you to watch the price action if crude oil got to $27.54. When it did, the en-
suing bearish engulfing pattern combined with the bearish divergence on the
stochastics confirmed and generated another textbook P3T sell signal. The
actual high was $27.69, a difference of only 15 cents from the target number.

FIGURE 6.8   Alert in crude oil. (*Source:* FutureSource. Reprinted with permission.)

This move might not seem to be significant or dramatic at first glance, but if you look closely at this chart, you will notice that this was a decline of nearly $1.25 per barrel in less than 24 hours. That figure equates to $1,250 on a single futures contract.

This next example is from a specific trade recommendation made in the *Weekly Bottom Line Newsletter* for the week ending May 10, 2002. In that recommendation, I explained fully how to examine and develop an exact P3T trade signal for the July cotton futures contract. Looking at the data from the prior week ending May 3, 2002, the high was 35.70 cents, the low was 32.85 cents, and the close was 33.52 cents. Using the pivot point calculations, the projected weekly target low for S1 was 32.35 cents, and the calculation for the R1 target high was 35.20 cents.

Because I always do the monthly analysis, let me include that also. During the month of April the high was 40.71 cents, the low was 34.30, and the month ended at 34.71. Doing the pivot point calculations again to project the monthly targets for May, the S1 key support figure was 32.61 cents, and the monthly target for R1 resistance was 39.02 cents. Using figures from both the previous week and the previous month, you now have the potential projected price ranges for those time periods.

I cannot stress enough why using the pivot point calculations to project two different time frames is important. If you think about it, in any given month there normally are four full weeks and 22 business days. Every week and every month will have an established price range. The high for the month will usually be made on one day, and it also will be the high for that week. The low for the month will usually be made on one day, and it also will be the low for that week. At the end of the month prices will usually settle somewhere in between.

If you have a target level to alert you to focus on that market if and when prices trade near that level, it gives you an edge in the market, allowing you to act rather than react to the market. More specifically, if both the weekly and monthly numbers are close to each other, then more close examination to find an opportunity to place a trade and to develop a game plan in either futures or options is warranted.

Figure 6.9 is the cotton chart and following are my comments and the exact trade recommendation as they appeared in the *Weekly Bottom Line Newsletter* for the week ending May 10, 2002:

> *The monthly support is 32.61 and Friday's low was 32.85, which is close enough for me, especially after a continuous price decline from being at nearly 41.00 cents four weeks ago. Bullish divergence and a hammer formation on the candlestick improve the odds that a short-term bottom is in place and a bounce is due. Look to buy near 33.25 to 32.65 and use 32.20 stop close only.*

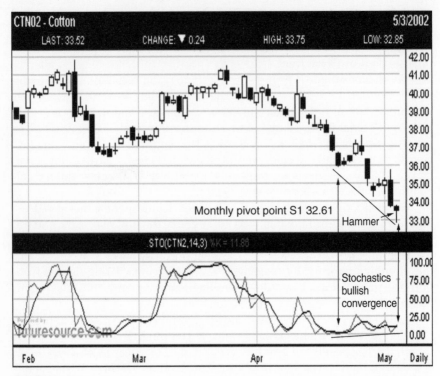

FIGURE 6.9   Hammering in a bottom in cotton. (*Source:* FutureSource. Reprinted with permission.)

By having both the monthly and the weekly pivot point calculations in addition to a bullish stochastic divergence, a hammer formation on the candle chart, and the fact that the market had plunged nearly 800 points in about 17 days, I was willing to map out a specific trade for the following week. If you do your calculations at the end of trading on Friday, collecting the data for all the markets you have an interest in tracking, then you have Saturday and Sunday to develop your trading plans. That analysis is what I provide in my advisory service.

Now let's look at Figure 6.10 for the results. During the next trading session on Monday, May 6, the low was 33.05 cents. In the next trading session on Tuesday, the low was also 33.05 cents. If you missed the trade recommendation even after those two days, you still had an opportunity to enter the position near 33.25 cents on Wednesday, May 8. Let's say you established a game plan and placed an order to buy. With your target risk factor set, the hardest part of this trade would be to decide where to take a profit.

The monthly projected R1 resistance targeted the high at 39.02. The actual high was 39.65 on the last day of the month. The market came within 24

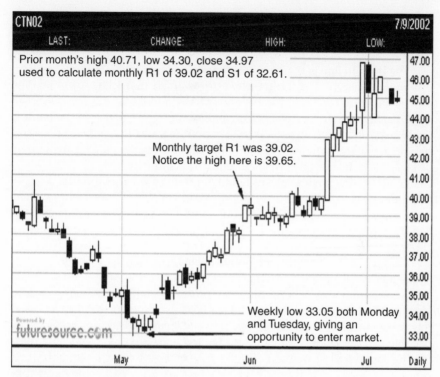

FIGURE 6.10 Prices take off! (*Source:* FutureSource. Reprinted with permission.)

points of the targeted monthly S1 low number and 63 points of the monthly R1 high target—really not a bad margin of error, wouldn't you agree?

These are facts—hard-core black and white indisputable facts—of how these numbers work. Again, not all the numbers work this well, but it is impressive to even an analyst such as myself to see how they still work for different time frames and on different investment vehicles and products as in this cotton example.

The initial performance bond requirement for cotton futures at the time was $1,000. If you had bought at the high end of the recommendation, which was 33.25 cents, and rode it to only, say, 38.50 cents or just shy of the 39.02 monthly target number, you would have captured a 550-point move in fewer than 20 trading days or $2,750 per contract!

Keep in mind the stop or risk factor that was targeted was about $500. This particular loss factor was on a stop close only basis, which is different than a regular stop. To get stopped out, the market would need to close below 32.20 cents. However, you should know there are significant increases in risk and loss amounts associated with stop close only orders. For instance, the market could trade limit down and not fill you at all, or it could close significantly below 32.20 and give you a greater amount of loss than you wanted.

The bottom line is that even ordinary stops do not guarantee a specific loss amount. Stop close only orders are used so that I know the market proved me wrong by trading lower and staying at that low price on the close. A regular stop could be triggered on an intraday move, and then the market could snap right back up and take me out of the trade. In essence, I could be right in my analysis and still lose money using regular stops. This method of order entry is discussed in further detail in Chapter 10.

Other trading tactics such as liquidating half of your positions at a target price and then moving stops up as the market moves in your favor (known as *trailing stops*) could have been employed. Or maybe you would have ridden the market for the entire 1,400-point move, which would have equaled about $7,000.

Taking the devil's advocate point of view, you may be wondering why, if this method is so good, would anyone in their right mind want to share this information with others? Simple. You can use many methods to trade. Most methods have a solid foundation of followers and credibility. So does this method. I believe the act of teaching and sharing ideas only helps me to become a better trader by instilling a higher degree of confidence and reinforcing sound trading methods. The key for success for any method to work is not only believing in it but also acting on that information and executing or following through with the necessary action.

If you are a novice or inexperienced in futures trading, or even if you are an experienced trader looking to expand your knowledge in technical analysis, it might pay you to learn this trading method and incorporate it into your trading style so you can survive this business and, more important, profit from it.

CHAPTER 7

Day-Trading, Swing Trading

Acting on Analysis

Anytime there is change, there is opportunity.
So it is paramount that an organization get
energized rather than paralyzed.
— Jack Welch, CEO, General Electric

I love Jack Welch's statement! It is so true and applies so well to the trading industry. A trader needs to adapt and change with the ebb and flow of the markets. Sitting on a position, cutting out of a trade early, or not taking action on a well-thought-out trading plan all lead to emotional paralysis. Understanding the potential opportunities and then having the confidence to act on a belief in them will no doubt result in positive energy and, thus, build your trading skills.

With that admonishment in mind, I want to introduce you to another valuable lesson using the pivot point method of price forecasting. By taking the daily, weekly, or monthly numbers, you can target a price level and then wait for confirmation from a recognized chart pattern. This combination of techniques can help you take advantage of the price swings from market reactions off those numbers. By having the calculations based on different time frames, you can use them whether you are day-trading or swing trading.

When the market trades near these pivot numbers, the reaction can be a significant bounce from a support number or the market can simply stall before blowing through the support number and then continuing the trend lower. In my experience there is usually a reaction from the numbers; the longer term the calculation, the bigger the reaction. The only thing you really need to do as a trader is to get in the market, capture a significant price move, and then get out with a profit.

113

Figure 7.1 is a 60-minute chart from July 16 to July 30, 2002. Pivot point analysis, based on the weekly numbers in one of the biggest down months in S&P 500 index history, targeted the support level for the low within 9 points. The week ending July 19, 2002, had a high of 929.5, a low of 840, and a close at 844. The fundamental backdrop was extremely pessimistic with all the corporate accounting scandals, doubts that the economy could sustain growth, Middle East tensions flaring, and earnings coming in weaker than expected. Not many indicators were calling for a low or a turnaround in the equity markets.

However, there were a few positive indicators, and pivot point analysis targeted 781.67 for the S2 low number for the week ending July 26, 2002. The hourly candle chart not only showed a version of a morning star formation but the actual low on the morning of July 24, 2002, was 771.30. The market stayed at that level for less than two hours. So why is this important? If you only had access to the daily or monthly numbers, then you missed out on the weekly projection for what turned out to be an important and powerful turnaround in stock index futures history.

FIGURE 7.1   Performing in volatility. (*Source:* FutureSource. Reprinted with permission.)

As you look carefully at Figure 7.1, it also may reveal what I call a "trade signal rich environment." Notice the inverted head-and-shoulders formation that developed? This formation may have helped to add conviction that a bottom was in place and that higher prices were coming.

Using the data from other markets also may help to give you more confidence in the strength or credibility than the target numbers for the S&P alone may have. For the week ending July 19, 2002, the Dow futures had a high of 8720, a low of 7945, and a close at 7998. Working out the pivot point calculations, the S2 number was 7446. The June Dow futures were projected to have support about 552 points lower on the week because they had closed at 7998 on Friday, July 19 (chart not shown). Another thing to keep in mind is that the Dow had closed at 9392 on July 5, so that would mean a decline of 1,946 Dow points in 10 to 15 trading days to test the S2 target area of support. The actual low: 7450!

Now I know most investors were panicking, and I am sure some went short, thinking the stock market was going to zero. Being armed with this information may not have prompted you to go long, but I am sure that, if you had the numbers in front of you and were trading, you would not have sold short at the low.

Figure 7.2, the hourly chart for Nasdaq 100 index futures, is not as exact as the previous example, but it helps to illustrate the point of alerting you to a selling opportunity or at least not getting trapped into buying highs. Remember, most successful traders do not get into the habit of buying highs. Taking the range for the previous week (August 26, 2002), the high was 985, the low was 873, and the close was 912.5. The weekly price target for the R1 number was 974, using the pivot point formula.

On the first test of the 974 R1 number, the actual high was 973 so, in essence, the RI target did stop the market's advance initially. The next formation was a variation of a dark cloud cover. On the third try to advance beyond the 974 R1 resistance number, a variation of an evening star formation developed. It was not a textbook pattern—the star looked more like a spinning top formation than a shooting star—but it did warn of an impending top.

It was with that second formation that stochastics generated a bearish divergence. At this point you might consider a short position. A sell signal was confirmed by the continuation of the bearish divergence from the stochastic oscillator, and the market was unable to maintain momentum above the 974 R1 level for any substantial period of time.

The next example (Figure 7.3) again comes from July 2002, one of the most volatile time periods ever for the stock market. To have a reliable tool to help discover a target price or forecast a high for the range in this period was invaluable.

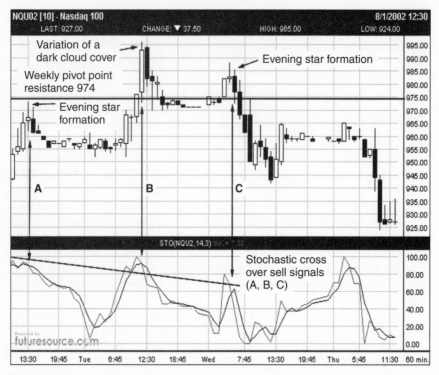

FIGURE 7.2   Nasdaq signals. (*Source:* FutureSource. Reprinted with permission.)

Taking the numbers from the prior week ending on July 26, 2002, the high was 856, the low was 771.30, and the close was 853.70. Those numbers produced the projected price range for the next weekly trading session (week ending August 2, 2002)—882.7 for the R1 first target resistance number and 911.70 for the R2 second target resistance. A bearish harami cross formed on Monday, thus generating a critical early alert that the market's price advance was slowing or coming to an end.

That pattern, combined with the weekly pivot point calculations, would have prevented you from buying at that level. Why would anyone even be thinking about buying there? Well, the market was bouncing off a major five-year low, it was significantly oversold, and many investors were convinced that the lows were in. After all, S&P 500 futures had experienced their single biggest monthly price decline in July, dating back to the inception of the futures contract. The actual high was 916.

Let's examine one more chart of the S&P 500 index, using the data from the week ending May 3, 2002 (Figure 7.4). The high was 1091.8, the low was 1063.5, and the week closed at 1073. Applying the pivot point formula to

FIGURE 7.3   Preventing a buy in S&P. (*Source:* FutureSource. Reprinted with permission.)

calculate the target numbers for the next week, the weekly target number for S2 was 1047.8. The weekly target number for R1 was 1088.7. Keep these two key prices in mind.

I also calculate the monthly price target range numbers for the top 24 markets to help give me a longer-term outlook for major support and resistance levels on those markets. Using the range numbers from April for S&P futures, the high was 1149.9, the low was 1063, and the month closed at 1077.2. After working the pivot point formula, the analysis projected the S1 monthly target low number at 1043.83. The R1 monthly target high number was calculated at 1130.23.

Both weekly and monthly time frames had calculations that were close to each other, reinforcing the significance of that area and requiring an alert trader to focus special attention on that price level as a potential turning point or buying opportunity.

The weekly and monthly pivot point numbers, combined with the bullish harami cross, provided the basis for a specific trade recommendation to go long.

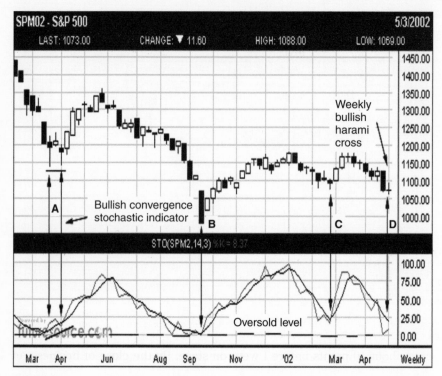

FIGURE 7.4   Forecasting an S&P reversal. (*Source:* FutureSource. Reprinted with permission.)

Here is my specific recommendation from the *Bottom Line Financial and Futures Newsletter:*

> *Technically, the weekly and monthly support numbers are near converging plus the weekly stochastics indicator is showing the market is in an oversold condition and it is at a level almost hooking into a crossover buy signal. The chart pattern could potentially turn into a major double bottom formation from the post-September 11 low. I will look to buy near 1048; use 1033 as your stop. Option traders can look to price out buying the June 1100 calls if the market trades near that level.*

There is a funny human-interest story behind that specific week as well. On Saturday, May 4, I finished the newsletter and posted it on the web site earlier than normal due to preparations for the Las Vegas Money Show. I was a keynote speaker, scheduled to go on stage on Tuesday, May 7, at around 5 p.m. Pacific time, specifically talking about swing trading using candle charting in conjunction with pivot point analysis.

This was a major investment event. All the big-name analysts and investment firms were in attendance. I had already passed out about 300 copies of the newsletter on the first day of the event, Monday, May 6. This simple trading method and my reputation were on the line.

By the close on Monday the S&P 500 was down big! Remember, on Friday it had closed at 1073. On Tuesday morning the talk of the show was how the equity market was in a nosedive going to zero. I had already passed out my research newsletter that advised buying the S&P 500 if it got down to 1048. You don't want to present a seminar in front of a large crowd teaching the validity of a trading method and be wrong.

John Murphy, the well-known technical analyst and author, came by the booth around 1 p.m., about the time the regular S&P 500 trading session was closing in Chicago. The market was at the 1047 level. I go on stage in less than four hours, and it's not looking so good for me. I asked John what he thought. I was hoping for a sign of encouragement from one of the industry's top-ranked technicians who wrote the bible on technical analysis. His opinion? "The market is going considerably lower!"

Whoa! But the show must go on and so I did. Thanks to positive comments after the closing bell from technology giant Cisco, the S&P 500 recovered about 10 points before I went on stage. By the close of business on Wednesday, May 8, S&P 500 futures had recorded one of the biggest one-day rallies of the year, up nearly 40 points in a day.

I want to acknowledge that, over the long term, John Murphy was right. But for a swing trader doing a weekly newsletter, I sure caught a lot of investors' attention. The best part of it all is that people benefited from my class.

Study Figure 7.4 a little more. Notice the dashed line at the bottom, indicating the stochastics oversold value range. The double arrow marked "A" back in March indicates a nice bullish divergence signal. Points B, C, and D reflect significant reactions when the stochastics had readings at or under 25 percent.

The week ending May 3, 2002, formed a doji. Although I have faith in dojis at market tops for sell signals, I personally do not trust dojis as the holy grail of buy signals. They do warn me of impending bottoms or indecision in the downtrend, and I will question if the move will continue. Based on that knowledge and with the pivot point analysis, I was comfortable with a decision to buy. After all, for this specific trade recommendation, I was willing to risk 15 points.

Now let's turn to the daily S&P 500 chart for the same period provided as Figure 7.5. The long white candle represents Wednesday, May 8, the day with nearly a 40-point range. Remember the two key numbers using pivot

FIGURE 7.5   The S&P market responds. (*Source:* FutureSource. Reprinted with permission.)

point analysis to project the weekly range, S2 support at 1047.8, and R1 resistance at 1088.7. The chart shows the actual low was 1045.8 (arrow) and the actual high was 1089.9, being 2 points off the low number and 1.2 points off the target R1 weekly high.

Figure 7.6 demonstrates how, in a given month, one day marks the low and one day marks the high and somewhere in between those points the market closes. Thus, a range is established.

When you examine this chart further, you will notice that the market indeed bounced off the 1044.83 support area twice during the month of May. By Friday, May 10, and the following Monday, the price had dipped back down to retest that low. Notice the bullish divergence that developed in the stochastics. It is not a classic divergence because the futures price did not make a lower low, but a buy signal was generated. In addition, using candle chart pattern recognition, notice the bullish belt hold pattern that developed.

Combining all those signs with the monthly R1 support calculations and the stochastics signal, all three signals triggered another P3T buying opportunity.

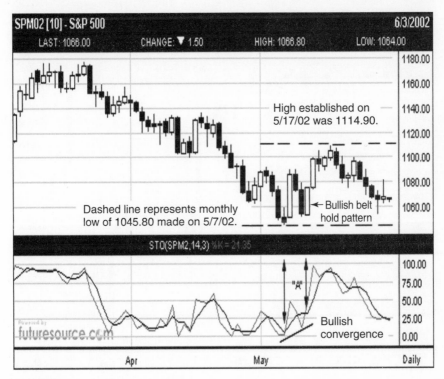

FIGURE 7.6   Making a P3T buy. (*Source:* FutureSource. Reprinted with permission.)

MULTIPLE TIME FRAMES

Let's take a closer look at the importance of using pivot point calculations from different time frames, mainly the daily, weekly, and monthly target ranges. Figure 7.7 is a 15-minute candle chart of the S&P 500. Taking the calculations from data for the prior week that ended on August 30, 2002 (high 956.3, low 902.8, and close 916.1), the weekly S2 target support was 871.57. Knowing and applying candle chart pattern recognition techniques, you would have been able to identify a powerful double combination of a bullish harami and a tweezers bottom formation. A weekly support number had already alerted you that this was an important price level. Add the candle pattern and you have the start of a trading plan for a long position.

This chart provides another example of a trade setup. Keep in mind that the market closed on Friday of the prior week at 916.1, so it is tremendously oversold by Thursday of the following week when this chart was printed. Another factor to consider is that Monday was a holiday that week so, in essence, just three trading days took the market down by nearly 45 points.

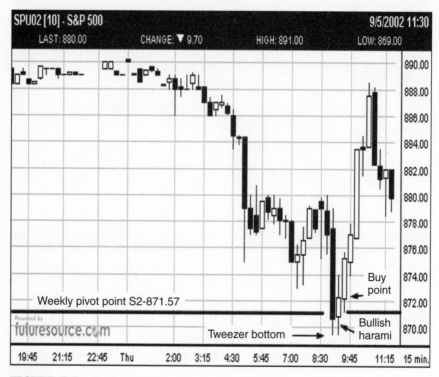

FIGURE 7.7   Bouncing off target support. (*Source:* FutureSource. Reprinted with permission.)

Within 30 minutes after trading begins on the New York Stock Exchange, S&P 500 futures collapse. A long dark candle breaks below the 871.57 support calculation and establishes a low at 869. That is roughly 2.50 points of slippage below a weekly target number, an important time period. Notice the lower shadow on the candle, indicating signs of buying near 870. The very next candle opens higher than the close and forms the bullish harami and a tweezers bottom. Right then and there a trading decision can be made. Enter an order to buy at the next time frame's open with a stop below the established low, which was 869.

For argument's sake, let's say you bought at 874. Your risk is below 869, so let's say 867 for the stop. That is initially a 7-point risk. On one e-mini S&P contract, that is seven times $50 per point, which comes out to $350 per contract. As a day trader, I see a move within two 15-minute candles that extends up to near 883.50. The third candle after the buy entry point appears to form a doji followed two candles later by a bearish engulfing pattern. I have several choices where to take a profit. The market in this example gives us nearly 45 minutes between 882 and 888 to get out or move stops up to at least break even or higher. Let's say we get out late at 882 or 880, still a profit of $300 or $400.

With the evidence we had from an oversold market condition, a weekly support number, and the candle pattern, we had a low-risk trade setup. Initially using a 7-point stop, we saw the market rally nearly 19 points from 869 to 888.50 within six 15-minute candles or an hour and a half.

SUPPORTING A TARGET

Because there is a tremendous increase in active day traders in stock index futures, especially the e-mini S&P 500, I want to show several more examples of how using the daily pivot point numbers could help in the analytical process. Once the target numbers have been calculated and then plotted on a chart, you can formulate a trading plan when you identify a candle with significant characteristics of a buy or sell signal.

On the 60-minute candle chart for S&P futures from late January 2002 (Figure 7.8), 1138.93 was the R1 resistance level. After prices reached that

FIGURE 7.8   Turning back at target resistance. (*Source:* FutureSource. Reprinted with permission.)

level on Thursday and then fell back, a shooting star candle formation developed on Friday. This candle has bearish implications and might have prompted you to establish a short position, placing the stop loss above the R1 level. The hard part would be to decide where to take a profit.

A nice bullish harami formed and a variation of a morning star formation also developed on the 60-minute S&P 500 futures chart from August 26, 2003 (Figure 7.9). Although not a textbook example, that pattern might have given you a bullish bias, causing you to establish a long with the stop loss below the 929 level, which is slightly below the daily S1 target low number.

One good point to make here, in all fairness, is that these numbers are not foolproof. The daily resistance for R1 was 956.83, based on the previous day's activity (box), and the actual high reached only 951.3, off by 5.50 points or so. Looking a little closer, you will note that the rally occurred late in the day. In fact, the high was made going into the cash market's close.

As a day trader, looking for high-probability profitable scalp trades is the main objective. If you had used this technique and hung on to the trade

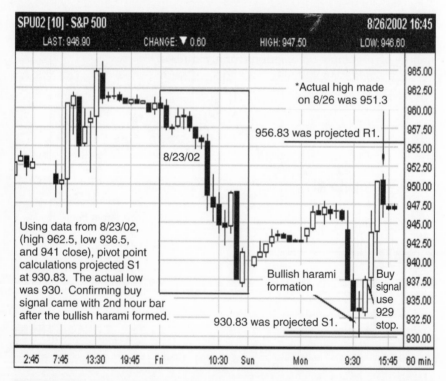

FIGURE 7.9 One that did not quite hit the target. (*Source:* FutureSource. Reprinted with permission.)

up to the very last minute waiting for the 956 number to materialize, you would have been disappointed in this case. Overall, however, waiting for a nice setup pattern to develop and confirming the pivot point target numbers is a great method to study.

PICKING THE MARKET

In addition to e-mini S&P 500 futures traded at the Chicago Mercantile Exchange, the Chicago Board of Trade offers Dow Jones Industrial Average futures contracts. Launched in April 2002, the mini-sized Dow contract valued at $5 times the index has been picking up volume quickly although still well behind the e-mini S&P, now the second most actively traded U.S. futures contract. Due to the general nature and volatility of the stock markets, these contracts reveal the increasing demand for smaller and electronically traded stock index contracts.

As new contracts are introduced, you may be wondering how you can watch all these different markets? I don't. I simply watch the ones where I have my trade alert signals set. By calculating the numbers and choosing 16 markets weekly, I narrow the field down. From those 16, I narrow the day-trading markets to the S&P, Dow, Nasdaq, and bonds, normally using 60-minute or 15-minute time periods for my studies.

The weekly numbers keep me focused on an important target for the week, and the daily numbers keep me focused on chart patterns to see if a recognizable setup is occurring. By watching the hourly closing time period to see if a bullish candle pattern appears at an important level of support or a bearish candle pattern at an area of resistance, I am able to determine a trading plan with a higher degree of confidence.

The 60-minute chart for the full-size Dow futures contract from late January 2002 (Figure 7.10) features several good examples of signals. In this case, using the data from January 24 (high 9855, low 9760, and close 9794), we calculated the S1 support for January 25 at 9751. During the second hour of trading on January 25, a bullish engulfing pattern formed and generated a strong buy signal. The opening of the third 60-minute period provided an opportunity to go long near 9790, using a stop below the low of 9735. In fact, a stop could have been placed below 9750 to bring the risk down to $400 ($10 times 40 points). Within one hour the market advanced to 9860 and gave an opportunity to move stops up or get out of a long position near the R1 resistance number of 9846. Three hours later the price advanced to a high of 9895, generating an opportunity to liquidate the long position near the daily resistance R2 of 9898.

The chart also points out why this analysis is not a precise science. With the S1 support target for the trading session at 9751, the actual low was

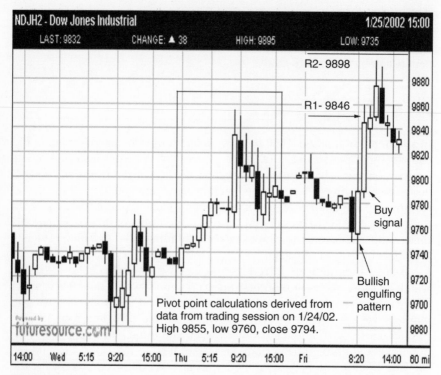

FIGURE 7.10   Finding the range. (*Source:* FutureSource. Reprinted with permission.)

9735. That is 16 ticks of slippage, which equates to $160 on the $10 per tick contract.

The 15-minute bond futures chart shown as Figure 7.11 is a P3T trade signal combining pivot point calculations with reliable candle patterns that also is an example of establishing risk factors or stop loss points that can help you attain a higher frequency of winning trades. At the very least, if you do your pivot point homework and watch the chart patterns at the close of each time period (15 minutes), then I believe you will not be selling the low of the range or buying the high of the range. When there are losers—and there will be—your loss amounts should not be as significant as they could be.

If you sold bonds near the low of the day near 110 because you were convinced the market was headed down and held on to that position up to the 111-16 level, the high of the day, you would probably agree it would have paid to have the pivot point numbers at hand. If you had them, you would have seen that the low was near the targeted low based off the S2 support number of 110 even. You may not have gone long at 110 because of your bearish conviction, but if you had the numbers, knew how to identify important

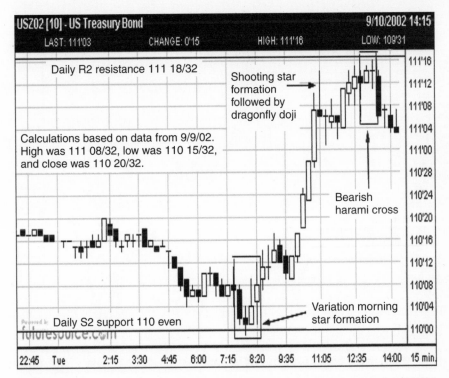

FIGURE 7.11 P3T trade in bonds. (*Source:* FutureSource. Reprinted with permission.)

candle formations, and practiced patience, you may have effectively gone short closer to 111-10.

The shooting star followed by the dragonfly doji signaled a top was near. Once the bearish harami cross formed, that should have given you ample conviction to sell short with stops above 111-18. The obvious question is: Where would you rather be short from, the 110 level or the 111-08 area? Of course, you'd like the 111-08 level. As a day trader you may have bought the low near 110 and placed stops below 109-31 once you had confirmation of the morning star pattern.

Here were two trade signals that were provided with candle chart formations at specific pivot point key numbers. Using effective risk management from proper stop loss order entry points is half the battle to consistent winning trades and wealth building.

Here, too, was a great opportunity for a short position at the 111-08 to 111-12 level. By the close of the market's open-outcry session, there wasn't much profit in the trade. But, because bonds trade virtually 24 hours, holding a short position overnight is manageable. Figure 7.12, a compressed 15-minute chart, shows the results of this trade and the effects that a shooting

FIGURE 7.12   P3T trade results. (*Source:* FutureSource. Reprinted with permission.)

star, dragonfly doji, and a bearish harami cross combination can have. The market fell to a low of 109-27 in less than 24 hours.

Once again, the hard part was deciding where to take a profit. If you don't remember, here is a solution to that problem: Move your stops down! The double bottom formation was a good spot to identify for taking nearly 1½ basis points or $1,500 out of the market.

Let's take on a more challenging situation, a 5-minute Dow futures chart with the price action on a day when an extraordinary event occurred (Figure 7.13). That was November 6, 2002, the day that the Federal Reserve policy-setting group, the Federal Open Market Committee, surprised the world with a 50-point decrease in the Fed funds rate, the first interest rate adjustment during 2002.

Was that a catalyst to incite volatility? You bet! But the pivot point numbers still identified the potential range for that day. Taking the data from the prior day's session (November 5, 2002, high of 8675, low of 8515, and close of 8648) placed the R2 resistance at 8771 and the S2 support at 8551, almost exactly on the high and low for the volatile trading day of November 6.

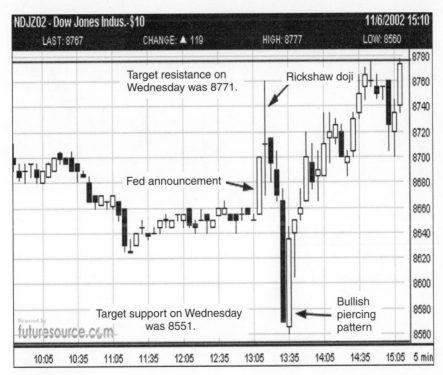

FIGURE 7.13 On target on an amazing day. (*Source:* FutureSource. Reprinted with permission.)

Take a look at the daily mini-sized Dow futures chart, starting with the actual low established at 7180 in October 2002 provided as Figure 7.14. Using data from the previous week ending October 4, 2002, the high was 7980; the low, 7450; and the close, 7550. That calculated out the S2 support at 7130, a small percentage margin of error. It was the bullish piercing pattern supported by the next long white candle's higher open that may have helped you catch a portion of that bottom price reversal.

Now look at the last three candles. The first two formed a bearish harami. That actually concluded the week on November 29, 2002, and, of course, ended the month of November. Taking the weekly range for the week ending November 29, 2002, the high was 8962; the low, 8660; and the close, 8870. The pivot point calculation reveals 9001 as the R1 weekly resistance number. On December 2, a Monday, the high was 9040, again a small margin of error of 39 Dow points. However, on that day, an extremely powerful doji candle formed. This particular doji, termed a long-legged doji or rickshaw doji, had helped to confirm the prior week's bearish harami formation as a sell signal. In addition, you had the weekly target resistance number of

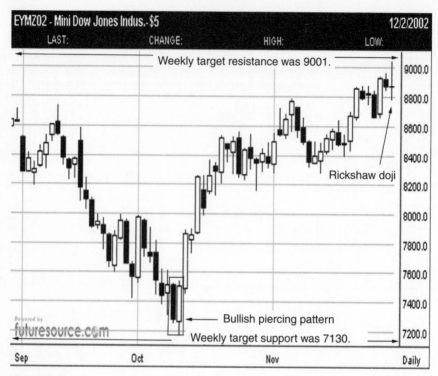

FIGURE 7.14   Reaching for the targets. (*Source:* FutureSource. Reprinted with permission.)

9001. That collection of indicators should have provided a wealth of sell signals in developing a proper game plan. At the very least it would have kept you from buying the high.

As the week finished and then continuing into the next week, the targeted S1 support was 8414. Again, that is based off the data collected from the week ending December 6—a high of 9040, low of 8485, and a close at 8657. If you were short, you may have earned nearly a 600-point decline for your trading account. The established low was 8441 on December 9 (Figure 7.15).

For the short-term or swing trader, action on the 15-minute Dow chart during this period on December 6 should be of interest (Figure 7.16). During the decline from the peak at 9040, the market did have some short-term correcting rallies. Using the prior day's figures from December 5 for the pivot point calculations (high 8828, low 8605, and close 8640), R1 resistance is 8777 and S1 support is 8468. Using the numbers from the prior week ending November 29 listed previously, S-2 support is 8528.The daily and corre-

FIGURE 7.15 Aftermath of doji top. (*Source:* FutureSource. Reprinted with permission.)

sponding weekly calculations, in addition to the bullish harami cross candle pattern, alerted a trader to a nearly 150-point Dow rally. This is another excellent example of how a textbook setup would help a trader identify an executable trade.

SUMMING UP TRADING TIPS

Here are some suggestions that may help you in day-trading or short-term swing trading:

- I use all sessions for the high, low, and close for the markets that trade 24 hours a day. Some quote vendors split the data between night and day. I combine both sessions as one day because that's what they are. Last night's high applies to the next day session's range, so I use that for my data in calculating the numbers.

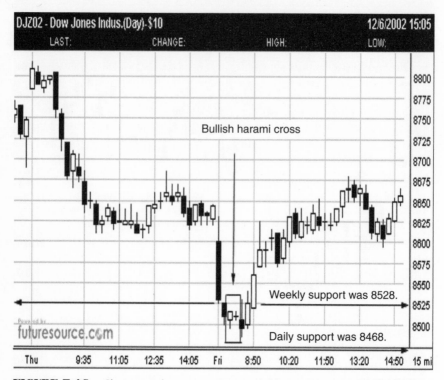

FIGURE 7.16   Short-term bounce. (*Source:* FutureSource. Reprinted with permission.)

- Tops take longer to form than bottoms so I will usually look for a second bearish candle formation at an important resistance number as a place to sell short.
- There are five business days in every week and usually four weeks in every month. One day within a month will mark a high, one day will generally mark a low, and the market will close somewhere between those points. That is what is called the range. The difference between a successful trader and a not so successful trader is the successful trader does not make a habit of buying the high of the range or selling the low of the range. When you are trading, at times it is hard to keep your emotions in check, so it is good to apply time and price logic in your thinking.
- Technical analysis is considered by most professionals to be an art and not an exact science. As technicians, we look at indicators or we rely on price pattern recognition techniques to give us clues to help interpret or anticipate the price direction or price movement of a market. Using these pivot point techniques combined with a discretionary method such as charting and chart pattern recognition allows a trader to have freedom of decision making while incorporating the flexibility of a me-

chanical trading method with prescribed numbers. This precise methodology will help eliminate and potentially solve the problem of trading on emotions and spur-of-the-moment hunches.

- Candle charting helps me clearly visualize chart pattern signals, and pivot point analysis alerts me to the potential highs and lows of a given time period of a particular market. Including other forms of technical analysis such as stochastics, moving averages, MACD studies, volume, and open interest helps me to make a logical, informed trading decision, where I can set my entry and exit points as well as define my risk parameters.
- As a trader, if you are out of money and have no more capital to work with, you are out of business. The elements necessary for generating profits as a trader are identifying and then acting on good trade signals. More important, when you are wrong, know when to get out, and act accordingly. These are the key elements for continuing to be a successful trader.
- Using pivot point analysis in your trading plans can help you not only plan your trades but also help establish and pinpoint entry and exit points as your personal target trading techniques. Most traders who are not familiar with using pivot points become excited and amazed at its consistency in predicting support and resistance in different time frames and for most markets.
- To stay on top of your technical analysis skills, I strongly recommend that all readers expand their knowledge and continue to learn new techniques as well as take a refresher course on the old ones.

CHAPTER 8

Technical Indicators

Confirming Evidence

The three purposes of thinking are to solve problems, to create opportunities, and to enrich the human condition.

—Abraham Lincoln

L incoln's statement was made long ago, but it really is the essence of this trading business. Which way will the market go? What indicators do I have to rely on? What influences are there on the market from a fundamental perspective? How can I benefit from this knowledge? Is the risk worth the reward? If I'm right, how much can I make? All of these questions require thinking.

To put more light on your analysis that will help you form an opinion about market direction, I would like to introduce you to other forms of indicators that can be applied in conjunction with pivot point and candle chart analysis—trading tools related by the use of mathematical formulas. Let me emphasize up front what follows is not a comprehensive explanation of all the indicators available. There are dozens of indicators, and some may be more valuable to you than those I describe. However, these are the indicators I use most frequently in my analysis.

MOVING AVERAGES

A moving average is defined as dividing the sum of two or more figures by the number of figures. In trading, that means adding up the price inputs for a given number of time periods and then dividing the sum by the number of time periods. Thus:

$$\text{Moving average} = \frac{(\text{Price 1} + \text{Price 2})}{n}$$

where n = the number of time periods.

Calculating simple moving averages can be useful for trend analysis and even in advanced computer trading systems. They are also used for identifying levels of support and resistance. Traders can use one moving average or combine a few different ones to overlay on their charts. By using short-term, intermediate-term, and long-term averages on top of a chart, you can see the trend direction of market prices from a different perspective. Typical time periods for multiple moving averages are 4, 9, and 18 periods, but today's software allows you to use any number of periods you want.

Linearly weighted moving averages can be calculated by taking, say, a five-day time period and multiplying the close of the last time period by five, multiplying the close of the previous time period by four, multiplying the close of the time period before that by three, and so on. Add the sum of all five time periods and then divide by five to get a weighted average that gives more significance to the most recent price action.

Exponential moving averages are calculated from complex formulas and have become the most common averages used today by many quote vendors, analysts, and traders as they also are weighted to give more importance to the latest data from current market conditions, and older data that becomes less important as time passes are eventually filtered out.

Calculating all of these numbers by hand or even with a calculator is tedious and time-consuming, but, fortunately, computers can now figure all of that out for us. I believe in the KISS method—keep it simple, stupid.

Many rules can be applied in moving average analysis. Different time periods can be used from, say, 3 minutes to 200 days. Generally speaking, longer-term time periods in moving average calculations will generate fewer trade signals than shorter-term time period calculations will. Different price points or averages of an average can be used. For example, you can take the average on a closing basis, or you can include the high, low, or even the range of a given time period average in an average.

Here are the simplest rules for trading moving averages:

- If the market is trading above the moving average, you should be long.
- If the market is trading below the moving average, you should be short.
- When the market has been trading below a moving average and then breaks out above it, you have a buy signal.

- When the market has been trading above a moving average and then breaks out below it, you have a sell signal.
- Buy or sell signals can also be generated when a short-term moving average crosses over a longer-term moving average.

Moving average techniques are numerous, from the simple to the complex trading system that a programmer can create for a computer to generate signals based on crossovers or price breakouts of moving average points of interest.

First, however, you should realize an important aspect about moving averages: They do not work well in volatile, choppy conditions or in markets that are in a trading range. In these trading range conditions, buy and sell signals will be generated every time the market gyrates above and below the moving average lines. Responding to this activity will simply kill you and your trading capital. A market spends most of its time in a consolidation phase and only about a third of its time in a trending mode, so that is a factor you have to keep in mind before relying on moving averages too much.

A more proven method of trading moving averages is the *dead cross* that occurs when a shorter-term moving average falls below the longer-term average and a downtrend is initiated. When a *golden cross* occurs, the short-term moving average crosses above the longer-term average.

Moving average crossover signals can get you positioned for some nice trends, as shown on Figure 8.1, the weekly crude oil chart showing moving averages of 5, 10, and 20 periods. You can watch various time frames, but my favorites are 3, 9, and 18 periods for most markets on a daily basis. The most popular longer-term moving averages for equity markets and individual stocks are 50, 100, and 200 days.

Most of the time the point of crossover is a significant point of resistance or support for future reference points of interest. Why? Because this is the actual point from which traders see a signal generated. Whenever you look at a chart, it is easy to see the old highs or lows. But to examine where the breakdown of support and the breakout of resistance occurred, overlay the 3-, 9-, and 18-period moving averages on a chart. A lot of time you will see that a market does not rally to test the old highs but, instead, goes up to test the point of the moving average crossover.

Does this move to a crossover point guarantee a winning trade every time you sell when a market revisits the old crossovers? Of course not. What it can do is illustrate a potential turning signal. It is wise to have other forms of verifying analytical methods to increase your odds of a successful trade. Note on Figure 8.1 that the crude oil market shows both a dead cross before a price decline and a golden cross before a price advance.

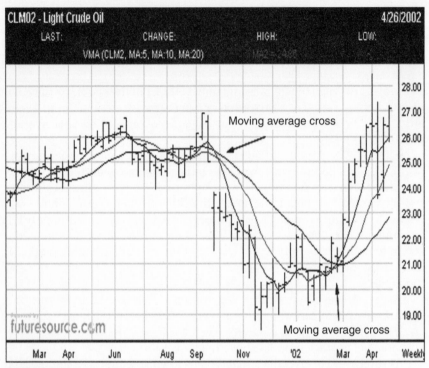

FIGURE 8.1   Crossing over. (*Source:* FutureSource. Reprinted with permission.)

Resistance levels such as this crossover point can have one of three qualities: (1) create a reversal level, (2) cause a pause in an advancing trend, or (3) have little effect at all. That is why momentum traders reverse their positions if an important resistance level is violated. Generally, you do see markets return to test old highs or lows—that is what creates the double tops and double bottoms. But, in other instances, the moving average crossover is the actual signal point.

Figure 8.2, the daily chart of crude oil, shows moving averages of 3, 9, and 18 days with the crossover point in March at or near $31 a barrel. This activity illustrates that a market tends to test the point of crossover, as it did in June, rather than the actual high.

In preparing my newsletter on Friday, June 6, I noted that not only was the week's pivot point resistance number $31.05, but it also was a monthly pivot point resistance level as well. Checking to see what relevant resistance there was near $31, I overlaid the 3-, 9-, and 18-day moving averages. Lo and behold, there was the dead cross that occurred back in March when the market peaked near $32.50. My expectation was for a significant reversal, based on the confluence of resistance points plus the dead cross. The

FIGURE 8.2   Test of moving average crossover. (*Source:* FutureSource. Reprinted with permission.)

recommendation was to sell near $31, using $31.49 as a stop. I also suggested looking at buying September 28 put options. (See more on the topic of options in Chapter 13.)

My analysis of the potential for a rally to test and then fail at or near $31 was an accurate decision based solely on these methods of technical analysis. The market did make a high the following week on Wednesday, June 11, at $31.15 and then proceeded to sell off nearly $2.40 per barrel to a low at $28.75 within two days. As a trader, I am only interested in capturing a trade, not a long-term investment in crude oil.

Arguably, the hardest part of this move would be to manage the exit point to determine a profit amount, right? Wrong. First, you should have moved stops down to the level above the 3-day moving average, which is $30.23. That at least locks in a profit. Second, if you were a multiple contract trader, you would get out of half of your positions as the market touched the 18-day moving average as that level will act as support—and it did! Rule of thumb: If you make 100 percent of your initial margin requirement, get out of the trade if you are a one-contract trader. Multiple position traders should move stops down and get out of half of their positions. Placing stops above the 3-day and even the 9-day moving average on the balance of positions is a smart placement level as these moving averages have a solid history of acting as a support or resistance level.

If the greatest story ever told is the Bible, I believe the second greatest story ever told is a chart. There are no opinions, only facts and pure price data. That is why they say charts don't lie.

The daily silver chart shown as Figure 8.3 paints a great story and helps to substantiate the lesson about moving averages. The beginning point of interest is the crossover that occurred in March around $4.67 an ounce. Note that this is where the market paused (Point A) after testing the crossover resistance point. It actually helped to generate a small 12-cent pullback, co-incidently right back near the 18-day moving average (Point B). Then a belt hold (or benchmark) candle blasted through that resistance level (Point C).

Earlier in this chapter I mentioned that once a significant resistance level is violated, momentum traders may reverse positions. Also, I mentioned that

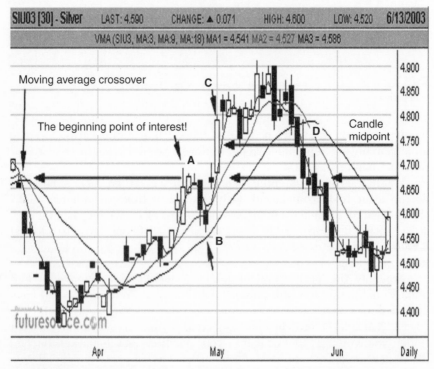

FIGURE 8.3   Testing reference points. (*Source:* FutureSource. Reprinted with permission.)

the midpoint of a benchmark candle will offer a first support level on pull-backs—after all, isn't the midpoint the average of the range? Figure 8.3 shows an example as that candle's midpoint served as a strong level of support for nearly 13 trading sessions. Once that failed, the market continued lower. That final break below the candle's midpoint was also about the time when the 3-period moving average formed a dead cross, confirming that the bull trend had ended.

You can analyze the same silver chart to point out where silver prices might stop descending and find support (Figure 8.4). Recalling that a support or resistance level may act as a reversal point or a pausing point or fail and do nothing at all, here is how I analyzed this situation in making a recommendation to go long in my weekly newsletter for the week ending June 13. I like to use other methods of analysis, as you may have guessed, particularly pivot points. The weekly pivot point support was $4.49, the monthly support number was calculated as $4.39. The moving average crossover in early April occurred in the $4.45 area. Plus a gap existed near that level. Silver made a brief low on Wednesday, June 11 (coincidentally, the same day

FIGURE 8.4 Signs of the end. (*Source:* FutureSource. Reprinted with permission.)

crude oil made its high). It rallied 16 cents from that low to the high of $4.60 two days later—certainly not a substantial move, but it was a nice trade after spotting the potential reversal signal from the 3-period moving average crossover level.

My most fervent advice: Use the pivot point numbers on a weekly and monthly basis when they coincide with a moving average support or resistance level or a crossover intersection. Act on the signal with an appropriate stop or risk level. Generally, that should be a point established below the actual low or high in relationship to the area of the moving average crossover.

For example, based on the weekly pivot point number, the buy signal on the silver chart (Figure 8.4) was $4.49. The moving average crossover was at $4.45. The previous low was $4.38. A good trading plan would be to buy near $4.45 up to $4.49 with stops below $4.38. Once the market moves off that low, manage the trade by monitoring the price action and moving stops up to the breakeven point. As silver prices move higher, adjust your stops to start protecting a profit.

Never—I mean never!—keep your stop at breakeven all the time. My reason is that once you establish the trade, you enter a risk situation. Once the trade moves to breakeven, you still need to keep your stop at the original loss amount. You do not want to be stopped out prematurely. Besides, the market really hasn't moved. However, once the market finally does advance, look to adjust your stop from risk to breakeven.

Remember the rule of thumb: If you make a 100 percent return on your initial margin requirement, liquidate half of your position, especially if the move occurs in a short period of time such as a day or two. This book is about trading, which is another way of saying base hits. Futures is not about long-term investing or waiting for each trade to turn into home runs.

Victor Niederhoffer gave a great word of advice on my radio program on June 18, 2003: "Don't try to be number one always looking to be in the top 25 percent." His point was not to get too aggressive and to take profits.

MOVING AVERAGE CONVERGENCE/DIVERGENCE

More commonly known as MACD, moving average convergence/divergence in simplest terms is an indicator that shows when a short-term moving average crosses over a longer-term moving average. Gerald Appel developed MACD as we know it today, and it is my understanding that he developed it for the purpose of trading stocks.

MACD includes three exponential moving averages (EMA). The initial inputs for the calculations were 9, 12, and 26 periods. Because traders are now more computer savvy than ever before, it is easy to change or tweak the variables in the original calculations. You can increase the time periods in the moving average calculations to generate fewer trade signals or shorten the time periods to generate more trade signals.

The 12-period and 26-period EMAs are usually based on closing prices (you could choose some other price component). When you subtract the 26-period EMA from the 12-period EMA, you get a difference known as the *fast* MACD line. Then you use the fast line to calculate a 9-period EMA, which gives you the *slow* line. When the fast line crosses above the slow line, a buy signal is generated. When the fast line crosses below the slow line, a sell signal is generated.

MACD signals react quickly to changes in the market. That is why many analysts including myself use this indicator, which helps to clear the picture when moving average crossovers occur. One of the most useful clues provided by this indicator, as with a number of other indicators, is known as *divergence*. This is a condition where the market price makes a low that is lower than a previous low but the underlying MACD pattern makes a higher low. This divergence indicates that the low is weak or a false bottom due to less selling pressure and signals a potential price reversal. The same is true in an uptrend when prices make a higher high but MACD makes a lower high, indicating a potential change to lower prices.

The weekly S&P 500 cash index provides an example (Figure 8.5). Prices made a lower low in September than in the March/April time frame (A), but the MACD made a higher high, which signaled the low was exhausted and was a false bottom. The market moved higher for about six months before the next wave lower formed a potential new setup for a bullish divergence buy signal (B).

A relatively newer method of using MACD features a graph called a *histogram*, which indicates the difference between the fast and slow MACD lines. I personally prefer the regular graph instead of the histogram when looking at this indicator, but the concept of the histogram is that if the bars are above the zero line, you should be long, and if the bars are below the zero line, you should be short. If the bars below the zero line are getting shorter or if the bars above the zero line are getting longer, it indicates that prices are rising and you want to trade the market from the long side. Conversely, if the bars above the zero line are getting shorter or if the bars below the zero line are getting longer, it indicates prices are falling and you want to trade from the short side.

Again, divergence is important, as Figure 8.6, the S&P cash index chart, shows. If prices continue to increase but the histogram bars above the zero line become smaller, then an impending change may be in store as the histogram suggests the uptrend may be running out of steam. Point C on the chart provides a good example.

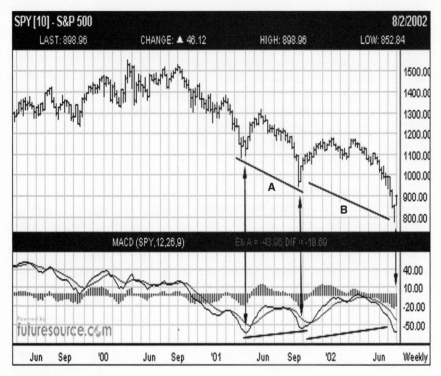

FIGURE 8.5   MACD, price convergence. (*Source:* FutureSource. Reprinted with permission.)

STOCHASTICS

George C. Lane is credited with creating the formula for a momentum oscillator indicator called *stochastics*. Here is another example of a person whose passion for the field of technical analysis motivated research into price behavior and resulted in a true master technician. George and his wife Carrie both are excellent teachers and truly care about their students. These are people that you want to meet and learn from.

Lane's stochastics indicator is a popular technical tool used to help determine whether a market is *overbought*, meaning that prices have advanced too far too soon and are due for a downside correction, or *oversold*, meaning prices have declined too far too fast and are due for an upside correction. The mathematical formula for stochastics compares the settlement price of a specific time period to the price range of a specific number of past periods.

The theory works off the assumption that, in a bull or uptrending market, prices tend to make higher highs and the settlement price usually tends to be

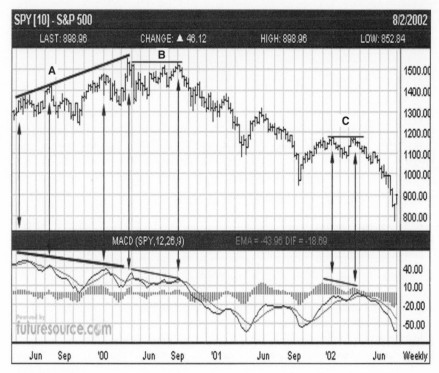

FIGURE 8.6 Divergence signals change. (*Source:* FutureSource. Reprinted with permission.)

in the upper end of that time period's trading range. When the momentum starts to slow, the settlement prices will start to fade from the upper boundaries of the range, and stochastics will show that the bullish momentum is starting to fade. The exact opposite is true for bear or downtrending markets.

The two lines in stochastics are referred to as %K and %D. These are plotted on a horizontal axis for a given time period, and the vertical axis is plotted on a scale from 0 percent to 100 percent. The formula to calculate the first component, %K, is:

$$\%K = (c - Ln/Hn - Ln) \times 100$$

where c = closing price of current period
Ln = lowest low during n period of time
Hn = highest high during n period of time and
n = number of periods

The second calculation is the %D figure, which is the moving average of %K. Here is the %D calculation:

$$\%D = 100(Hn/Ln)$$

where Hn is the n period sum of $(c - Ln)$.

Wow, isn't that something?! Is the formula worth knowing and doing by hand? No way! Fortunately, computers calculate stochastics for us, and most software vendors include stochastics in their services.

What is important is understanding the rules about how to interpret buy or sell signals:

- When the readings are above 70 percent and %K crosses over the %D line and both lines are pointing down, a hook sell signal is generated.
- When %K crosses above %D when the reading is below 30 percent and both lines are pointing up, a buy signal is generated.

Some people adjust the 30-70 parameters, and there are other techniques associated with using stochastics. One is a trading pattern called *bullish convergence*, which is used in identifying market bottoms. The market price itself makes a lower low than a previous low, but the underlying stochastic pattern makes a higher low, indicating that the low is a false bottom and can result in a price reversal.

Another signal is a trading pattern called *bearish divergence*, which is used in identifying market tops. The market price itself makes a higher high than a previous high, but the underlying stochastic pattern makes a lower high, indicating that the second high is a weak high and can result in a lower price reversal.

These patterns are similar to those of the MACD indicator. Stochastics can be programmed for trading on a one-minute, daily, or monthly basis. Short-term professional day traders and long-term traders can and do use this indicator. Stochastics do well in volatile or choppy market conditions, unlike moving average studies, which do not. However, in trending market conditions, stochastics may generate false buy or sell signals.

Visual observation of your charts combined with the help of computer-calculated price indicators can be powerful aids for traders. The general rule is to trade and use signals that coincide with the overall trend. For example, if the trend is down, wait for a correction and then watch for a sell signal to develop.

As seen in Figure 8.7, the trend is clearly lower on the S&P 500 futures chart in the first week of May when the stochastics generates a bullish divergence buy signal and the market shows a 50-plus point gain. By the end of

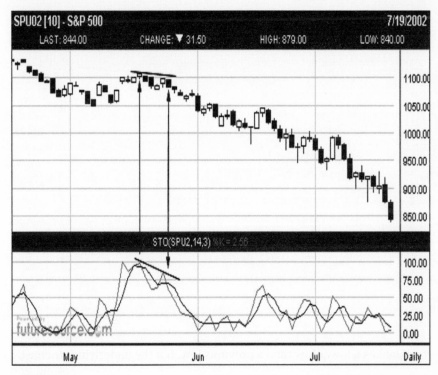

FIGURE 8.7   Stochastics show divergence. (*Source:* FutureSource. Reprinted with permission.)

May a bearish divergence developed as the market trend continued lower and stochastics made an even steeper decline. Notice that during the whole downtrend that followed, the stochastics indicator continued to generate buy signals. There are small gains that are tradable for a one-day or two-day swing trader, but the difficulty is that the only classic stochastics signal where the %K and %D cross over is the sell signal back in late May when the stochastics readings were above 75 percent.

Figure 8.8 is a classic example of bearish divergence on a weekly chart of the euro currency futures contract. A little background on the fundamentals will help you understand the importance of this chart. The U.S. stock market was in a severe decline, and foreign investors were pulling their capital out of the United States—things looked bleak. Remember, as the U.S. dollar declines, foreign currencies increase in value. Looking at the chart, notice how the stochastics signaled bearish divergence as the euro hit 101.80, a new high, in the week ending July 19, 2002, but stochastics did not make a new higher high.

FIGURE 8.8   Divergence at the top. (*Source:* FutureSource. Reprinted with permission.)

In addition to stochastics indicating a bearish divergence sell signal, euro prices for the following week, ending July 26, had formed a long dark candle and closed lower and below the previous week's close and low. Further, if you had the monthly pivot point price projections, you would have known that the R1 target high for the July time period was 101.40. The actual high was 101.80. Yes, this chart should be used as an example under pivot point analysis, but the stochastics bearish divergence was a powerful influence as well.

Look at the euro picture again a few weeks later as shown in Figure 8.9. After the combination of sell signals, the market tumbled back to the 96.00–96.50 level, failing to continue higher and consolidating in a lower trading range. This is a good example of how to use the verification from stochastics to exit long positions or, at the very least, to not enter a long position at the very top. Using candlestick charting may have given you the visual pattern recognition alert to help you identify a top or turning point in the trend. Combined with pivot point monthly analysis, these signals again provided a proven winning technique, verified by the stochastics signal.

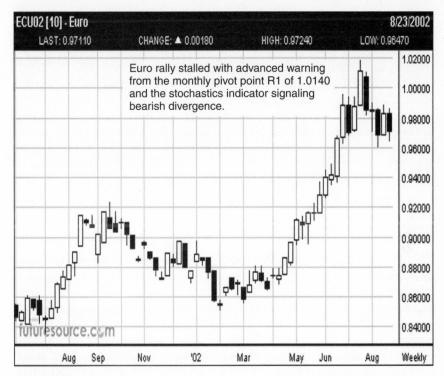

FIGURE 8.9 Stochastics verification. (*Source:* FutureSource. Reprinted with permission.)

GANN THEORY

William D. Gann was a trader in the first half of the 20th century who died in 1955 and left behind a legacy of instrumental and complex trading theories. His philosophy of trading was considered to be a mixture of mathematical, geometrical, and astrological analysis. Truly a legend, the secrets behind his trading tools and methodology consisted of two things, hard work and common sense.

Gann's techniques were based not only on measurements of price but also on time and cycles. Time turns or counts are as important and significant for the market's price behavior as cycles are for nature. Look at the changes from night and day, high tide and low tide, winter and summer seasons. These times can be determined by mathematical calculations, and Gann believed the markets could be as well.

Among the concepts Gann used were price corrections based on percentages derived by dividing the market's price action into eighths as well as thirds. He is also famous for developing the importance of a 45-degree trend-line angle, the Gann "Cardinal Square," and the timing of market events based on the degrees of a circle such as 30, 60, 90, 180, and 360 degrees. If the market made a bottom today, he would try to calculate the next turning point using these numbers to project into the future.

Gann also was big on anniversary dates of big events—for instance, 1 month, 3 months, and 12 months. There was also the 144-day period, the only square Fibonacci number. Some chartists believe in filtering out a lot of these calculations and just using the basics. Gann methods alone would make a book and are far too extensive to cover here. Gann wrote a book, *How to Make Profits in Commodities*, which would be a great place to start if you want further information on his teachings.

FIBONACCI NUMBERS

Thirteenth-century Italian mathematician Leonardo Fibonacci concluded that a number sequence reflected human nature and that patterns repeated themselves in a certain order. The *Fibonacci series*, as it is called, is an infinite series of numbers that adds each number to the previous number such that $1 + 1 = 2$, $2 + 1 = 3$, $3 + 2 = 5$, $5 + 3 = 8$, and so on to get a number sequence of 1, 1, 2, 3, 5, 8, 13, 21, 34, 55, 89, 144, ... These numbers are used to help cycle analysts time market turns and lengths of price moves. Major tops or bottoms are often calculated by starting with the event of a high or low and then calculating out in time and price increments that correspond to the Fibonacci series.

Fibonacci's work can be applied to trading in various ways. You can look at time cycles, searching for a coincidence of a reoccurring pattern that develops on a historic basis such as every 21, 34, 55, or 144 days or perhaps 3, 13, 21, 34, . . . weeks. If you do a little math, you will see that the numbers, other than the first few smaller ones, all have the same consistent ratio to each other. These ratios—0.382, 0.50, 0.618, 0.768, 1.00—show up often in analysts' research as price retracement levels, wave lengths, time projections, and in other ways. For example, you can take the distance in time from price peak to peak and then apply these ratios to help predict the timing of the next potential peak or smaller or larger peaks.

Figure 8.10, the S&P 500 futures chart, shows a five-month cycle count. Not only did the low on July 24, 2002, fall on the five-month number but also on the day of a full moon. The significance of the five-month cycle is that it is a Fibonacci series number and is approximately 100 trading days, which is a Fibonacci ratio figure and the length of a moving average that many traders watch. Not all of the lows on the chart are monumental lows, but more times than not they are distinctive lows. Pivot point analysis pinpointed the R2 target weekly low for the July low at 781.67, close to the actual figure.

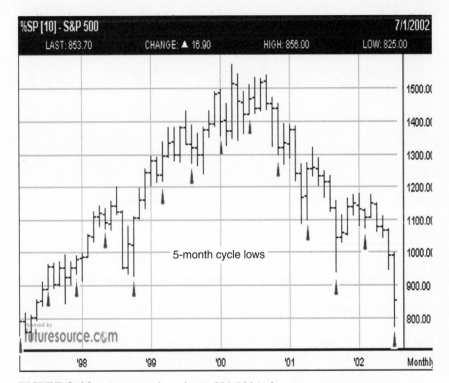

FIGURE 8.10 Five-month cycles in S&P 500 index. (*Source:* FutureSource. Reprinted with permission.)

This market had many good clues for a potential bottom to occur. However, keep in mind that picking bottoms can be hazardous to your wealth. This information might have at least kept you from selling short in the hole.

When looking for a cycle occurrence—in other words, a repetitive pattern—go back to historical price moves. This research may prove to be enlightening for your trading. Here is an example taken from an article that was e-mailed to clients and posted on my web site on Tuesday, July 23, 2002, the day before the Dow made a bottom at 7450 and the S&P 500 index low was 771.30.

The seven worst months for the S&P 500 since the inception of stock index futures in 1982 were, in calendar order:

1. October 1987, 152 points
2. October 1997, 148 points
3. August 1998, 175 points

4. April 2000, 201 points
5. March 2001, 182 points
6. September 2001, 219 points
7. July 2002 (as of July 23), 208.5 points (996.5 high to the low right now of 788)

Is it wrong buying near such an extreme decline, knowing what the results were every time the market experienced such declines of this magnitude? If you were wondering why I am not bearish now, it is because of historical standards. The market price usually dictates a substantial rally after severe monthly declines. Odds of being right that the market will rebound when the market declines between 150 and 219 points are good. In fact, all declines before the 201-point decline in April 2000 resulted in a continuation of a bull market. The April 2000 decline still resulted in sharp advances before the downtrend continued.

There are chartists who see the head-and-shoulders formation on a monthly chart, and that is one reason for their price projections to 550. It is possible, but I do not believe it will be this month or this year. Elliott wave theorists believe we will never see 10,000 in the Dow ever again. Well, that could be, but let me share with you one thought. Joe Granville (older investors may remember that name) was a major doom-and-gloomer back in 1980 when I got in the business. He was warning that the Dow would crash even back then. The Dow was at 900. As we know now, it is at 7700. That crash he warned about? Never happened.

What's my point? Try not to get bearish in the hole, and never follow the herd mentality. Use common sense and always—I mean always—use stops.

By identifying the five-month cycle low count and looking at the historical price record, I was able to make a keen observation and share it with my fellow investors. A good plan based on good analysis does pay off!

This book was not intended to go much into cycle studies. However, the amazing repetitiveness of another timing cycle is worth mentioning. The equities market seems to respond to what I identified as an 11-week cycle low back in late 2001. The relevance of the 11-week cycle is that it is approximately 55 trading days—the number 55 is a Fibonacci series number, and it is approximately half or 50 percent of the five-month cycle. The 50 percent Fibonacci ratio number also interacts as a reference with the 11-week cycle. So there is a connection with the Fibonacci series and ratio numbers.

Futures magazine printed an article I wrote in the December 2002 issue predicting that the week ending December 29 would be the date to expect a low to occur in the stock market. This article was written in the middle of October to make the printing deadline. There was no turning back—after all, who wants to be wrong in their predictions? Most analysts expected the traditional "Santa Claus rally" prior to the holiday season. The fact of the matter is that the market did make a low in the last week of December, as the 11-week cycle projected (Figure 8.11), and the S&P 500 index proceeded to gain more than 50 points (nearly 600 points in the Dow)!

An interesting point regarding this 11-week cycle: 11 is not a Fibonacci series number. However, it has Fibonacci connections, as previously noted. A good point to raise now is that shorter-term cycles within the Fibonacci framework do occur within longer-term cycles. The term referencing this tie is called a *harmonic timing event*. Cycles do not react exactly the same way. Not all moves will be proportionally equal. The charts with the 5-month and 11-week cycles will certainly point this out.

So why study cycles and use the Fibonacci series or time counts? In this case, they seem to have a bearing on when the equity markets rally. Once again, following a repetitive trend or pattern is what a technician is after.

FIGURE 8.11 Eleven-week cycles in S&P 500 index. (*Source:* FutureSource. Reprinted with permission.)

Back to Fibonacci methods. One more study Leonardo is credited with is the common *retracement* percentage figures. They are rounded off at 0.38 percent, 0.50 percent, 0.618 percent, 0.786 percent, 1.272 percent, and 1.618 percent. These numbers are actual ratios within his Fibonacci series. For example, 1 divided by 2 is 50 percent, 2 divided by 3 is 66 percent, 144 divided by 233 is 0.618, 0.786 is the square root of 0.618, 1.00 subtracted from 0.618 equals –0.382.

The theory behind Fibonacci price retracements is that, when a market makes an initial move from, say, a low to a high, it is normal for that market to make some corrections with retracements of 0.382, 0.50, 0.618, or 0.786 of that upmove and to then continue the original trend. These calculations are also good for establishing profit objectives, which are derived from a sound and reasonable mathematical application. The cattle futures chart provided as Figure 8.12 is a good example of a 50 percent correction in prices from a longer-term perspective on a weekly chart. The 50 percent retracement target price (dashed line) was established from the high in February near $71.00 to the low that was established in April at $59.92. The 50 percent

FIGURE 8.12   Fifty percent retracement in cattle. (*Source:* FutureSource. Reprinted with permission.)

calculation for the market to bounce back from the low provided a good price objective for planning a trade.

There are many Fibonacci experts. One such expert in Fibonacci ratio work is Joe DiNapoli of Coast Investment Software. DiNapoli was a guest on the "Personal Investors Hour" on August 6, 2003, and described a technique using Fibonacci ratios to help calculate potential price moves by extending out the value of a move and applying the ratio numbers to that figure. For example, let's say that prices move 10 points from Point A to Point B. The market makes a 50 percent retracement to Point C. Take the value of the A–B move (10 points) times the Fibonacci numbers 0.618 percent, 1.00 percent and 1.618 percent and then add the results to Point C to give you price projections or possible resistance levels that the market may test (Figure 8.13).

I have often used this method and find an uncanny coincidence with the pivot point calculations. When that occurs, it absolutely gives me a stronger reason to exit a position near that projected resistance and even gives me an idea that a reversal of my position may be in order from that area.

Figure 8.14 shows an application of projected Fibonacci measurements on a daily S&P futures chart. With a low at 957 (Point A) and a high at 1010 (Point B), the move was 53 points. The Point C low was 980. Multiplying 53 by the Fibonacci ratio of 0.618 and adding that number to the Point C low produced a target of 1012.75. Adding a full 100 percent extension of 53 points to Point C resulted in a target of 1033.

Applying pivot point analysis was slightly more accurate in pinpointing the high. Using the weekly target method, if you take the prior week's numbers—week ending September 5, 2003, when the high was 1028, the low was 1003.50, and the market closed at 1020.2—and calculate the pivot point formulas, you would have had 1030.97 for the R1 calculation and 1006.47 for the S1 calculation.

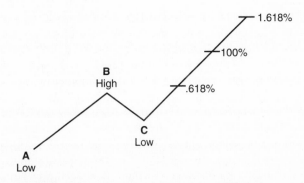

FIGURE 8.13 Projecting Fibonacci targets.

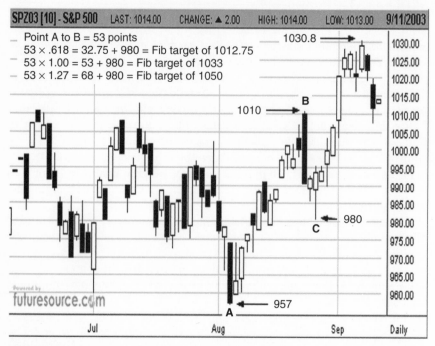

FIGURE 8.14   Reaching Fibonacci and pivot point targets. (*Source:* FutureSource. Reprinted with permission.)

The actual high was 1030.80. The last low before the chart was copied was 1009. The margin of error was quite a bit smaller using the pivot point numbers, but here was a phenomenal validating combination using the Fibonacci and pivot point analysis methods together.

Another method for applying Fibonacci ratios is in calculating an extension of a price correction. Sometimes markets may go beyond the traditional 0.50 percent, 0.618 percent or 0.786 percent move. They can and do retrace back 100 percent of a move. This action would be considered a retest of the low or the formation of a double bottom. Sometimes you may wonder why a market made a newer low, only to bounce back, and you swear that it only made the new low to hunt for your stops. Fibonacci price extensions can help solve that mystery. If you apply a Fibonacci ratio multiplier of 1.272 percent or 1.618 percent of the initial move, you can determine potential support beneath the market once it has taken out the initial low (Figure 8.15).

Using Fibonacci price objectives is similar in theory to pivot point analysis but does not have as detailed a mathematical equation. It deals with a relative length of a move rather than the time constraints such as a daily, weekly, or monthly range calculation that pivot point analysis needs.

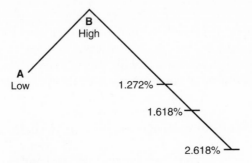

FIGURE 8.15   Fibonacci price support extensions.

The difficult part about using the Fibonacci ratios is identifying the points of peaks and troughs.

ELLIOTT WAVE THEORY

Ralph N. Elliott began to develop his theories and views that prices move in waves in the 1920s. He identified *impulse waves* as those waves moving with the main trend and *corrective waves* as those waves going against the main trend. Impulse waves have five primary price movements, and corrective waves have three primary price moves (Figure 8.16).

Elliott presumably used some of Fibonacci's work because of the way he described a wave cycle in a series of 5 and 3 waves, both Fibonacci numbers. The fundamental concept behind Elliot's theory is that bull markets have a tendency to follow a basic five-wave advance, followed by a three-wave decline. The exact opposite is true for bear markets.

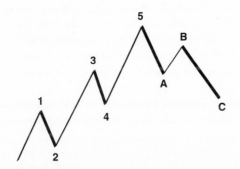

FIGURE 8.16   Basic Elliott wave pattern.

More experienced chartists, of course, might recognize that point five could possibly be considered the number one point of a 1-2-3 formation or the head of a head-and-shoulders formation. The one thing Elliott most wanted chartists to recognize is that his wave theory worked on long-term charts as well as intraday charts. A wave is a wave. Each wave contains lesser-degree waves while at the same time being a subset of a higher-degree wave.

Each wave has its own set of rules. Here are the basic ideas:

- The first wave is derived from the starting point and usually appears to be a bounce from a previous trend.
- The second wave usually retraces the entire previous trend. This is what technicians generally consider the makings of a W or M (1-2-3 patterns), double tops or bottoms, or a head-and-shoulders chart pattern.
- The third wave is one of the most important. It is where you see the trend confirmation occur. Technicians jump on the trend and place market orders to enter a position from the breakout above the number one wave. You usually see a large increase in volume and open interest at that point. One rule that needs to be followed: For the third wave to be a true wave, it cannot be the shortest of the five waves.
- The fourth wave is a corrective wave. It usually gives back some of the advance from the third wave. You might see measuring chart patterns such as triangles, pennants, or flags, which are continuation patterns and generally break out in the same direction as the overall trend. The most important rule to remember about the fourth wave is that the low of the fourth wave can never overlap the top of the first wave.
- The fifth wave is usually still strong in the direction of the trend, but it is also during this final phase that the price advance begins to slow. From the rule of multiple techniques, indicators and oscillators such as RSI and stochastics begin to show signs of being overbought or oversold and the market begins to lose momentum.
- Wave A is usually mistaken as a regular pullback in the trend, but this is where you could possibly start seeing the makings of a W or M (1-2-3 patterns), double tops or bottoms, or a head-and-shoulders chart pattern.
- Wave B is a small retracement back toward the high of wave five, but it does not quite reach that point. This is where traders exit their position or begin to position for a move in the opposite direction.
- Wave C confirms the end of the uptrend. When confirmation is made by going beyond wave A, then another cycle begins in the opposite direction.

Figure 8.17 shows an example of a bearish Elliott wave pattern. Using trendline analysis to help uncover the waves, you can see how clear the pat-

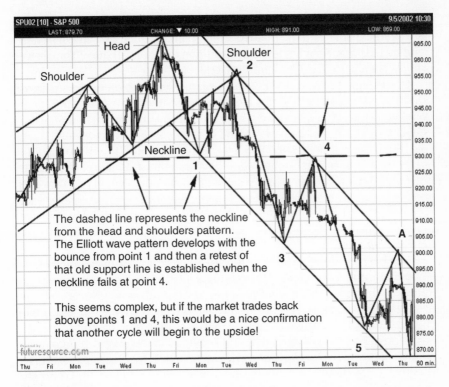

The dashed line represents the neckline from the head and shoulders pattern. The Elliott wave pattern develops with the bounce from point 1 and then a retest of that old support line is established when the neckline fails at point 4.

This seems complex, but if the market trades back above points 1 and 4, this would be a nice confirmation that another cycle will begin to the upside!

FIGURE 8.17 Elliott waves in trending channels. (*Source:* FutureSource. Reprinted with permission.)

terns can become. In using the theory in practice, you would look for a resumption of the uptrend to continue with a move above the neckline or the dashed line where Points 1 and 4 intersect.

For further research on the theory of Elliott wave analysis, *Elliott Wave Principles* by A. J. Frost and Robert Prechter would be helpful as would any other writings by Prechter.

SUMMARY

With all the tools and techniques I have mentioned, you might almost feel like a victim of information overload. That is true, but I believe it is helpful to become familiar with the more popular techniques and get a feel for what works for you, the individual investor. There are different types of technical indicators for different types of market conditions and for different types of traders.

Moving averages will eat you alive in trading range markets. Oscillators such as stochastics and the relative strength index will crush you in steadily trending markets. So what is the best trading technique to use? The answer is there is no perfect solution or holy grail.

One thing I do know is that I can't jump around from one system to another. If a system or method that has been consistent starts to fail and I abandon it and start to shop around for a new method, by the time I notice how effective and accurate the new method is, that is about the time when it runs cold. Stick to what works and when you run cold, take a break. Some of the biggest and best players in the game have gone bust. Some have even run years without a winning streak. What is important is that you can step back and reevaluate what is going wrong. Sometimes you just need to paper trade while you are retesting a system, method, or skills. Not only can paper trading help restore your confidence, but it also may keep your remaining working capital intact.

You can use these or many other tools or chart patterns to develop a setup that informs you it is time to initiate a trade and execute a predetermined trading plan. That plan includes setting target levels for risk and profit objectives. Pattern recognition, whether it is candles or traditional chart patterns, is a learned technique that does take time to study. The benefit of pivot point analysis is that it is based on calculations and gives immediate target price levels as does Fibonacci work. Moving average studies do offer a convincing alternative for a verifying technical tool, and stochastics can help determine the potential turn in trends.

These are what I personally look at when I am analyzing the markets on a technical scope. I review what the pivot point analysis looks like on a daily, weekly, and monthly basis. I look at the stochastic indicators beneath the actual bar charts and have an overlay of the 3-, 9-, and 18-period exponential moving averages on each of those three time periods. I also include MACD for short-, intermediate-, and long-term analysis. I examine bar charts and candle charts for these three time periods and include these indicators along with trend line analysis to help me in my price forecasting techniques.

Fibonacci is an easy tool as most software companies include the normal price correction ratios. It takes more specialized software to include the features of projections and extensions. For futures traders, Gecko Software provides an incredibly good graphic and detailed packaged product that includes many of the Fibonacci tools such as the arch, time count, retracement, and extension tools a trader might want to explore.

These are a few of the favorite technical tools I use to supplement my pivot point target numbers. They work for me. Maybe you will want to use some or all of these techniques in your analysis as well.

CHAPTER 9

Market Sentiment

What Traders Are Thinking

A professional is one who does his best work when he feels the least like working.

—Frank Lloyd Wright

Wright's comment is a long-time favorite of mine because it applies so well in the trading business. Trading demands discipline; it can be emotionally draining, particularly if it is not your full-time job. So we as traders or investors can fall into the trap of, "I don't have time to do my research so let's see what others have to say." If that has ever happened to you, then this chapter is for you. Finding out what "others have to say" about the markets is a form of a getting a consensus of the market. Just be careful to whom you are listening or whose advice you are following.

MARKET CONSENSUS AND CONTRARY OPINION

Because prices reflect the mass psychology of the marketplace, there always seems to be a great deal of interest in finding out what the other traders are doing. One means of getting this information is taking surveys or evaluating newsletter opinions to measure the market's sentiment or to find a market consensus. The key is getting a true reading that accurately reflects the sentiment.

In an uptrending bull market, a large portion of the market participants are interested only in buying and will commit money for positions in the market. If they become even more bullish and build up their positions, eventually they have no more resources to continue buying or no one may be left

161

on the sidelines who wants to buy at the inflated price levels. When the market is overcommitted on the long side, it is said to be *overbought*. The buying pressure to move prices higher subsides, sometimes after a last-gasp blowoff, and the market becomes vulnerable to a reversal. The same is true on the downside if the bears become overcommitted and the market becomes *oversold*. The ebb and flow of trading will bring markets back to normal.

Imagine that a boat is loaded with people, and they are all on one side. When enough people fall off as it begins to lean, the boat will flip to the other side. Essentially that motion is what can happen in the markets. When the first batch of bulls start to take profits, it may cause an avalanche effect and result in a sharply lower price correction. The exact opposite is true for bear markets.

MARKET VANE

If everyone is long or bullish, how can prices move higher? As mentioned in the previous section, that conclusion is the exact theory of market consensus or contrary opinion. A report called *The Market Vane Bullish Consensus* (P.O. Box 90490, Pasadena, California 91109) ranks a market's past historical level of bullish and bearish conditions against current conditions. This ranking can be very helpful in discovering whether prices have reached a climax top or whether there is more room to move higher. Earl Hadady, who was the founder of the *Market Vane* report, wrote a book titled *Contrary Opinion* on the subject that can give you some insight on this concept and market psychology.

Market Vane measures the market on a percentage ranking system based on polling a certain number of analysts, assuming that these analysts will influence a large number of people in making their trading decisions. The ratings start with 0 percent as a measure of extreme bearishness and 100 percent as a measurement of extreme bullishness. If the number is closer to the overbought figure of 100 percent, then the market is probably due for a downward price correction. The opposite is true for bear markets when the number is closer to 0 percent. Then prices could be susceptible to a price reversal higher. For me, I look at the number when the percentage reaches near 75 percent to 85 percent and a particular market has been trading in an uptrend for a prolonged period of time.

COMMITMENTS OF TRADERS

One technique for gauging the consensus is to use the *Commitments of Traders* (COT) report released weekly by the Commodity Futures Trading

Commission (CFTC). This report reveals who is doing what in the futures market or whose hands the market is in. Many investors who have traded stocks and have never traded futures think of using the COT information as being like insider trading. Well, not exactly.

The report breaks down the three main categories of traders and shows their overall net positions. The first group is called *commercials* or *hedgers*, the next group is the *large speculators* (sometimes categorized as the commodity funds), and the third group is the *small speculators*. Commercials and large traders tend to have large positions and, as a rule, whenever they trade above a certain number of contracts, these positions need to be reported to the CFTC. The number of allowable positions that needs to be reported varies by different futures contracts. If you compile the data and subtract these figures from the total open interest provided by the exchanges, then the balance is assumed to be from the small speculators. The data are taken from the close of business on Tuesday and released the following Friday at 2:30 p.m. for futures only and also for futures combined with options.

To understand the importance of the COT report, it helps to know the breakdown of the numbers and what they represent. Commercials are considered to be hedgers and could be producers or users of a given product. Because they will or do own the underlying product, they are trying to hedge their risk against adverse price moves in the cash market. When a commercial entity fills out its account application, it usually discloses that it is hedging. The exchanges recognize that hedgers are on the other side of the market from a cash standpoint and can usually support their futures position financially. Therefore, they set lower margin rates for those accounts.

Commercials are considered to be the so-called smart money or the strong hands because they are in the business of that commodity. They are supposed to have the inside scoop, so to speak. For example, by having access to internal corporate inventory reports, global production estimates, and projected customer needs, commercials have a better working knowledge of the fundamentals. Banks and institutions may have a better idea about the direction of money supply and corporate debt, for instance, and may want to hedge their exposure on current holdings against an upcoming adjustment in interest rates. For the most part, they are using the futures market to lock in prices to produce a profit or to lower their costs on the cash side of their positions.

The large traders category is considered to be the professional trader. Commodity trading advisors or commodity pool operators who manage a large fund are considered to be large traders if they hold a certain amount of positions. An individual trader who holds a substantial position in the market may also be classified as a large trader. Traders who have more contracts than a designated amount need to disclose those positions to the

CFTC. Each futures contract has a different number for its reportable limits. Just like margin amounts, that number can change on a moment's notice.

The theory is that if you are a large trader, you are committing a large amount of capital to a risky investment and have confidence in that position. You are either a very good trader who started small and built your capital up, or you are a professional trader with a good track record. Either way you look at it, professional traders with large reportable position limits are still speculating in the markets with the motive for profit. They are well-financed and typically have large amounts of money to defend their positions.

The last group is the small traders or speculators. These are regular investors, mainly members of the public trading on their own or using recommendations from an advisory newsletter service or a broker or a combination of all three. It is estimated that 80 percent or more of individual traders who enter the markets lose, so this is the category that you generally do not want to follow.

A couple of old sayings may explain why the preceding is good advice: "Even a blind squirrel can find an acorn sometimes" and "a broken clock is always right twice a day." Even the little guys win once in a while. I have found that a lot of individual investors have a good knack for calling market direction but have a hard time with timing when it comes to entering or exiting the market. The problem is they are usually undercapitalized and cannot defend their positions during periods of volatility.

One other difficulty is they sometimes refuse to take a profit when the market gives it to them. Due to the very nature of the market's moves, some novice traders invest with a buy-and-hold mentality. For that reason the sheer psychology and emotional makeup of individual investors needs to be addressed before investing in the futures and options market. For some investors managing risk is not as hard as managing a winning trade.

There are many variables behind why the individual speculator is often wrong in the markets and loses money. My concern here is that you realize who represents what when it comes to the CFTC COT report. It is also important to understand and watch the behavior of the market from Tuesday when the position reports are submitted to Friday's close. This behavior can change the interpretation of the numbers as the market participants have had a chance to adjust their positions, making the report lose its importance if market conditions have changed during that time period.

What you want to watch for in the COT report are the net positions for each category. If you see a lopsided market position and prices are at an extreme high or an extreme low, this condition could signal a major turnaround in price direction.

Here is an example of a situation to watch. The large traders are net long, the commercials are net short, and the small speculators are extremely long from a historical perspective or account for a large percentage of the open interest. To add to this scenario, the market is at an extreme high or has been steadily rising for a good period of time. Look out! A downside correction could be around the corner. Once the CFTC releases the data, it is like trying to run ahead of an avalanche; everyone is headed for the exit door and nobody wants to be last, at least from the large traders' perspective. If they see that the market is vulnerable to a price correction, all it takes is a few smart traders to start liquidating long positions and a sharp sell-off could result. It is important to review the COT report to see whose hands control the market.

MEDIA ATTENTION

What we see on television or in the newspaper is a good indicator for me, especially if the media is publicizing the market price level or reporting on the fundamental developments with lots of attention. If the local nightly news is reporting about a specific market situation when it would not normally discuss such topics, it gets my attention. This reporting usually tells me that the facts are out and the market price has already factored in this situation, which probably accounts for the old saying in this business, "Buy the rumor and sell the fact."

More than ever, the media is now involved in hype and showmanship. It has a captive audience: you. The more viewers/readers that mass media has, the more it can charge for advertising rates, its reward. It pays for the media to embellish on the past and promote what I call "the gossip for the game." You need to learn how to filter out the gossip-for-the-game syndrome versus acquiring a true market consensus.

It is a different situation when you listen to one person's opinion and follow that advice. It helps to know that person's record of accomplishment. If he or she is reasonably good, you may have more confidence as a trader to put on a trade. But remember, verify, verify, verify. Listen, form an opinion, check the fundamentals, verify that by looking at the charts, and then verify that by looking at some technical indicators. This is a technique that will help in your trading discipline and help filter out these opinions, which can distract you from making good trading decisions.

If you look for one opinion after another as if you are searching for the holy grail, then certain failure is probable. Another situation setting up for failure is when you act or invest after hearing hype or a tip from a media source. A great example of this is reading a financial paper that has a big write-up on a market that had a spectacular market move. The story seems to embellish how bullish or bearish the market conditions were. Then, when you listen to the television commentators, they also mention this same market move. All of a sudden, market experts are coming out of the wood-work talking about this particular market move. It seems everyone is an expert, and some inexperienced investors can't help but fall for the trap.

There is truth in another old saying, "By the time it gets on the news, the move is probably over" because it is most likely factored into the market. In a bullish market, the buyers have already bought, and there are no more new buyers coming in to play except those latecomers who buy the top—generally the inexperienced trader or investor or broker who doesn't want to miss the opportunity. The simple laws of supply and demand dictate that prices cannot sustain extreme levels for long.

During the 2000 Bush/Gore election campaign, I recall many television financial stations interviewing so-called experts on how the markets would react if Bush were elected. The debates went on and on. The general consensus was that, if a Republican president were elected, it would be bullish for stocks and bearish for bonds. We all know the outcome of the election, but the outcome of the predictions certainly did not materialize. The point is: Be careful what you believe when it comes to another person's opinion about price direction in the markets.

MARGIN RATE CHANGES

Some analysts believe another good sentiment indicator is watching changes in the margin requirements that are set by the exchanges. I discussed the importance of margin requirements and their function as a good-faith deposit or performance bond in the futures market in Chapter 1 and noted that exchanges can change those requirements quickly. If you examine the reasons behind the increase or decrease in margin requirements, you will learn that it is a direct relationship to the expected amount of risk you may assume in that market.

Some analysts believe that when the price behavior is bullish in a steadily rising market and the exchange raises the margin, it may indicate that the market is near a top and that a price correction is close. The reason for this belief is that the higher prices move, the more vulnerable a price correction would be for smaller investors who would need more trading capital to afford such losses. So the idea is that if you want to enter a position, then you would need more trading capital.

On the other side of the coin, if the market price of a futures contract is at an extreme low, the exchange may lower the margin as it concludes the risk factor is lower. The theory is that when the exchanges lower the margin requirements, it may signal that a market may be near a bottom as it encourages more traders to take more positions. Once again, this is strictly a theory. However, I personally have seen several monumental market reversals within days or a week after a margin rate increase and decrease, and I do watch for margin changes.

PUT-TO-CALL RATIO

The put-to-call ratio theory is another method of measuring the market's sentiment. When trading options, it is important to form an opinion about the underlying futures market price direction. Traders who are bullish may choose to buy calls; traders who are bearish may choose to buy puts. In the futures industry we can track the level of open interest and volume on the strike prices for both puts and calls. If the majority of traders who buy options are bearish, then the put volume should increase and the level of calls should stagnate or decrease. Analysts can, therefore, monitor the volume of puts and calls to determine a level of bullishness or bearishness in the marketplace.

The Chicago Board Options Exchange (CBOE) has been trading stock options since the 1970s. It has a put-to-call ratio index based on volume figures from S&P 100 options, better known as the OEX. These figures are published on the CBOE web site (www.cboe.com) and in *Barron's* weekly financial paper. The statistics use the volume of put options for x amount of strike prices below the underlying market and then divide that number by x amount of strike prices above the underlying market.

The figure or ratio calculation is then used to gauge the market's sentiment. A figure that is increasing is considered to be indicating a bearish market tone or a downtrending market, as evident from a higher volume of puts than calls. A figure that is decreasing is considered to be indicating a bullish market tone or an uptrending market, as evident from a higher volume of calls than puts. An extremely high reading of the put-to-call indicator can usually signal a market bottom or a price correction. An extremely low reading of the put-to-call indicator can usually signal a market top or a price correction.

This ratio is a popular indicator for those who track and trade the stock indexes as well as for advisory services and those who publish financial newsletters.

VIX

The volatility index, otherwise known as the VIX, is a relatively new indicator that the CBOE introduced on January 19, 1993. It gained tremendous popularity at the height of the stock market price boom in 1999–2000. The

CBOE lists and tracks this indicator as a measure of the level of implied volatility for stock index options. It is simply used as another measure of the overall volatility of the U.S. equity markets or the amount of market turmoil that breeds fear. As a result, the VIX is sometimes known as the fear indicator or the fear factor gauge.

The VIX was originally calculated by taking a weighted average of the implied volatilities of eight S&P 100 index (OEX) calls and puts based on the Black-Scholes option pricing model. These options normally have an average time until expiration of 30 days, and the VIX is calculated and reported on a minute-by-minute basis in real time.

The most widely used application of the VIX involves a reading between, say, 24 to 20, a signal that volatility is low and suggesting there is complacency in the market. This low reading generally occurs when the market is at a high and is accepted as a sell signal. Moreover, if the stock market is rising, the more confident investors are convinced that the trend will never end. This condition is when the market is most vulnerable to a downturn or correction.

Historically, readings below 20 are considered a red flag or a warning signal to bulls, especially when the markets are in a rallying mode. Simply put, a low VIX reading means that sellers of options prevail and are aggressive and confident that the market will most likely not move. Buyers are not interested in acquiring puts for protection against their core cash positions, causing a decline in demand for options. In essence, the VIX acts like a contrarian indicator. When there is a consensus that the market won't move or that volatility will remain low, a believer in contrarian theory would conclude that the opposite would be true.

This observation brings up an important point: A rise in volatility could be from price increases as well as decreases. This point is important because a low VIX reading does not always signal that prices will drop; prices could rally and increase the volatility level. When prices of the stock market were at extreme lows, the VIX was as high as 45 and even reached an intraday high of 56 in July 2002. Based on VIX theory, as the markets declined, the volatility increased as did the fear in the market. This high reading was construed as a buy signal, indicating that the downturn was nearly complete. At the very least, it was another warning not to get bearish in the hole.

The CBOE overhauled this index and began using a new formula on September 22, 2003. This new formula provides the market's expectations of volatility directly from index option prices rather than from the algorithm that involved calculations of implied volatilities from the Black-Scholes option pricing model. The new VIX is calculated using options on the S&P 500 index and now uses a wide range of strike prices. The original VIX is now called the VXO and uses implied volatility from an option pricing model. The

VXO will still be calculated and the information provided in real time on the CBOE web site.

There is a slight difference in the way the two stack up. Using an annual comparison basis, the old VIX (now the VXO) had a daily closing high in 2002 of 50.48 and a low that year of 19.25 while the new VIX put the high at 45.08 and the low at 17.40, according to CBOE officials.

The CBOE was scheduled to launch its first futures contract on this newest derivative product in March 2004. As of December 4, 2003, the VIX had hit a low of 15.77. According to theory this low reading may indicate that volatility will rise, and traders can use the new VIX futures to start placing bets on the actual price of the index itself.

How useful will this instrument be for speculators or even for those looking to manage risk? Time will tell, but I believe a good bet is that volatility will remain a constant in the stock markets. Maybe adding a volatility component to a portfolio will work out to be a so-called sure thing. Of course, remember the advice about something that sounds too good to be true. It will be interesting to see how this market performs after the first year in business.

SUMMARY

The COT report, *Market Vane*, the put-to-call ratio, or the VIX are all based on the concept of finding a market consensus or measuring the market's sentiment to determine if prices have reached an extreme and are at or near turning points. In other words, a trader uses these as a means to determine a contrary opinion.

Market consensus is not something they usually teach you in an economics class. The bottom line: When everyone is bullish, don't join them. Remember these sayings, too: "Buy low, sell high" and "Buy it when nobody wants it, and sell it when everybody has got to have it." These are sheer psychological trading techniques that you can use to your advantage.

CHAPTER 10

Order Placement

Executing the Plan

*The price of success is hard work, dedication to
the job at hand and the determination that,
whether we win or lose, we have applied the best
of ourselves to the task at hand.*

—Vincent Lombardi

Lombardi's comment sounds like a tall order to accept—that we have
applied the best of ourselves, especially when it comes time to learning
new methods and means for doing something. Executing orders and
online trading platforms can require a little hard work and discipline. Being
dependent on connectivity and a reliable Internet connection can be scary.
It is the outside unforeseen influences that we have no control over that can
disrupt any individual's mental state and focus.

But framing the order you want to accomplish what you want is something over which you do have control, and it must be done carefully. Placing
orders is and will be an integral part of trading. Which orders are accepted,
when to use a stop to enter or exit a position, when and where to use order
cancels order orders—these are all questions for which you need answers
so you can put all the hard work from your analysis into action. The order
process is so important that I'm devoting a separate chapter to it.

ORDER ENTRY SELECTIONS

Understanding the mechanics of the market is an essential element of trading. Knowing which order to place is like having a specialty tool to get the

right job done. If you have ever played golf, you know there are different clubs for different shots. I don't think you would use a pitching wedge for putting. Understanding market terminology is critical when entering orders as well.

Let me put it this way. Some traders like using market orders to enter a position and to liquidate the position. This order lets them know they are either in or out of the market at all times. If that is all you need to know and you are comfortable with it, then that is great. However, you must understand that this approach requires nerves of steel, constant monitoring of the market, or a bundle of cash to help fund those really bad days when the market moves against you.

First things first. Every trader should be familiar with the more frequently used terms and what you need to say in what sequence to place orders correctly over the phone. There are about 14 different types of orders you should know about, including what they do and in what market conditions you should use them. This knowledge will help you in your judgment of trading decisions and give you more wisdom about how to implement them. One note: Different exchanges accept only certain types of orders and under certain market conditions. Different rules apply with different exchanges and, like many things, these rules can change without notice. Contact your broker for the current information on what orders you can use in various markets.

Because the majority of the futures industry is now using the Internet and Web-based technology to transmit orders, most traders are now moving to online trading platforms for order entry. The main concern here is that you make sure you read the computer screen carefully before clicking the final "OK" on the enter order button. It can be as simple as checking whether your screen says "Buy" or "Sell" or remembering not to double-click on the "enter order now" icon so you enter the same order twice. Most platforms do have safety features such as, "Is this the correct order? If so, click YES."

If there is any single problem that makes many online traders nervous, it is the connectivity issue. Will you have a connection to enter orders when you need it most? Connectivity could involve links to your Internet service providers or problems that may arise at the brokerage or exchange end. Even the Globex terminals do go down at the Chicago Mercantile Exchange (CME) once in a while. Some trading firms have an overload capacity on their servers, and that can cause you to lose connections. In that case you need to log off and then log back on—pretty straightforward but when you clicked "enter," was your order accepted? Are you in the market or not? If you need to exit a position and the connection goes down, frustration and panic can set in quickly. The solution is to work with a brokerage firm that offers support and allows you to call in orders without a tremendous increase in commission rates.

The e-mini S&P contract is attracting traders from all backgrounds and has become one of the favorite online trading contracts. The policies for the CME's Globex system as well as the latest information regarding system updates and news events can be found at www.cme.com/globex. There have been situations where erroneous orders have affected trading and elected stops in the market due to "fat finger" issues (typing errors). For example, rumors have it that a trader intended to sell 100 contracts and entered 10,000. This mistake caused the order system to sell until all 10,000 contracts were filled, and any stops that were under the market would subsequently be filled. Some firms may not accept actual stop loss orders but hold orders on their order desk if they are off the market by a large amount.

The point I am making is that the markets are reliable but not infallible. To ensure the integrity of the marketplace, the CME has a "bust trade policy" so that when and if these problems arise, it can reconcile differences. Trades that would normally not have been filled may be taken off the books. Ask a representative at your trading firm if it has this policy on hand. Generally speaking, the markets change, thus driving the demand for policy changes, so it is best to keep the link to your broker bookmarked on your favorites list for easy access on the web.

Exchanges can and do have system outages. When a breakdown occurs, you are exposed to market risk, which may leave you wondering what to do. You could spread the risk off in a large open-outcry product or get to know what market you can easily hedge it against. For example, the mini-sized Dow trades about the same dollar amount as the e-mini S&P does. If the Chicago Board of Trade system is operating and you are in a couple of e-mini S&P contracts when Globex goes down, you could balance the risk by entering the opposite side of the trade in a like product that has a fairly close monetary value on a tick per tick basis. This situation, though rare, has happened, leaving traders at the CME with no access until the next day's trading session while the problem was being repaired. If you trade actively, you always need to have an emergency backup plan for every step of the trading process. Smaller, less frequent traders may want to consult with a firm that offers different trading platforms to determine whether the costs warrant the access of such online order entry systems.

Some traders make it a point to deal directly with larger futures commission merchant (FCM) clearing member firms instead of trading at the smaller companies registered as introducing brokers (IBs) that clear through an FCM. In some cases, traders at an IB can have advantages over those at the FCMs. For example, independent IBs can utilize the best of one, two, or more FCMs. The IB's clients may get not only more personalized services, but also better execution services from a selected FCM. Not so long ago an FCM was purchased by another firm, and some clients could not trade or close accounts until the books were transferred. If you happened to be a client limited to that firm for handling your trades, you were not a happy camper! An account with an independent IB may give you the flexibility to continue to trade without being affected by regulatory red tape.

There will be certain times when order entry needs to be done over the phone. For instance, if your power goes out or you wish to place a trade at night or you want to trade markets other than electronic products or you want to trade contracts for which you might need special permission, you may have to call your broker.

No matter whether you trade online or on the phone, you need to know market terminology and procedures you should follow. Before you place an order to initiate a position in the market, you should have made a decision about which direction you believe the market may move. If you are bullish, you will want to go long the market, meaning you are speculating that the price will go up. If you are bearish, you are speculating that the price direction will be down and would want to sell short. When offsetting a long position, you need to sell that exact same contract to liquidate your position—a September bond contract is not the same as a December bond contract or the same as a September T-note contract. Offsetting makes you *flat* the market or out of a position. If you were short the market, you need to buy the same contract to *cover* your short position to make you flat the market.

Most brokerage firms have a certain format they want their customers to use when they enter an order over the phone. The broker or order-taker is filling in a ticket by hand or typing the order on the computer, so following this standardized format is more likely to get your order executed correctly. Here is a common format:

1. Name.
2. Account number.
3. Clearly state, BUY or SELL.
4. Number of contracts.
5. Contract month (and perhaps year for distant contracts).
6. What contract (perhaps indicating exchange as well).
7. Type of order.
8. Price at which the order is to be activated (not necessary for market orders).
9. Time duration of the order.

For example, when placing an order over the phone you would say: "Hi, this is John Person, account number 12345. Buy four June T-bond futures at the market." If this were another type of order, you might have said, "Buy four June T-bond futures at 112 stop, good until canceled." Your broker will repeat the order, so listen carefully. Make sure what the broker repeats is exactly what you said and intended. The broker or order clerk should conclude with something like, "Is this order correct?" If it is, you need to respond, "Yes, it is," or if you were not paying attention, ask to have the order repeated again. When you are sure it is correct, the broker or order clerk will give you a confirmation ticket number that refers to that order in case any follow-up action is required.

Once the order is placed and executed, you are at risk for whatever happens. Errors that were made by placing orders over the phone usually occur because one individual or the other was not paying attention.

One specific error that stands out for me involved a colleague of mine who had a client who called to buy two U.S. bonds at the market. At the time the broker had two phones. His client was on one ear, and he was placing the order to the floor with the phone in his other ear. Another broker sitting near him made a derogatory remark because his voice was loud. Just before the floor clerk repeated back the order as he heard it, my colleague turned to the nearby broker to tell him not to interrupt, in so many words.

Just that split second of distraction cost my friend about $4,000. You see, the floor clerk heard, "Buy ten at the market," not "Buy two at the market." It was at that moment that Federal Reserve Chairman Alan Greenspan was being quoted by the financial media, and the market nose-dived a half point. Right as the fill was reported, my friend remembered hearing, "You paid even for ten" (floor talk for you bought ten contracts at 106-00). He told the floor clerk, "I think you got the wrong guy." The floor clerk said, "No way! I heard ten, I repeated buy ten, and you bought ten at 106 even." With the market at 105-16, the loss was $500 per contract. My friend's client wanted only two so he had to eat the balance of eight contracts with a loss of $500 apiece.

Murphy's Law is always at work, right when you least expect it. The rule for errors is simple: Just cover them immediately. Don't stay with errors. They usually only get worse, and the cost increases against you. Figure out who's in the wrong later. By getting out of a mistake immediately, you reduce the chance for the market to continue to move against you. My friend argued for another 20 or 30 seconds instead of taking care of the mistake immediately, and it cost him, all because he did not pay attention and listen when he should have.

In addition to verifying the accuracy of the order when you enter it, also remember to listen carefully when the fill on the executed order is reported. Did you get exactly what you wanted (allowing for slippage, of course)? Errors cost money and, more often than not, you are the one who has to pay. Getting into good habits from the beginning can help you in your trading career.

Entering orders online follows essentially the same steps, but no one is there to catch errors you may make except you and your computer. The order is reviewed at the brokerage firm, but if it has all the right elements, it will be executed as you directed—no one will question, "Is that what you really mean?" That's why you must be very careful to review the order before you hit that final "enter" key. Sometimes if you modify an order, the computer makes a change you don't notice, like going back to a default for buy when you intended to sell. Check and double check.

You also should be keeping track of all the details of your order on some type of trading log such as the sample shown as Table 10.1.

MARKET CONDITIONS

In addition to order terminology and procedures, you also should be aware of market conditions as your order may be handled differently in certain circumstances or certain orders will not be accepted at all at times. You don't have any input in ruling what market conditions are in effect. The exchange determines that, but you need to understand the types of situations in which you may be operating. If you are trading any market, it is important to be aware of your trading surroundings and to know what the market conditions are before placing orders to initiate or offset a position.

Normal Market Conditions

"Normal market conditions" describes the usual state as trades are occurring at a normal pace and the price fluctuations are not in a wild erratic state. There is a fluid market for buyers and sellers, and the competition for bids and offers is flowing smoothly. Most orders that are entered should not be delayed in execution, and fills should be reported back to you quickly. Liquidity is fluid and there are plenty of bids and offers to make trades.

TABLE 10.1   Sample Trading Log

Date	Buy/Sell Cancel	Quantity	Month	Future/ Option	Price or Strike	Ticket Number	Time Entered	Fill Price

Fast Market Conditions

"Fast market conditions" describes a hectic and busy condition when orders are coming in too quickly to be handled smoothly in a balanced market and prices are usually very erratic. When the herd mentality takes over in a down market, for example, more people are willing to sell at a certain price level than there are people willing to buy. This imbalance creates competition for any order to get filled first at specific price levels. Traders and floor brokers can be frantic and overwhelmed by the sheer volume of incoming orders. They are trying to get orders executed at the best available prices but are deluged by the heavy volume and can't keep up.

Then several events take place: (1) Incoming orders are given preference over reporting filled orders, primarily because the floor broker needs to sign or endorse each filled order and doesn't have time. (2) Because everyone is working faster and at a heightened stress level, this is a time when errors are more likely to occur. Exchange officials recognize this situation and declare a "fast market." (3) An "F" designating the fast market condition appears next to the last trade price on both the exchange floor quote boards and most quote vendors' screens. (4) The rules of trading officially change at that point. Floor brokers are not held, meaning they are not responsible for bad fills, good fills, or filling your limit orders at all, even if the price trades through your order. Obviously, you need to be aware of these little rules before engaging in trading.

Limit Up

Not all futures markets have a "limit" provision, but this is the maximum price the market may move up in a given trading day from the previous day's settlement price. Trading can occur at or below that price but not above it. "Locked limit up" refers to a situation when there are no offers to sell at the limit-up price, only bids to buy. If you are long the market, it is a good situation, of course. However, if you are short, it's not good. You cannot cover your short position by buying unless the market trades off the limit. To buy, there has to be a seller. When there are no offers, that means no sellers are present.

Limit Down

"Limit down" is the maximum price the market may move down in a given trading day from the previous day's settlement price. Trading can occur at or above that price but not below it. "Locked limit down" refers to a condition when there are no bids at the limit down price, only offers to sell. If you are short, you'll like it. But if you are long, you won't be able to liquidate your position unless the market trades off the limit. To sell, there has to be a buyer. When there are no bids, that means no buyers are present.

After-Hours Trading

Some markets trade electronically around the clock so there is no open-outcry pit trading. E-mini S&P 500 futures, for example, do not trade on the floor. Traditionally, the open-outcry session is considered the "day session" or "regular trading hours," and the after-hours session is considered to be any time before or after that. For example, the floor session or day session may be 8:30 a.m. to 3:15 p.m. Central time. Many futures markets now trade almost 24 hours a day. For example, as of the end of January 2004, the e-mini S&P session starts at 3:30 p.m., takes a maintenance break from 4:30 p.m. to 5:30 p.m., and then continues around the clock until 3:15 p.m. the following day.

However, just because trading is available does not mean it is advisable to trade in the middle of the night in the United States. Trading may be very thin with wide price gaps between trades in the overnight session. You want a liquid market where orders can be filled quickly and efficiently, and you may have to limit your trading to the more active day session hours in some markets, even if trading at 3 a.m. sounds interesting because you also have a day job.

FOURTEEN ORDER CHOICES

The following list of order types gives you plenty of alternatives for entering and exiting the market in a number of different ways. Read the descriptions carefully to see if a particular type of order will achieve what you want. Keep in mind that not all brokers and not all exchanges accept all orders. Only a few types of orders may be allowed for some electronically traded contracts—for example, you may not be able to enter open or good 'til canceled orders. Table 10.2 lists the types of orders that U.S. futures exchanges will accept.

Market Orders

At the market is a common order instructing the broker to buy or sell a specific quantity, contract month, and futures position at the next best available market price. That price could be better or worse than what you see on your quote machine. The process is similar whether orders are executed in an open-outcry pit on the floor of an exchange or an order-matching com-

TABLE 10.2 Orders Accepted at U.S. Futures Exchanges

Exchange/ Market	Limit	Market	MOC	FOK	Stop	Stop Limit	SWL	SCO	SLCO	MIT	OCO
CME											
All products	Yes	Yes	Yes	Yes	Yes	Yes	Yes	Yes	Yes	Yes**	Yes
CBOT											
All products	Yes	Yes	Yes	Yes	Yes	No	No	No	No	No	No
COMEX											
All products	Yes	Yes	Yes	Yes	Yes	Yes	Yes	Yes	No	Yes	MOC
NYMEX											
All products	Yes	Yes	Yes	Yes	Yes	Yes	Yes	Yes	No	Yes	Yes
NYBOT											
Cotton	Yes	Yes	Yes	Yes	Yes	Yes	Yes	Yes	No	Yes	Yes
O.J.	Yes	Yes	Yes	Yes	Yes	Yes	Yes	Yes	No	Yes*	Yes
USD Index	Yes	Yes	Yes	Yes	Yes	Yes	Yes	Yes*	No	Yes	Yes
Coffee	Yes	Yes	Yes	Yes	Yes	Yes	Yes	Yes	No	Yes	Yes
Sugar	Yes	Yes	Yes	Yes	Yes	Yes	Yes	Yes	No	Yes	Yes
Cocoa	Yes	Yes	Yes	Yes	Yes	Yes	Yes	Yes	No	Yes	Yes
NYFE products	Yes	Yes	Yes	Yes	Yes	Yes	Yes	Yes	No	Yes	MOC
KCBT											
Value Line	Yes	Yes	Yes	Yes	Yes	Yes	Yes*	Yes	Yes	Yes	Yes
Wheat	Yes	Yes	Yes	Yes	Yes	Yes	Yes*	Yes	Yes	Yes	Yes

MOC = market on close; FOK = fill or kill; SWL = stop with limit; SCO = stop close only; SLCO = stop limit close only; MIT = market if touched; OCO = order cancels order.

*not held; **no meats.

puter at an exchange. In layman's terms it means, "Get me in or out of the market right now at any price." You use a market order to be sure your order is executed as fast as possible in any market condition.

Market If Touched

A *market if touched* (MIT) order is specifically designed to turn into a market order if prices trade at or through your specified price level. It could be filled at that price or the next best available price that the floor broker can execute.

Market on Open

Market on open (MOO) is a market order that specifically means you want to be filled in the opening range. A buy order is typically filled at the high of the opening range, and a sell order at the low of the opening range. You usually need to get this order to the floor at least 10 to 15 minutes before the market opens to ensure that the filling floor broker has enough time to organize his or her "deck" (the term that refers to all orders the broker is holding).

Market on Close

Market on close (MOC) is a market order that specifically means you want to be filled in the closing range. A buy order is typically filled at the high of the closing range and a sell order at the low of the closing range. You usually need to get this order to the floor at least 10 to 15 minutes before the market closes to ensure that the filling floor broker has enough time to organize his or her deck and execute the order to those specific instructions.

Limit Orders

Limit orders have specific price instructions, requiring them to be filled at the designated price or better. For example, if you enter a buy limit order, it needs to be filled at or below that price and cannot be filled at a higher price. In effect, you are saying you will pay x price but no more. If you enter a sell limit order, it needs to be filled at the specific price you designate or higher. The fill cannot be at a lower price, but it could be higher than you specified, depending on price action at the time.

These orders set specific prices where you want to enter or exit the market. Generally, the market needs to trade through your price area to ensure a fill. If you absolutely must have a fill, you may want another type of order as there is no guarantee that a limit order will be filled, even if your designated price is touched. You should also be aware of the fact that floor brokers are typically not held to execute these limit orders during the opening and closing ranges. For example, if you placed a limit order before the open to buy 10 contracts of March Corn at 2.18 and the low of the day was 2.17, you could expect to be filled on your order—unless it was in the opening or closing range or in a fast market condition.

Stop Orders

Although they often are called *stop-loss* orders and are associated with getting out of a losing position, a *stop* is an excellent order to use to either enter a new position or get out of a current position. A *buy stop* is an order that is always placed above the current market price. If the market trades at or above your specific price, it turns your stop order into a market order to buy at the next best available price. A *sell stop* is an order that is always placed below the current market price. If the market trades at or below your specific price, it turns your stop order into a market order to sell at the next best available price.

A small detail should be noted here. Some exchanges rule that the market does not need to actually trade at your price. Rather, a bid at or above a buy stop can elect your order, and an offer to sell at or below your sell stop can elect your order. That factor may not mean much to you now, but when your sell stop gets elected and is the low of the day or your buy stop is filled at the high of the day, it will. Check regularly with your broker for current rules and specific market conditions of each exchange and the products that you wish to trade.

When a stop order is used as a stop-loss to get you out of a position, it is often a mechanical order to get you out of the market if a certain target price is hit. There are no guarantees that this type of order will get you out of the market, mainly due to certain market conditions, and there are no guarantees that you will be filled at the price you specify in your order. The market could reach your price, activating your order, but the next price available might be some distance away—a phenomenon known as *slippage*, which you must expect in your trading. A stop order in a fast market or a limit-down period or in thin overnight trading especially may or may not be filled at a good price or filled at all.

Under normal market conditions this is still a good tool and you should be in the habit of using stops for risk management purposes. *Trailing stops* usually refers to moving the price of your stop order up or down as the market moves in your favor and you want to lock in a profit or reduce a loss.

Entering a market position using a stop is effective when trading technical chart points. If prices appear to be in a channel and you only want to buy if the market trades above a resistance point, then you might place a buy stop above that area to enter a long position if the market moves that high. In other words, you are waiting until the market proves that it may go higher by surpassing a certain price or chart point.

Of course, the opposite is true for a sell stop. If you only want to sell once the market price trades below a support point, you would place a sell stop below that area to enter a short position, waiting until the market proves that it may go lower by surpassing a certain price or chart point.

Stop Close Only

Stop close only stop orders are elected only if prices in the final closing range (usually the final minute of trading) are below your sell stop or above your buy stop. This is a specific order that some traders use to make the market prove they are wrong when exiting a trade. It can also be used for entering a trade if the market is closing above or below a certain point. It can be a dangerous order financially as the market could move significantly above or below the intended price level on the close.

Stop Limit

Stop limit (SL) is a two-tiered price order generally used to limit slippage. The first part of the order is the stop price level; the second is the limit price level where you are willing to allow the filling floor broker to execute your order. The danger here is that the order may not get executed at all if the momentum of the market is severe and the price moves dramatically beyond your limit order level.

Straight Cancels

The *cancel* order is a simple command to remove your order from working in the marketplace. I mentioned earlier that, when you place an order, the order is repeated back to you and you get an order ticket number. This order number is used as a reference when you want your broker to just scratch your existing order if it has not been filled already. Sometimes the process of reporting fills can be delayed. When you use a straight cancel order and your order has been filled, you will get a report back that says, "order filled, too late to cancel."

One point here: Never assume that your order was cancelled and is out of the market, and do not cancel an order to see if you can get a quicker fill report—you may get what you ask for. By canceling an order that may be due a fill, the last command usually will hold up and the filling floor broker will be off the hook for making any adjustments from orders that may be due a fill. In volatile market conditions if you intentionally want to remove your order and you want confirmation as soon as possible that you are out, then you need to ask for a "cancel and confirm" that the order is dead, out of the market, and not working. You will get a call back with either a "too late to cancel" message, meaning that your order was filled, or a confirmation that your order is out of the market.

Cancel, Replace

If you want to change the quantity of your order from, say, 10 contracts to only 5 or if you want to change your limit price order to a different price level or change it to a market order, you want to do a *cancel replace* order. This order would ensure that you do not get a double fill from canceling one order and placing a new order without confirmation that the original order is out of the market. One aspect that cannot be changed is the contract month. That type of change would need to have the old order straight canceled and confirmed out and then a new order entered once you receive confirmation.

Order Cancels Order or One Cancels Other

Bracket trading or profit and loss parameters can be established all on one ticket with this order. An *order cancels order* or *one cancels other* (OCO) may involve two orders with one goal—getting into or out of the market, whichever order is executed first. Say you enter a long position and want to liquidate it at a specific limit price above the current price level to take a profit. At the same time you are working a stop-loss order below the current price level in case prices decline. The OCO will automatically cancel one order if the other is filled.

One problem with OCO is that only some exchanges accept this order and under certain market conditions. Check with your broker for current rules of each exchange on the conditions of accepting this type of order and for each product being traded at that particular exchange.

Fill or Kill

A *fill or kill* (FOK) is a "let me know right now" kind of an order. If you want to buy or sell a specific quantity at a specific price and know the results immediately, you might use an FOK order. When this order gets into the floor filling brokers hand, it needs to be filled or canceled and the results reported back immediately. If it is not filled, it is a dead order, and a new order would need to be placed.

Open Orders, Good 'til Canceled

As a matter of clarification first, when you place an order, it is always automatically assumed to be a day order. That assumption is a universal understanding in trading. If your order is not filled at the end of the day, it is canceled and considered a dead order. A new one would need to be reentered the next day.

The purpose for an *open order* or *good 'til canceled* (GTC) is that it remains working for the life of the contract or until you cancel it or it is filled. An open order or GTC is usually placed as a limit or stop order. Under most circumstances you can cancel and replace the order in situations where you would trail your stop or move a limit order. Make sure that you state that you wish to continue using a GTC with the replacing new order.

The procedure that most firms utilize is to first identify yourself and state your account number. Next instruct your broker that you have an open order that you need to cancel/replace and give him or her the order number. That way they can access your information from the list of working GTCs or pull your information off the computer screen, saving valuable time by allowing the broker to process your request as soon as possible.

Remember, always make sure you communicate your intentions clearly. Errors do happen when traders forget they have placed open orders. The most common example is when you enter a position and use an open order (or GTC) as a stop loss. You may see an opportunity to exit the position and use a market order to do so. Unless you cancel your GTC order, it is still working. As time passes, this order could come back to haunt you as you may get a fill when you do not want to be in the market.

Checking your open orders once a week is a good practice for active traders to get into. Reviewing working orders online is another method you can use to avoid the error that happens with open orders—checking your account status is just one click away.

Spread Orders

Commonly referred to as the purchase and sale of the same or similar instruments in different months simultaneously, *spreads* have their own trading patterns and conventions and require experience to become familiar with them. Some New York market traders refer to spreads as a *switch* or *straddle* order.

The concept of a spread is to buy and sell the same or related product, different products, different months, different exchanges, or some combination of all of these. The goal is to profit from the difference in the price movements of the two sides.

The two sides of a spread order, the buy side and the sell side, are usually called *legs*. You can enter a spread one side at a time, called *legging into a spread;* you can enter both positions with market orders; or you can enter a limit order specifying the exact price difference between the two sides. Common examples of spreads include the S&P 500 and Nasdaq, gold and silver, Chicago wheat versus Kansas City wheat, July soybeans versus November soybeans (new crop/old crop spread) and cattle versus hogs. The list goes on and on.

Exchanges recognize a number of spreads, generally offering reduced margin requirements. For example, the historic Chicago Board of Trade-Chicago Mercantile Exchange common clearing link that became fully operational on January 2, 2004, cleared the way for substantially lower margin requirements and more effective clearing procedures for spread trades involving e-mini S&P and mini-sized Dow futures, an outstanding benefit for retail traders. Usually the same futures contract that is traded in different delivery months has substantially reduced margins, based on the idea that all contracts for a given market will tend to move together. Some spreads are not recognized and do not get a break on margin rates. Check with your broker for the list of intermarket and intramarket spreads that are recognized by the exchanges.

A common misconception is that a spread is not as risky as trading an outright single position. The fact is that spreads can sometimes be just as risky, if not riskier, because the trader is in two separate positions.

Typically a spread trader is trying to profit from the strengthening or weakening of the price difference between the buy side and the sell side. Another reason for spreading is that a trader may be entering a new contract month and closing out an old position that is approaching delivery or expiration. This shift to a new month can be done on the same order ticket at the same time, a process called *rolling over* your position.

Another reason for spreading is to *spread off* a current position to reduce risk exposure or to defend a position to avoid a margin call. For example, a trader who is long one December S&P 500 futures may want to sell one March S&P 500 futures against it to provide cover over the weekend. Then the trader can lift one side of the spread or leg out of the short March futures side Monday morning. This action would, in effect, make the trader net long one position.

Whether placing a spread order by phone or online, its order form looks a little different than just a straight buy or sell. Start off by telling your broker that you want to place a spread order so he or she can prepare the right ticket or punch up the right computer screen. In addition, specify if it is an open order as well.

Start with the buy side first, giving the quantity, contract month, and the market. Then give the same type of information for the sell side, the quantity (which usually should match the quantity as the buy side), the contract month, and the futures contract. Then, if it is a limit order, indicate what the price difference should be or say that it is a market order.

If you do not have an equal amount on the buy side and sell side, then it would not be a true spread order and might not qualify for lower margin rates. You may have a reason for an imbalance if you are rolling out of one contract month into another and want more or less positions. For example, if you are long five December euro contracts and want to have only three when you roll into the March contract, you would buy three March and sell five December all on one ticket and most likely at the market.

Again, you need to check with your broker to see if the floor filling broker will accept a specialty order such as that in the first place. It is better to ask questions than to place the order and find out later that it did not go through. I have known brokers who have placed orders for clients, only to learn that the floor would not accept the order due to a change in market conditions, or it may have been rejected as a bad order and not reported back at all. Then, when the broker calls the client, the broker finds out the client has left for the day or is out of reach, thinking they were in a position when they were not.

Never assume. Always ask questions when placing any order that might be a little different and check in with your broker from time to time when you are working a special order.

SUMMARY

Order entry procedures can be as important as determining and analyzing the market direction itself. Imagine being right in predicting the market move but not being able to participate because you were not filled on your order. Worse yet, maybe you entered a stop order to enter a position using a breakout method instead of a stop limit order and the resulting slippage caused a loss instead of a potential profit. The combinations for errors are too great to mention.

Although online order entry is becoming increasingly popular, novice or new investors in the futures market should consider the benefits of having a licensed, full-service broker accepting their orders. For one, they usually are familiar with the investor's account, different trading philosophies and strategies, and the trading terms and phrases taught in different trading courses. For another, full-service brokers can give investment advice, and they usually have experience to help catch common mistakes that could cost an inexperienced investor thousands of dollars. In fact, they can be a fine mentor in the initial stages of a trading career.

I would also recommend interviewing brokers. Think of a broker as an employee. If you think about it, they really are working for you! Ask questions about how long they have been in the industry, what would make them want to help you, and how they would help. Ask if they provide specialty services such as faxing or e-mailing charts or preparing special market reports. You may want to find out if they offer a hotline recording or an online voice-activated chat room for market analysis. Most important, tell them what you need and what you want them to provide for you. Most experienced full-service brokers accept discount clients even though they may be experienced and proficient traders on their own. Brokers will be there for you and may be able to respond quickly to answer any questions or concerns you may have. Even the great Tiger Woods has a coach. Why wouldn't you want one on your side?

If you want to place your own orders, that's fine. Many traders do. Just remember that unlicensed phone clerks are generally prohibited from giving clients investment advice and special services. They usually do not have the experience that a broker has, and they may not have passed the Series Three exam. Registered brokers are licensed by the National Futures Association and are regulated by the government. They even submit themselves to taking ethics exams and attending refresher courses and seminars. Clerks generally just take your order, even if they realize you are making an error.

Online order entry can be a valuable tool. However, it is not foolproof, especially if your local Internet service provider is busy or down or you have other connectivity problems. Placing orders online as an inexperienced trader may not be the answer. If you are comfortable with it, great. Just make sure you have a backup plan and accessibility to an experienced broker who will work for you.

Know the rules of the game, and use the tools you have to do the job right. Weigh the benefits of using an experienced broker versus a discount order clerk or placing orders from an online platform by yourself. Also remember to be organized, write down your activity, and listen to what your broker repeats back to you with your order ticket number. Or, if you are trading online, read what you are entering and be careful not to double-click when entering your orders. These seem like simple steps, but they require discipline, commitment, and a strong arm. I say that because to write a trade log requires lifting that 400-pound pencil or pen. Get in the habit of taking an inventory of your performance, whether it is good or bad. That way, you can try to replicate what went right and learn from what went wrong.

CHAPTER 11

The Mental Game

Inside the Trader

Nothing can stop the man with the right mental attitude from achieving his goal; nothing on earth can help the man with the wrong mental attitude.
—Thomas Jefferson

To succeed as a trader, you have to get your conscious and subconscience mind working for you. You must have a winning attitude, which can be achieved by surrounding yourself with positive events and introducing yourself to self-motivating or positive attitude tapes or books. This chapter is devoted to helping you identify problem thinking and develop an optimistic way of thinking. I not only want to help teach you methods that may improve your awareness of solid discipline and confidence, but also to help you conquer your fears by presenting examples of how traders can correct or monitor themselves when times get tough.

In my experience, successful traders seem to possess the uncanny ability to correctly anticipate the needs and trends of the marketplace. Some call such ability an inherent feel for the market. Even better, they have the ability to act swiftly and execute a trading plan. I believe that these are talents that you develop and are not born with. Successful traders were, are, and always will be students of the markets. They are achievers who continuously study, in perceptive detail, people's actions, the processes of events, and the products in the markets they trade. When they place a trade, it is an educated decision, not merely a guess, and they know it. That knowledge gives them the confidence to execute and act on trading decisions.

Confidence or thoroughly believing in yourself may come naturally or from the secure feeling you had when growing up. It may have been developed from achieving success from previous experiences or in being successful in some other aspects of your life. Other ways to gain confidence in yourself might have come from overcoming an obstacle or having a successful experience in conquering some adversity in life. You consciously know that you have achieved or overcome challenges and can succeed due to a past experience. Building confidence in yourself and in your trading skills is extremely important in stimulating an optimistic winning attitude.

The other common feature that successful traders seem to have is they are not afraid to be wrong. They realize that anticipating a market move will always include an element of risk. They act, not react, to market conditions. This means they place orders before the market moves rather than wait until after the market reacts to a situation or event. In my experience, those who hesitate or wait or are not prepared seem to have the most trouble capturing the element of success when it comes to trading futures.

This chapter really describes the common emotional weaknesses for most unsuccessful traders. I illustrate how this negative mental attitude develops and offer methods that can help solve the problem if you experience losses and are a victim of these symptoms. Think of this as the problem-solving chapter. At first it might seem like negative thinking, but if you don't examine your troubles and face your fears head on, you will not be able to become an effective problem solver.

WHO ARE YOU?

The first step to improving your trading results requires the ability to examine your actions and do a thorough, honest self-evaluation. Let's call it taking an inventory of your actions and how you react emotionally to a situation because, after all, you are the most important part of the trading equation. When I interviewed Mark Douglas, author of *The Disciplined Trader* and *Trading in the Zone*, on my radio program, he offered the idea that every outcome of a trade decision based on a technical chart pattern is a random act. It is not a 100 percent guarantee that a chart pattern that resembles a bull flag will extend higher every single time. The problem is not the chart or the market but the actor, Douglas contended.

In my career as a broker, I have found one popular phrase that often leads investors down the road to the poorhouse, either from actual monetary losses or from missed opportunities. I heard it from all different types of people. It did not matter what gender they were or what part of the country they were from. The fact is a lot of people used it. The phrase was:

"I'll think about it."

A trader needs to take action rather than wait and see and then react to the market. As a trader, you need to be quick. A sudden brain spasm spawned by fear, doubt, or greed will most likely not bring consistently good results. Hesitation is a trader's enemy. That is the message in the guideline, "Plan your trade, and then trade your plan."

Let me give you a few examples of when *"I'll think about it"* happens. An investor identifies a trade opportunity and looks to buy near a significant support level if prices decline to the planned entry area. The trader establishes a risk factor based on a monetary loss or on a technical violation of a support level. Things are pretty good so far, as it seems the trader has done the necessary homework. Now comes the time to place the trade. Ah, *"I'll think about it"* pops into mind, and the trade is never entered. What happened? A lack of confidence in analytical ability, self-doubt that the trade will work, or fear that the trader's pride will be hurt if the trade prediction does not work? Maybe the trader is afraid of losing money or if the trade is a loser, a humiliating experience.

So the trader decides to wait a day or two to just watch the market. You know that if the trade had worked out as planned, the four famous words *"I'll think about it"* would be forgotten. What fearful traders do think and say is, "I should have done that" or "I knew that was going to be a winner" or, better yet, " Boy, I don't know what got into me. That would have been a great trade."

Remember the "plan your trade, trade your plan" axiom? Even if a trade does not work out, isn't it better to take a risk and fail than to never take a risk at all? After all, not every trade will be a winner. That is why you are—or should be—using risk capital when trading. Hopefully, applying the P3T signal method of trade setups may help give you the confidence you need.

Another great example of *"I'll think about it"* is when a trader has a long position in the market and has a small or respectable profit built in the trade. The market condition may be changing. For example, supply or demand factors or an upcoming fundamental event such as a government report may cause the upward momentum of the price advance to stop. The trader is looking for even more money out of the trade. Maybe the trader is breaking even or has a small profit. Deep down, the trader knows the trade is not working and the position should be exited. Then *"I'll think about it"* enters the picture.

This is where I have seen traders and clients turn large, small, or no profits into substantial losses. Sometimes this business is not about the risks we take for each trade that needs to be managed as much as it is what we do with the profits we have in a trade. A profit is only a profit when you exit a position. Until a position is offset, it is only a paper profit. Emotions such as greed or complacency can be disastrous. They can keep you in a trade longer than the market invited you to hang around.

If you took a poll of investors, floor traders, brokers, and retail customers and asked them, "What does it take to be a successful trader?" what do you think the answer would be? Timing. Pure and simple, timing. Timing your trade entries and exits. So do your homework, plan your trade, and execute that plan by entering your orders. If the trade does not work out, examine what the results were so you can learn from the experience.

Here's a trading thought to share with you: "It's okay to lose your shirt in this business, just don't lose your pants because that is where your wallet is." In other words, it is okay to lose, but don't lose everything because then you have no equity to come back with. Losses need to be minimized and examined. Study what went wrong and use your findings as experience for the next trade.

As Jesse Livermore and other famous traders have observed, you are out of the game if your stake is gone. Don't lose it all in one shot. That is where money management techniques can prove to be vital for your survival in this game. That applies to both losers and winners. Profits need to be taken. If you believe in managing risks, you need to manage profits, too, because the markets giveth and they definitely taketh away.

GETTING IN TOUCH WITH REALITY

One question that new investors ask me a lot is, "Why do I do better at paper trading than I do when I trade with real money?" The answer is easy. Fear, doubt, complacency, greed, anxiety, excitement, and false pride can all interfere with rational and intellectual thoughts. When dealing with real money, you are faced with the realization that you and your money can actually be separated.

It is a sad feeling to lose a bunch of Ben Franklins quickly. (It's more like depressing!) When you are paper trading, you know that your winnings are fictitious so you let them ride. However, when it comes to real dollar trading and you have a $2,000 or $3,000 winner in a short period of time, it is extremely hard not to look at your account balance and then call your broker or get online and say, "Get me out!" So when you get out and a week or so later the same position turns into what could have been a $20,000 or $30,000 winner, I don't know how a human being cannot say, "I should have stayed in!"

Try not to get into the buyer's remorse syndrome. That's when you buy a specific product and are still price shopping six months later to make absolutely sure that you got the best deal in town. That is another situation that creates negative emotions and you need to guard against it. Most traders know the saying, "Any profit is a good profit, no matter how small." It is hard not to look back, but you always have to think positive and be grateful that you picked the right market and did make some money. You should also feel confident and comfortable knowing that your system, method, or skills may allow you the opportunity to do it again. Hindsight trading is easy; being a mature, professional, and optimistic trader is hard.

Fear can cause paralysis and lead to inaction. "When in doubt, get out!" These are five famous words to remember. Do not vacillate or contemplate a decision to get out of a position in the market. Just do it! When the markets are acting differently than what you would expect or when the information you are analyzing and the trading signals you are getting are confusing, it is important to reevaluate your trade or position.

For you golfers, maybe it's like losing your swing one day after being able to hit like Ben Hogan the day before. It is confusing and frustrating because you know you can hit the ball correctly. You just did it yesterday. So you take some practice swings to try to get your motion or swing back. As a trader, if you are not sure about the price behavior or the way the market is acting, then simply get out of your position. Take a look at the market from a distance on the sidelines. Some investors like to watch and wait; others will hope things change. The better or more experienced trader will simply get out. Sometimes this simple approach will save you from losses and give you a better time to reenter the market.

Maybe you can identify with problems such as "Greed and the undisciplined trader" or "I'm-scared-so-I'll-think-about-it trader." I associate greed with the trader or investor who desperately wants to trade to make a quick buck. This type of trader personality profile is certain to realize failure when trading. Such traders have no discipline, acting on any rumor, story, or so-called hot tip. They are checking research web sites and jumping from one source to another to search for the winning trade. There is a common denominator with this type of investor: They constantly do the same thing over and over and over again, generally resulting in losses.

There is an old definition for insanity: repeating the same actions and expecting a different outcome each time. I'm not talking about the casual trader who asks his broker, "What's new today?" I am referring to the investor who has traded at different firms and jumps around and loses each time.

Even worse are those investors who do not even follow their own advice or research. In the brokerage business we call them screen "watchers"—those who stare at a computer and analyze the market without putting their thoughts and analysis into action. They always have an opinion and think of themselves as experts. These kinds of traders may be brilliant market analyzers but lack the emotional or financial resources to carry out their thoughts and put them into action to achieve the desired results, a winning trade. Life is too short to fall into that trap. There are better ways to spend your time and achieve nothing in return for your efforts. Trading requires hard work, effort, and time. If I am investing my time in a project or a job, I want to get paid for it.

GETTING DOWN TO BUSINESS

Trading should be considered a business. Treat it as such. Here is a suggestion: Work with one market and become a specialist in that market. Once you have achieved that, then move to another product until you have maybe 10 or more markets that you are comfortable trading.

Here is another suggestion: Start a trading worksheet. You can do this by hand or by computer. Figure 11.1 shows how I set up a daily worksheet. As the age of computers has evolved, many different software programs have been developed. If you want to start a worksheet by computer, getting started is easy. All you need is the raw data. To get the information, you may use several sources. One is the newspaper, another is the brokerage firm's web site, another is subscribing to a quote service that provides analytical software. But remember the saying, "You get what you pay for." Software can be inexpensive or even free. Other software vendors can be very expensive. Most trading firms will place on their web sites needed information such as charts and price quotes as well as technical studies. Some will provide market commentaries or even information such as daily, weekly, and monthly support and resistance numbers to their clients. I do it and continue to offer it to clients free of charge.

What you really want to accomplish is gathering information for a daily worksheet and taking the time to fill it out. This practice forces you to make a quick study of the market and get into the habit of a daily routine. Consider it like a daily investment diary. All you have to do is fill in the blanks. You can make up your own field requirements, or you can use the ones shown in Figure 11.1 A daily worksheet will not guarantee that you will have profitable trades, but it will get you to do your homework and get you into a disciplined trading preparation sequence.

Fill in the data. Form an opinion based on technical information. Outline a trade. Establish a risk factor. Determine a profit objective. Make a reasonable trade based on specific facts and tangible data. You do not have to base your trade on emotions or a feeling. If you lose, then at least it was a calculated loss. If the trade turns out to be a winner, it is a very satisfying feeling of accomplishment, not to mention putting a profit into your trading account. Either winning or losing, keeping a worksheet helps you track the process and allows you to review the results any time.

TRADE WORKSHEET

Trade Date	06/19/01	
Commodity	**Bonds 30 year**	
Margin	2,025 initial	
Tick value	31.25	
Yesterday high	$101^{12}/_{32}$	
Yesterday low	$100^{27}/_{32}$	
Yesterday close	$101^{02}/_{32}$	
Last week's high	$102^{01}/_{32}$	
Last week's low	$100^{04}/_{32}$	
Last week's close	$101^{03}/_{32}$	
Five-day trend direction	down	
Stochastic reading (daily)	%K = 66 %D = 75	
Relative strength index	53	
3-day moving average	$101^{2}/_{32}$	
9-day moving average	$100^{31}/_{32}$	
18-day moving average	$100^{19}/_{32}$	
Pivot point	$101^{3}/_{32}$	Buy/sell: Buy at $100^{18}/_{32}$
Support 1	$100^{26}/_{32}$	Stop loss: Sell at $100^{08}/_{32}$ stop
Resistance 1	$101^{11}/_{32}$	Profit objective: Sell at $101^{10}/_{32}$
Support 2	$100^{18}/_{32}$	Results: Winner! High of day was $101^{10}/_{32}$
Resistance 2	$101^{20}/_{32}$	Contingencies: Once one side is filled, cancel other

Notes: Market has been down for five days; technicals are showing an oversold market condition. Look to buy near Support 2 since the primary support is projected to be lower than the previous day's low (100-27). Risk ten points $10 \times 31.25 = 312.50$ plus commissions. Profit objective: Look to sell near 101-10 (near today's price from Resistance 1 and below yesterday's high of 101-12). If filled at 101-18, a $500 profit is generated at 101-02 and $750 profit at 101-10.

Trade followup: Once filled on the buy side at 101-18, watch market to move stop. Move stop up to break even if bonds trade up to 100-28.

FIGURE 11.1 Sample daily trading worksheet.

On successful trading days it will be good to recap your successes so that they can be repeated. Of course, on bad days recapping can allow you to focus on what went wrong so you can improve and stop repeating the same mistakes over and over again.

A DOSE OF REALITY

When you fill out your worksheet and study the markets you select, make sure you have a realistic grasp of what you can accomplish with the resources you have. One of the major sources of strain for you may be the amount of capital you have to trade. Overreaching or taking on more than you or your account can handle can be a major cause of discouragement and defeatism, the opposite of the attributes you want to develop to be a successful trader.

Be realistic about the amount of total capital you have to trade compared with the margin requirements you need. Study the markets you are familiar with and can realistically afford. If your trading account is only $10,000 or less, studying or charting the Nasdaq 100 index futures with an initial margin requirement of close to $20,000 would not be considered a realistic approach and would most likely be a waste of your time.

Here is a guideline for what you might be able to trade. Assume your starting balance is, say, $10,000 and you want to trade five contracts of a commodity where the initial margin is $2,000. For each full position, you are using $10,000 of margin money ($2,000 × 5 = $10,000). That's 100 percent of your investment capital for one trade. If the market moves against you only a small amount, it could wipe out most or all of your account.

Some money managers suggest using only 50 percent of your investment capital in any one trade and then risking 20 percent of your initial capital in that trade. With this formula you would be using $5,000 in margin on a $10,000 account, risking $2,000 on your first trade. That is more realistic than thinking you can trade five contracts. Throwing the dice and putting all your capital in one trade idea is a crapshoot and sounds like a long shot. This is not to say it can't be done, but you need to be able to accept the consequences if you lose your entire trading account in that one trade.

Use only risk capital to trade. Specifically, that means only money you can afford to lose. Then accept the fact that you will lose on some trades, maybe all of your money or even more than was in your account. If you don't realize this, then you might be trading scared money, and fear of losing will keep you from placing well thought out trades or, worse, cause you to hesitate and get in the market late after the move is over.

UNDERSTAND YOUR EMOTIONS

Fear, greed, doubt. These three emotions can hinder your trading. Every investor should analyze his or her own emotional makeup and the resources available for trading. Many books have been written on this subject, but the conclusions are mostly a matter of self-analysis that depend on each trader's personal characteristics.

Fear of losing can cause traders to make bad trading decisions, and doubt can cause the same results. Greed can cause some traders to allow good profits to erode back to breakeven levels or even losses as they hope for even bigger gains. Putting on too many trades searching for the "big kahuna" or "mother lode" also stems from greed. Sometimes it is best to just have a series of base hits rather than going for the grand slam. I certainly do not have the patent on this cliché, but it has been said, "It is better to have a million profitable trades rather than one profitable trade that makes a million."

Understanding your emotions is a very important subject that needs to be addressed and examined. Trading can produce an increase in your heart rate and your blood pressure. Make sure you are physically fit to handle the demands that trading in the markets may produce. You need to monitor your trading behavior and actions while under stress or while dealing with what I call the adrenaline rush. When you are wrong, do you freeze up and get the feeling of butterflies in your stomach? Do you become unduly irritable or feel panicky? I hope that you are aware that these conditions are not conducive for successful trading.

Lack of confidence and fear are your enemies. Avoid putting yourself in a situation that will cause you to be skeptical or afraid before you trade. Also, do not trade while going through major personal events such as buying or selling a house, moving, illness, a change in careers or loss of a job, a breakup in a relationship or divorce, a death in the family, or loss of a friend. Try to make educated decisions, and make sure you have the time to invest in your work before putting on any trades.

TAKE A BREAK

Whatever your emotional makeup, trading can be a very emotionally draining experience, especially when you are wrong and lose money. There is nothing more humbling and crushing to an ego or confidence level than getting beat up in the market. If it ever comes down to the point that you are frustrated and not happy with your trading results and you lack desire or the faith that you have the ability to succeed, stop trading immediately!

Take a break. Maybe two weeks or sometimes a month or more will help. Getting away from the trading action will give you a fresh perspective on the markets and allow you to refocus your game plan once you return. To attempt to be successful, you have to be prepared and in a confident frame of mind. To be on top of their game, athletes train hard, work out, and are in fit condition before competing. I don't think Tiger Woods would play a round of golf competitively if he pulled a muscle in his back. He would take time out to let the injury heal and then get back into the swing of things. If you are emotionally beaten or your confidence is down, you are not going to be in tip-top shape to trade. In that state of mind mistakes may easily be made. Remember, preservation of capital and equity growth are the most important aspects of trading. If you are not in the right frame of mind and lose your confidence, you may increase your chances for losses.

If you have been on a losing streak, take time off to let your psyche heal. Use the time off to reexamine how you feel and act under stressful situations. If you are wrong too often and do not see some profitable results or you have the "eat like a bird and crap like an elephant" syndrome (when a trader takes extremely small profits and lets devastating losers ride), stop trading. Reexamine how you are doing when you are trading before you put on another position.

On the golf course the thrill of hitting a 300-yard drive straight off the tee and having the ball roll right down the middle of the fairway, skydiving, surviving a high-tech roller-coaster ride, and trading futures and options can generate major adrenaline rushes. That rush is what drives some people to those events. Only the last one will be an expensive ride if you are wrong too often. Reevaluate why you are in the game. Hopefully, it is to make money and to have fun. If it is for the rush and you lose money, seek professional help. Only you can determine what it is that you are doing.

YOUR TRADING TO-DO LIST

Here are some techniques you can try that may help you stay on top of your game and keep you in peak performance. Remember, if you continue to learn in life, you will continue to grow, and your life may change as a direct result of the effort you put forth. So try these physical and psychological exercises to help improve your thinking and frame of mind. Do this so that you can consistently try to make money and cope or accept things better if they do go wrong. Hopefully, you will be able to identify what is not going right and respond quickly to correct it. Following these suggestions may not lead to success; not following them, however, may increase your chances of failure!

1. Write down your trading goals and identify your focus. Be realistic; start with small goals. For example, resolve to commit 15 minutes a day to your analysis. Start by filling out the worksheet with the indicators that I demonstrated or choose your own. You may want to start with chart pattern recognition and focus on identifying those for a few commodities. Eliminate tracking the futures products that you would not trade due to circumstances such as margin requirements or liquidity concerns. If you do not have the capital to trade Nasdaq futures, natural gas, or platinum, don't waste your time studying or analyzing those markets. Don't bother looking at the euro/yen spread or the Fed funds contract or fluid milk futures. Those are not highly liquid markets that you are likely to day-trade or swing trade anyway so stay away from those markets as well. Study the markets within your immediate financial grasp.

2. If you have the ability to be a good analyst but can't pull the trigger, then try this exercise with your broker or brokerage firm if you trade online. When you are ready to trade, you should have formulated a game plan that includes your entry and exit points. The exit point should consider the risk as well as the profit objectives. I write a weekly newsletter on Saturday or early Sunday with my entry and exit points. The analysis is done in a calm state of mind where I am not disturbed and can focus on work. On Monday mornings I place open orders (GTC) for clients based on that research, both entry and stop-loss orders. The next step is to sit back and wait.

The process is all mechanical; no emotions hinder me. Win, lose, or draw, the orders are executed, and most times the hard part is contacting the clients to find out where they want to take a profit on the winning trades. The losers are stopped out, and the orders that are not hit or executed are canceled at the end of the week. You can use the same approach. Do your homework on a daily basis. Place your orders before the market opens with instructions for your broker to call you once the orders are filled. Then monitor the trade. You should not get stage fright in placing the orders because the market won't be open yet.

3. Reward yourself once in a while. After achieving a goal—devoting 15 minutes a day for a week to some project or completing a successful trade, for example—I will usually compliment or treat myself to something. It could be as simple as telling myself, "That was a great job," to maybe buying a Godiva chocolate or a nice cigar. On really good times, it may be scheduling a vacation, especially where there are golf courses.

4. Positive affirmations are extremely important to help improve self-confidence, especially in trading. This exercise requires physical exertion. What you need to do is to pick up that 400-pound pen or pencil and write out these words 10 times a day: *"I am a positive, fearless, and a successful trader"* or *"I am succeeding in making money trading the markets."* By doing this activity, you are reaffirming your subconscious mind that you are a successful trader. You are then only going to focus on the positive forces and work on combating the destructive negative emotions that can and usually do interfere with being successful in trading. This technique can be applied to other aspects of your life as well.

5. Utilize visualization techniques, taking quiet times during the day, meditation, and other steps to achieve relaxation. All of these methods may sound silly or absurd. However, they have all been proven methods to help in different areas of different people's lives. Practice them and apply them in your trading life. Take a few moments a day to visualize yourself as a successful trader. Close your eyes and take a moment to project in your mind the steps that you would take from doing your chart work and analysis to entering your order and taking a profit. Get your mind prepared for being a winner and making money. Sometimes people become what they think they are. So tell yourself that you are a successful trader and practice these principles while you are trading. Take quiet times during the day to focus your attention on the business at hand. Not everyone can be staring at a quote screen all day—that is, unless you are a professional trader or a broker. Even then, you need to walk away for a moment.

You will have daily distractions from your job. Take a few moments out for yourself. Take a few deep breaths and tell your subconscious that you are a "positive and fearless trader." Try a meditation technique when you feel unusual stress developing or just do it everyday on your way to work, in an elevator, or sitting on the "throne." Take a long, deep breath and hold it for about 10 seconds. Then exhale slowly and at the same time concentrate on saying to yourself, "I am calm and relaxed" or "I am a successful trader." Repeat at least 10 times.

Stress can cause muscle fatigue and tense back muscles. Learn to relax. Get a massage or take a hot bath or a long shower when you get home. Treat yourself in moderation, maybe to some ice cream or your favorite candy bar. Spend 15 to 30 minutes a day working out doing exercises. These are ways to decrease the stress levels in your life as a trader.

6. Do not be too demanding of yourself and do not become obsessed. Life is about balance. Another phrase applies here: Work hard and party hard. I believe in self-rewards, serenity, and financial security. Getting the most out of life is great. Going to extremes is a difficult way of life that generally catches up with you. Complete isolation and compulsive reclusive studying are not the answer for me nor do I believe they are for most people. Be flexible and shoot for consistency. I believe in consistency and progress rather than obsessive behavior and striving for perfection. Consistency is rewarded by confidence. Success is not measured by how much you made in one trade but by being able to make money consistently over time and keeping what you made.

The purpose of this chapter is not to entice the trader who is losing money to think he or she will make money by following these techniques. I do not want to give you a false sense of hope. I just want to show you what has worked for me through the years when I have gone through cold spells. Other extremely successful traders that I have known and listened to have gone through cold spells. They spent thousands of dollars seeking the advice of professional counselors or mentors or took time off from trading just to improve their self-confidence and discipline levels. You are not alone if you are going through a period of losing trades, and you certainly are not unique. Many superior top-ranked traders have all suffered through their times of bad trades.

If you have not had to experience any dramatic losses yet, knock on wood! But there may come a day when nothing goes right and your "equity keeps on slipping, slipping into the futures" (sung to the tune of the Steve Miller song, "Time Keeps on Slipping"). If that day comes, do not panic. Stop trading, reread this chapter and put it into action. Remember, it is all right to be wrong; just don't be wrong all the time and make the same mistakes over and over again.

Successful trading is all about diligence and hard work and having a winning attitude! Keep that in mind and evaluate yourself in 30 days after having tried some or all of these exercises to see if you are a better trader.

CHAPTER 12

The Tactical Trader

Tips and Techniques That Work

The harder you work, the luckier you get.
—Gary Player

I want to introduce you to some of the techniques that professionals use so you can incorporate and apply them in your trading plans. I have done a casual survey in the industry by interviewing brokers over the phone and in person. What I discovered was that some were not actual brokers or traders but were "equity raisers" or licensed solicitors with little or no market knowledge or actual trading experiences. Clients of mine have admitted that they thought they were more knowledgeable and experienced in the field of investing than their previous brokers.

That admission gives me two reasons to reinforce the fact that investors need to read this book. First, at the end of Chapter 10, I explained why it is important to ask questions so you can choose the right brokerage firm and broker for you. Conducting a simple interview by asking a few select questions may save you money and, more important, aggravation. Your broker is really your employee so make sure you get a qualified and experienced one. You should be getting what you pay for. If you are using a full-service broker who is charging a higher rate of commission for service and experience, make sure he or she actually has experience and knowledge and can help tutor or train you in tactical trading techniques.

If you are a seasoned trading veteran, you may be trading with a deep-discount brokerage firm. What the firm will allow you to do during the open-outcry (day) session versus after-hours trading may be different from what

you expect. Here are some things you might want to find out that could affect your trading style:

- What is the day-trading margin policy? Some firms have more flexibility in day-trading margin requirements than others, so day-trading multiple positions may offer you more leverage than you expect, which may
  be good or bad depending on how you handle it.
- Can you margin your account with securities such as gold or silver
  certificates?
- Will the firm allow you to trade if you have U.S. Treasury bills in your
  margin account?
- Are services such as real-time quotes, research reports, newsletters,
  and the like free or is there a charge?
- Can you place orders over the phone or online 24 hours a day, seven
  days a week?
- How is the firm's support staff when you need them?
- Does the firm even have a customer service department to answer
  questions you may have regarding your account statements?

These questions illustrate what I mean by finding out what services a brokerage firm has to offer. You may be able to add other needs and questions,
but these are some things I think you want to know.

The second reason why I firmly believe traders with different levels of
experience can benefit from information in this book is because they can
learn—or at least refresh what they may already know—about practical
market strategies, trading tactics, or target trading techniques used by professional traders.

Previous chapters covered the basics of futures and the mechanics of
the markets as well as technical analysis techniques to identify potential
buy and sell signals. I also covered measuring techniques that chartists use
to gain insight on how far a market may move based on chart pattern recognition and mathematical formulas. I touched on the subject of measuring the
temperature of the market by using sentiment and consensus readings as
well as explaining different market conditions and dealing with emotions.

The focus in this chapter will be on how to apply different techniques
and tactics in your arsenal of trading tools and knowledge. To elaborate
on this subject, I would like to illustrate from the book, *Technical Analysis
of the Futures Markets*, written by John J. Murphy, the three important elements of successful futures trading. They are price forecasting, trading
tactics, and money management. I cannot put it any better so I will simply
quote from his explanation:

Trading tactics, or timing, determines specific entry and exit points. Timing is especially crucial in futures trading. Because of the low margin requirements and the resulting high leverage, there isn't much room for error. It's quite possible to be correct on the direction of the market, but still lose money on a trade if the timing is off. Timing is almost entirely technical in nature. Therefore, even if the trader is fundamentally oriented, technical tools must be employed at this point to determine specific entry and exit points.

The simplest way to summarize the three different elements is that price forecasting tells the trader what *to do (buy or sell), trading tactics or timing helps decide* when *to do it, and money management determines* how *much to commit to the trade.*

The techniques discussed in this chapter really have to do with the element of timing your entry and exit points and using different methods to capitalize on price direction.

PYRAMIDING

How to build a market position is a popular topic. More experienced traders have had success and acclaim the value of pyramiding. New investors inquire about this trading method because it has the get-rich-quick mystique surrounding it. Writers have published articles about it, and there is information on the Internet advertising how the "smart money traders" use this method and why investors should incorporate the secrets of this "time-tested" method into their trading plan to "create wealth quickly."

With all the attention that pyramid trading has gained, no wonder this seemingly get-rich scheme attracts novice traders. I will explain only what I have gained from my own experience after clients have asked about it. A lot of new investors want to find out if there is a pyramiding opportunity. Of course, there is always the chance for opportunity in futures anytime you trade, but remember that there is always the opportunity for loss as well as profit. Pyramiding can create massive profits when the market trend direction moves in your favor. However, massive losses can mount up as well if the market price corrects against you.

I am only going to present hypothetical examples of what pyramid trading is in a perfect-world scenario. As we all know, this is not a perfect world. The illustrations are for educational purposes only. I do not want you to go out and start trading like this without further investigating. This is a technique that I consider to be leveraging leverage using more leverage.

The following is an exact example of formulating a trading plan using a specific trading tactic that incorporates a sound money management technique. However, every trader is responsible for his or her own actions and finances. Do take the time to do your homework and work out the numbers on any other futures contract before using this technique.

This example uses soybean futures. A long-term chart should paint the picture as to the normal price range of the market (Figure 12.1). I chose soybeans for several reasons: (1) The margin requirement was relatively low ($1,000 per contract at the time of this analysis). (2) At $4.20 per bushel, the price was near a historic low. (3) There was relatively little downside risk and a lot of upside profit potential if the market moved higher. (Although those conditions existed in early 2002, they have not existed since then so that is why this must be labeled a hypothetical example.)

The total contract value of one soybean futures contract at the time was $21,000 ($4.20 × 5,000 bushels.). If the price went to zero, that is all you could lose if you could never exit the market for whatever circumstances. I consider that position to have relatively little downside risk. Another factor to keep in mind is that the lowest price for soybeans since 1973 was about

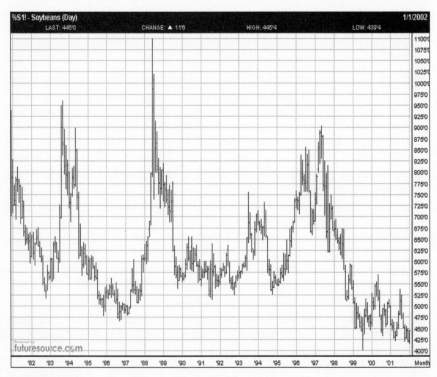

FIGURE 12.1   Base for a pyramid. (*Source:* FutureSource. Reprinted with permission.)

$3.45 per bushel, only 75 cents below the price on January 2, 2002, which is the basis for this analysis.

Limit buy orders were used, and the concept is that you do not add orders if the market does not move higher. You add positions every 20 cents higher. I used a 20-cent price swing mainly because the dollar value was equal to the initial margin requirement. This tactic virtually trades using money made from the market rather than your own capital. This example does not account for slippage from trailing stops, commissions, or other fees associated with trading. I used a standard minimum account balance of $5,000.

This technique may seem complicated, but it really is simple if you just write down the figures and do your math. Using professional money management techniques, I started with one contract, risking 20 percent of my initial investment of $5,000, which is $1,000 or a 20-cent stop loss. The soybean chart seven months later (Figure 12.2) shows nearly a $1.80 advance that would have made any pyramid trader happy. As you can see from Table 12.1, my risk shifted from loss to no risk to having positions on and stopping

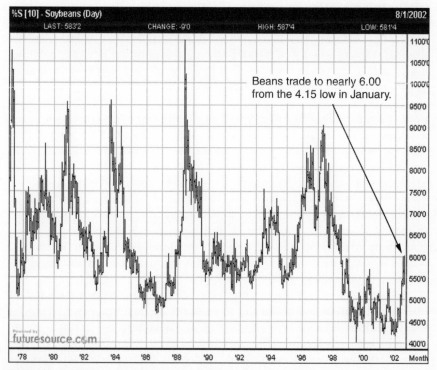

FIGURE 12.2 Seven months and many dollars later. (*Source:* FutureSource. Reprinted with permission.)

TABLE 12.1   Soybean Pyramid Plan

Starting Equity	Entry Level	Stop Loss	Position	Risk	Results
$5,000	4.20	4.00	Long 1	−$ 1,000	0
$6,000	4.40	4.20	Long 2	−$ 1,000	+$ 1,000
$7,000	4.60	4.40	Long 3	$ 0	+$ 3,000
$8,000	4.80	4.75	Long 4	+$ 1,000	+$ 6,000
$11,000	5.00	4.95	Long 5	+$ 4,000	+$10,000
$15,000	5.20	5.15	Long 6	+$ 7,500	+$15,000
$20,000	5.40	5.40	Long 7	+$14,000	+$21,000
$26,000	5.60	5.50	Long 8	+$16,000	+$28,000
$33,000	5.80	————Take Profits————			+$36,000

myself out with profits. By adding one contract each time the market advanced 20 cents, I wound up with eight contracts when prices reached $5.60. When the price moved from $5.40 to $5.60, for example, I had seven contracts working for me, earning $7,000 in profits.

At the point of taking profits, my account balance (not including the transaction costs and commissions) would be near $41,000 ($36,000 plus the original starting amount of $5,000). Buying one contract at $4.40 and holding it until $6.00 would have resulted in a gain of only $8,000 for a balance of $13,000 before commissions and fees.

I could have added more than one position, liquidated half of the positions at any time, or let the market ride and continued to trail the stops. There are many variables that could be done with the add-one technique. Play around with the numbers yourself and discover how pyramiding works.

Another variation of pyramiding is to buy several contracts at the $4.20 level and scale back on the number of contracts with every purchase above your initial entry level (Table 12.2). This style of pyramiding is what most people feel is the more standard method because you are long more positions from the bottom of the market so it's like the base of an actual pyramid rather than an equal amount as in the previous example. The problem is that you will be risking nearly your whole account if the market stops you out in the first stage of the trade.

One other point is the stops are trailed or adjusted as the market moves upward. The trader has to set stops based on varying factors such as prior support and resistance levels or profits or losses accrued in the account. Some investors will move a stop up just to protect a profit, which in this style of trading is usually against the main principle of the let-it-ride type of mentality that is necessary for pyramiding.

TABLE 12.2 Soybean Pyramid Plan Variation

Starting Equity	Entry Level	Stop Loss	Add On	Position	Risk	Results
$ 5,000	4.20	4.00		Long 4	−$ 4,000	0
$ 9,000	4.40	4.20	Add 3	Long 7	−$ 3,000	+$ 4,000
$16,000	4.60	4.40	Add 2	Long 9	+$ 2,000	+$11,000
$25,000	5.00	4.70	Add 1	Long 10	+$12,500	+$29,000
$35,000	5.20	4.90		Long 10	+$24,000	+$39,000
$45,000	5.40	5.00		Long 10	+$29,000	+$49,000
$55,000	5.60	5.40		Long 10	+$49,000	+$59,000
$65,000	5.80	5.50		Long 10	+$54,000	+$69,000
$75,000	6.00			————Take Profits————		+$79,000

This is a specific game plan strategy that requires discipline and the ability to be able to risk the entire account value to achieve the targeted results. I use the stop placements here as both a reasonable capital preservation maneuver and as a responsible trader looking to take money out of the market. Always remember, though, that stops do not guarantee anything due to market conditions, as discussed previously.

Extremely large profits can accrue quickly with very little investment capital. However, you can lose it just as quickly. Several events could happen and need to be addressed: Stops need to be adjusted carefully. You might be tempted to continue to add positions beyond a top indicated by your analysis. The exchange could raise the margin requirements while you are in the trade, forcing you to deposit additional funds or liquidate some or all of your positions earlier than you would want.

Certainly no trade is ever this predictable, and a move in soybean futures from $4.40 to $6.00 was a tremendous price move for a short period of time. These are some factors that I did not include in my example, so do a reality check of the market you are trading when you estimate how high a market could rally in a specific time period. You need to control your greed factor as well and trail those stops. Just try to develop a game plan before you trade and see for yourself if this trading tactic could help in your knowledge of trading futures and options. Even if you apply a portion of this technique in another market and a smaller move occurs, you may boost your trading capital better than you expected.

Whatever you do, you do not want to get into a reverse pyramid arrangement where you get cocky after the market goes up and gives you money to work with. You may be tempted to add multiple contracts at higher and higher price levels, setting up a situation where even a small price setback could wipe out all of your profits.

SCALE TRADING

Scale trading is another popular style of trading that tries to capitalize on a market that is at historically low price levels. It involves entering multiple contracts and staggering your positions at different entry levels. Some analysts and professional traders prefer to use this method with physical futures contracts rather than financial products because with physical futures there are finite price levels that affect supply/demand, and there will always be demand for the product at some price. Financial products are paper assets with no real physical value and are susceptible to complete devaluation.

Charts for physical commodity futures will show an absolute low value from an historical price perspective as well as from a cost of production point of view. It is that belief and theory that gives scale traders confidence not to get scared out of a market but to increase their holdings and to cost average as prices move lower. Coffee may be an example of a market that has gotten about as low as it can go in the early 2000s (Figure 12.3).

Prices could trade lower or stay at a low level for an extended period of time, but I don't believe coffee producers will give their product away for free. It costs too much in labor, delivery, and storage to harvest a single coffee bean at too low a price. When the burlap bag it is carried in costs more than the raw product, producers, exporters, or roasters will be forced to shut down their operations. The result will be that supplies will tighten, and prices would then tend to rise to ration demand.

After all, isn't that what happened to crude oil in 1999 when prices were trading near $9.80 per barrel? A cut in production by the Organization of Petroleum Exporting Countries and continued strong global demand caused a spike in prices, a great example that shows how prices go from one extreme to another. In less than two years crude oil prices went from below $10 to nearly $36 a barrel (Figure 12.4). Some analysts call this *supply complacency*, a phase that occurs when end users believe prices will always remain low and don't commit to buying and holding supplies.

Scale trading generally takes the guesswork out of timing when to go long a market—to a certain degree—especially when prices are near historic lows. If you want to be a scale trader, you need to lay out a plan and have a large reserve of trading capital while you wait for your plan to work.

The idea in scale trading is to set a base price at a point near previous lows or when prices seem to be about as "low as they are likely to go." You begin buying at that price. You may be early and prices go lower, but instead

FIGURE 12.3 Coffee: Setup for a scale plan? (*Source:* FutureSource. Reprinted with permission.)

of getting out of your position, you set up your plan to buy more contracts at specified increments below your starting price—like averaging down in buying stocks. You do not use stops. You keep buying on the way down until prices hit a bottom and begin to turn back up. They do have to go back up, don't they? Once the market price rebounds, you simply sell positions back to the market that you have accumulated from lower levels.

On the oil chart (Figure 12.4), for example, you might have started buying on a scale trading plan at $15, below the 1995 low. You bought more at $14, more at $13, more at $12, more at $11, more at $10—who ever expected prices to go that low? Eventually your plan paid off, but you can imagine how much money you would have had to put up to hold your positions.

In addition to large amounts of reserve capital, one hazard of scale trading is market timing. You may have to roll out of one contract month into another multiple times before prices begin to move up, and the new contract may be at a different price level. Undercapitalized trading accounts can experience large drawdowns in equity, and you could be blown out of positions by not meeting margin calls.

FIGURE 12.4   Oil: Foundation for a scale? (*Source:* FutureSource. Reprinted with permission.)

OTHER TACTICS AND TECHNIQUES

There is certainly never a guarantee that any trading strategy will produce substantial, if any, profits, but it is a good idea to understand the techniques and the methods behind what other traders may be doing.

Here are some other techniques and tactics I have used or observed in recent years. The amazing thing is they continue to work with relatively little notoriety, meaning not many people discuss these trading tactics. That's good because by the time the news is out about them, things will change.

- Utilize the S&P 500 Friday 10:30 a.m. rule. This is a directional time rule. The trend from 10:30 a.m. until 12 noon will be the trend going into the close of business on Fridays. My suspicions for the reason behind this phenomenon is that I believe traders are determined to follow the trend right into the close of business for the week. Traders don't want to be the last one holding the proverbial bag over the weekend. The trend that starts at 10:30 could be due to Fed time (when the Federal Reserve

makes adjustments in the banking system by adding or depleting funds
with its borrowing program) or margin call liquidation time (margin
calls that are not met are discovered when wire transfers are not received). The trend of the day is sometimes reversed from the day session open until 10:30. Sometimes the trend starts out on a strong up
note but then drifts and reverses lower. In any case, the trend that forms
from 10:30 until noon is the trend that continues through the close. Day
traders may want to wait until that time to trade with the established intraday trend. The S&P daily chart (Figure 12.5) illustrates 12 weekly
closes when the market closed darn near the actual low or high of the
daily trading range session. All but two examples are picture perfect.
Those two were holiday trading sessions (July 3 was a Thursday rather
than a Friday trading day because the market was closed on Friday).

- Chart patterns are hard to visualize for some traders. When you are having a hard time interpreting bullish or bearish patterns, turn the chart
around and upside down. You may gain a different perspective that will
enable you to visually identify a particular formation.

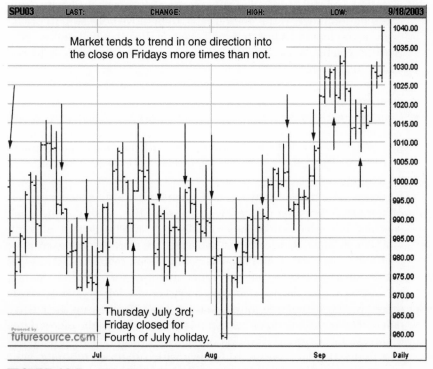

FIGURE 12.5   S&P trends on Fridays. (*Source:* FutureSource. Reprinted with
permission.)

- Watch your entry prices on stops. Be careful not to place stops at certain levels—for example, 08/32nds, 16/32nds, or 24/32nds in bonds and 10-year notes. These numbers are equal to quarter, half, and three-quarters. You generally want to put your buy stops above these levels and your sell stops below those levels as those prices can act as support and resistance on an intraday basis. Grain markets act the same way. Do not use 0.5 or 1-cent levels for stops. In meats, 0.25, 0.50, and 0.75 act in the same manner.

- Whenever you have a signal that is so strong that you think it can't fail— I mean, 10 different indications—and you are so sure the market just can't go the opposite way, then use a stop reversal. Odds are if the market looks that good, it probably looks that good to every other trader. What everyone else knows isn't worth knowing sometimes. If the market fails and stops you out, then it will fill you on a reversing stop, and the momentum of the price move could help offset a loss in the original position.

- Trade in multiple contracts, and get out of half of your positions when the market gives you a decent profit. That way, if it continues in your direction, you still have half of your contracts that can participate in the continuation move. If the market fails, then move your stop to break-even so you have a chance to break even on the other half of the trade. Because you booked a profit on the first half, it becomes difficult to lose money on a winning trade. This strategy requires action to maintain your position. Buy-and-hold strategies make it hard to build capital in some markets.

- Compare market analysis and cycle analysis to see if they correspond with each other. In some economic environments you will see bonds go up and equity prices decline. Know your markets. This is a great technique, especially when trying to verify a position or strategy that may not be working out.

- Be aware of first notice day tricks. Brokers often want speculators out of markets before first notice day, because of the inability of the small speculator to make or take physical delivery from a financial standpoint. More times than not, prices move in agriculture markets on the day after first notice day. Floor and professional traders, realizing that the pie will be smaller to share once the retail investors are out of the market, are willing to take the risk of trading a market in a delivery period. Their secret is that if they are long a market, they "freshen up their entry dates." Deliveries are made against positions based on the oldest dates of those long positions. If you get out of a long position two days before first notice day and reestablish your position the next morning, your chances of getting a delivery notice are slim. The exchanges release these dates of notice every morning so traders can gauge how long they can ride the market without risk of getting a delivery notice. This is not a tactic for everyone, but if you believe the fundamentals exist for a supply shortage in the nearby futures contract and prices will carry higher, then it may help you. Take up this technique with your broker.

These tips and techniques are updated in my advisory service.

CHAPTER 13

Options

A Primer

*There is no future in any job. The future lies in
the man who holds the job.*

—George Crane

I believe George Crane captures the reason why so many people are interested in trading: They want to take control of their own financial destiny. After all, you are your own boss when it comes to trading. You hold your own future in your hands because you hold your own job as a trader. You have the opportunity to succeed.

If you are interested in becoming that trader who controls his or her own destiny but are still concerned about the volatility and risk in futures, one way to trade that may be more palatable to you is with options, an alternative that might fit your trading style better. If used at certain times, buying options can be a great and powerful investment tool for any trader.

If you are right about market direction, very few, if any, investments in a government-regulated trading vehicle can offer the leverage and profitability with limited downside risk that buying options offers. The possibility exists for tremendous gains, especially with the increasingly volatile market moves.

However, options do have a negative connotation for many investors. Many industry experts estimate that 80 percent to 90 percent of the time, options expire worthless. Many individual investors who have traded them have found that to be true—the hard way, of course. However, if you think about it, a wrong opinion about market direction will result in a loss any way you look at it, whether it is in a futures position or an options position. Some believe that when you are wrong about the market, trading futures is like a quick death while buying options can be like a slow "bleeding to death" type of trade due to the time until expiration. But, wrong is wrong, any way you look at it.

So I think options may have been given a bad rap and abused by traders. If 80 percent to 90 percent of the options expire worthless and traders lose their premium money, the answer must be to do the opposite—that is, you must write or sell options to make money eight out of ten times by selling option premium. The probabilities seem to be in your favor.

However, there is one glitch when writing options: Your profit potential is limited and your risk is unlimited. Therefore, options writing usually involves more risk capital, as there are generally margin requirements that have to be met. It is the two times out of ten when you are wrong that selling options can kill you and wipe away any trading profits.

Of course, no method can be guaranteed to trade profitability. The unpredictability of the markets and the severity of market moves require investors to be more knowledgeable and diverse in their trading techniques when they trade options. At the very least, though, traders should become familiar with options.

The key to making money in any investment, first of all, is to be in the market and to establish a position before the market moves. Timing the entry or exit is most of the battle; having the right amount of contracts is the rest. Again, the important element is timing. Being in the market before it moves and participating with a good balance of instruments relative to your risk capital is considered establishing a position. In futures and options, that could be two positions for small traders. For an extremely large trader, it could mean having a thousand positions. For an investor in options, timing is one of the key elements in calculating the value of an option. Being in the market too early will result in an option expiring worthless.

Positioned properly, options can be very helpful in certain situations. In the following pages, I explain some of the basics of using options on futures, give examples of different strategies, and demonstrate how options can be combined with a futures position to act like an insurance policy.

OPTIONS 101

To start, there are two types of options: calls and puts. You can be a buyer or a seller. The price at which an option is bought or sold is called the *premium*.

A buyer or long option holder of a call has the right, but not the obligation, to be long a futures position at a specific price level for a specific period of time. For that right, the buyer of a call pays the premium. A buyer or long option holder of a put has the right, but not the obligation, to be short a futures position at a specific price level for a specific period of time. Again, for that right, the buyer of a put pays a premium.

For option buyers, the premium is a nonrefundable payment, unlike the good-faith deposits or performance bonds required for a futures contract. Premium values are subject to constant changes as dictated by market conditions and other variables.

A seller or option writer of a call or put grants the option buyer the rights conveyed by that option. The seller receives the premium that has been paid by the buyer. Sellers have no rights to that specific option except that they receive the premium for the transaction and are obligated to deliver the futures position if assigned according to the terms of the option. A seller can cover his or her position by buying back the option or by spreading off the risk in other options or in the underlying futures market if market conditions permit.

A buyer of an option has the right to either offset the long option or to exercise the option at any time during the life of the option. When a buyer exercises the option, he or she gets the specific market position (long for calls and short for puts) in the underlying futures contract at the specific price level as determined by the strike price. Options are generally exercised when they are in the money. In fact, in the futures market, if an option settles in the money at expiration, it will automatically be exercised for the buyer unless the buyer gives an order to abandon the option. In that case, the option premium will be lost, and the option writer will be released from his or her obligation to accept the opposite position.

Three major factors determine an option's value or premium:

1. *Time Value.* Time value is the difference between the time you enter the option position and the life the option holds until expiration. An option that has a longer life ahead is worth more than an option that is soon to expire, other things being equal. The reason why the term *wasting asset* refers to an option is because as the option gets closer to its expiration, it is worth less than it was when it had more time value.

2. *Intrinsic Value.* Intrinsic value refers to the distance between the strike price of the option and the price of the underlying futures contract. If an option's strike price is closer to the underlying futures contract, it will be more expensive than an option that is further away from the strike price. For example, a call option, which gives the buyer the right to be long the market, will cost more if the strike price is lower or closer to the actual futures price. The reverse is true for put options. A put option will be more expensive if the strike price is higher and closer to the actual futures price. If the strike price of a call is above the price of futures or if a put price is below the price of futures, the options are considered to be *out of the money* because neither is worth exercising. When the

strike price of a call is below the price of futures or the strike price of a put is above the price of futures, these options are *in the money*. A 5.00 soybean call is out of the money when the futures price is $4.45, for example, but a 5.00 put would be considered in the money.

3. *Volatility Rate.* Volatility is based on price fluctuations in the activity on the underlying futures market. The wider and faster the price movements are, the higher the volatility level is, and the higher the volatility, the higher the premium for the option, other things being equal. *Implied volatility* is a figure used to rank the volatility percentage that explains the current market price of an option. It is considered the common denominator of option pricing as it helps compare an option's theoretical value under different market conditions. *Historical volatility* refers to the measure of the actual price change of the futures product during a specified time period. Using mathematical calculations, historical volatility is the annualized standard deviation of daily returns during the period.

Other variables are also used to calculate an option's value such as interest rates and demand for the option itself. For instance, if you bought a call option and if the underlying futures market is moving up toward your strike price, then the option's premium may increase in value as option writers or sellers will want more money and buyers will have to pay more for the option.

One of the first things to know about buying options on futures is that you do not need to hold them until expiration. Option buyers may sell their position at any time during market hours when the contracts are trading on the exchange. Options may be exercised at any time before the expiration date during regular market hours by notifying your broker. This is called the *American style* of option exercising. The *European style* of option exercising means you can only exercise your option on the day the option expires. This method usually refers to equity options traded overseas. The references in this book are only to options on futures that are traded in the United States.

You also need to know that most options on *deliverable* futures expire about a month before their respective futures contract months. For example, a July call option on corn futures will expire around June 20. Cash settlement products such as stock index futures have their options expire on the same day as the main underlying quarterly contract months: March, June, September, and December. Stock index futures also have off-month options that expire on the third Thursday of every month.

If you buy an option and the market moves in the direction of your strike price, then the value may increase to the point where you may realize a profit after commissions and fees. If you are long a call or a put option, all you need to do is sell it. If you believe that market conditions have changed and your opinion has changed, or if you think the option has gained about as much as it can, then get out. Provided there is a liquid market for the option, you should receive at least some premium back if there is time value left and if the strike price is still close to the underlying futures price.

The purpose of this chapter is to give you a better understanding of the mechanics of options trading. I want to acquaint you with the everyday relevance of options trading for the individual trader and include my experiences and observations. I would rather help you understand when and how to use options than try to explain the complex details of the formulas and mathematical computations that determine the theoretical value of an options premium. The Black–Scholes model incorporates the current underlying futures price, expected volatility, time until expiration, interest rates, strike price, and so on. That type of computation is what computer programs are for, and we'll leave that for the brokers and software vendors who provide these services and can tell you the effect of different scenarios for volatility, time, and the magnitude of the price move.

Although some elements of options pricing may seem to be complex, you should be familiar with what are known as *the Greeks:*

- Delta is the amount by which an option's value will change relative to the change in value of the underlying futures contract.
- Beta is a measure of an option's price movement based on the overall movement of the option market.
- Theta is the estimate of the price depreciation from time decay.
- Vega is the measure of the rate of change in an option's theoretical value for a certain percentage change in the volatility rate.
- Gamma is the rate of change in an option's delta based on a certain percent change in the underlying futures contract.

Options and option strategies can be made simple or extremely complex because options are an extremely versatile investment instrument. What has made options trading so popular is that investors are now realizing that there are a wide variety of strategies and combinations that can offer the ability to maximize leverage and define risk parameters. Options can be used as a surrogate futures position, or they may be implemented as a hedge against a futures position, which, in turn, could be a hedge against a cash position.

The complex options strategies usually involve spreading two or more positions and are considered a multiple-leg spread strategy. Generally speaking, the more complex the strategy, the more legs that are involved. That complexity can mean more transaction or commission costs as well. You need to examine and include these costs in a trading strategy to weigh whether the trade is worth initiating. Consider it like evaluating whether the cost of doing business is worth the effort. If there is not a lot of room for profit and the risks outweigh the rewards, then reconsider initiating the trade. Once you learn to understand this simple concept of weighing your alternatives, I believe trading in options can be a lot less stressful, and the result might be a more rewarding trading experience.

After determining a trend direction or a price move in the underlying futures contract, I like to explore the different avenues to discover which strategy works for me to capitalize on my opinion. For example, I will look at the costs, the risk, and the potential reward. Unless you try to figure what is the best method, you won't know how to get the most bang for your buck. Analyze what will work best for you.

Education provides enlightenment and helps give you the confidence you need to experience new things. Humans seem to have an inherent natural tendency to be afraid to try new things due to fear of the unknown. What can cause more fear than investing in an industry that claims that 80 percent to 90 percent of investors lose money? But let me show you how to examine the markets and formulate your own opinion before you invest using options. Then you can make an educated, rational business decision on your own before you place an order using options.

OPTIONS TRADING STEPS

To begin with, you have to have an opinion about what you expect the underlying market to do. Simple. You have three choices: up, down, or sideways. Now all you have to do is your homework, analyzing support and resistance, technical indicators, or whatever you want to use in your analysis to arrive at a decision. After doing your homework, you decide you want to go long, say, coffee futures. You arrive at this conclusion based on the fact that the price is at a 30-year low and your technical indicators are generating a buy signal. You expect a move from the 40-cent level back to at least the 80-cent price range, which would be a 50 percent correction level derived from a 2-year high. You conclude that it may take at least 6 months to see the trade mature.

Great, this is the first step in planning a trade. Now let's see how you can trade a plan by exploring the alternatives incorporating the use of options. I like to use options combined with futures as a hedge or insurance against adverse moves. This is one situation where that may be a good choice.

First, you need to know what it takes as a good-faith deposit to margin a futures contract. You see that the initial requirement for coffee at that time is $2,450 (may change with market conditions) and the maintenance margin requirement is $1,750. Every point move in coffee is $3.75. A move from 45 to 46 cents is a 100-point move, which is equivalent to $375.

An at-the-money 45 March put has a price of 280 points so, with each point worth $3.75, the cost of the put is $1,050 before commissions and related fees. The March put expires on February 8, providing 72 days of protection from today's date, November 28. If you buy a futures contract at 46.60 cents and pay a premium of 280 points, the cost of the option and the difference between the strike price and the futures price is 440 points (times $3.75 equals $1,650). Until the expiration of the option, that is your risk and your margin requirement. To break even at expiration, you need coffee futures to be at 49.40 cents.

If coffee falls to, let's say, 10 cents for the first time in 30 years, all you could lose is the initial dollar amount of $1,650. This is, in essence, a limited loss/unlimited profit spread position. The only way you can lose is if coffee goes down or does not move at all for the next 72 days. The profit opportunity that exists, if coffee rallies, is unlimited if the price reaches above 49.40 during the next 72 days.

All right, that is scenario number one. Or, as I tell investors, start playing the Monte Hall television game show, "Let's Make a Deal." That is what is behind door number one. Let's start looking behind doors number two and three.

You now know what the costs are, what the risks are, and what the potential rewards are. Let's shop around and see what is behind door number two. First, you'll price call options. You are trying to figure out what you can get for the same amount of money with the same or better returns if the price of coffee rises—within the realm of reality, of course. For example, you do not want to buy a call with a strike price of 100. That is not in the realm of reality. Prices could reach that level, but it would mean the price of coffee futures would have to more than double in a relatively short period of time.

You will also compare how much a May call option is versus a July call option. Another determining factor that I use is the amount of time there is until expiration on the option and the price difference between the same contract month of the futures contract and the options month. Also, are May and July futures and options a liquid month? Would an options spread be beneficial?

Start working the math on the different costs associated with different strategies and watch what the parameters of the option strategies are. The characteristics like limited risk/unlimited reward or limited reward/unlimited risks should be explored and understood.

When trading a futures contract, you need to analyze which direction the market may go and when it is going to move. When dealing in options, especially when buying calls and paying premium, you need to know not only which direction the market may go and when it is going to move, but you also need to add another factor, an estimate how far the market will move.

Remember, when buying call options, you need to cover the cost of the premium plus commissions and transaction fees to make a profit at expiration. This is a situation where you could be right about the direction of prices but still lose money if the market does not move beyond your strike price at expiration.

For this example, though, a July 55 call option seems to be a better choice, weighing all the factors of cost, leverage, and risk/reward ratios. These options expire on June 14, providing 198 days until expiration. The premium is 500 points so, at $3.75 per point, the cost of the call is $1,875. The underlying futures contract is at 50.55 cents, which is 445 points out of the money. So you can use a call to buy an equal amount of coffee that will give you about the same amount of leverage and risk parameters as entering the market with one futures contract combined with a put option. The benefits are you have 2.75 times more life until the option expires using the outright long July 55 call option instead of the March futures and options strategy.

In doing the math and analyzing your costs, look at what the probability is that the market will hit your targets and look at the possibility of the market moving in your direction. Now look at the risks and ask yourself if you can afford to lose if you are wrong. And then ask if the trade is worth the reward. If you follow this line of thinking, then you may have a better understanding of what you are doing.

Because options on deliverable futures contracts generally expire the month before the month of the futures contract itself, it is a good idea to use the half-and-half rule when buying options outright. If half of the time value or half of the premium value erodes, reevaluate the position. Either get out of the options or salvage some premium by liquidating a portion of your position. You could also adjust your position by adding on more of the same options to lower your average premium price or you could buy other options that have more time value. This approach could be considered cost averaging, but some pundits consider it throwing good money after bad. Sometimes it pays not to give up on the product or the investment idea; just admit the timing was wrong and reevaluate.

OPTIONS STRATEGIES

There are so many different option strategies available that it would be difficult to cover them all. I explain here a few of the more common strategies that individual investors use, and you can see both the advantages and disadvantages for yourself. Again, some strategies use the concept of spreading, which involves the act of simultaneously buying and writing or selling multiple option positions. Remember, the more legs or combinations involved, the more commissions and fees are involved, and you need to include these costs in your calculations for risk and reward parameters.

Most of the following strategies can be combined with different strike prices and even options with different calendar months. I hope the names will help you identify the different characteristics associated with each strategy so you can use them for a quick future reference.

Bull Call Spreads or Debit Spreads

The terms *bull* and *call* imply a bias toward an upward price direction, so you can assume this strategy involves a spread that goes long the market by using calls. *Debit* implies that you are paying for the trade and that the costs are being debited from your account.

Other courses or books may refer to this as a *vertical bull call spread*. What is usually involved in this strategy is the purchase of a close-to-the-money or an in-the-money call and at the same time the sale of a further away strike price call option of the same expiration date. The close-to- or in-the-money call option may cost a great deal of money as it is near or lower to where the underlying futures contract price is trading, especially if there is substantial time remaining until the option's expiration. Traders spread this cost off by selling or writing a further out-of-the-money call option. When you sell or write a call, you collect premium or receive a credit to your account. This credit reduces the cost of the close-to- or in-the-money call option.

The profit/loss profile for this strategy is a limited risk and a lower expense for the investor as premium costs are reduced by the sale of the higher strike price call. The short call is covered by the long call so there is a predetermined risk factored in this trade and no unnecessary risks associated with option writing. The profit potential is limited to the level between the two strike prices minus the premium costs, the commission, and fees.

For example, if March silver futures were trading at $4.10 on November 28 and you expected the market price to rise to at least $4.75 by January, then you might look at buying a March 425 call and at the same time selling the March 475 call. The strike price difference is 50 cents. If each penny move in silver futures equals $50, then this is a $2,500 maximum spread difference. If the cost of doing this trade is, say, a net of $500 for the premium, $65 per option (times two) for commissions, and $5 per option for fees, then your total cost is $640. That is your risk and maximum loss amount. Your maximum profit is $2,500 – $640, or $1,860.

Your risk/reward ratio is almost 1 to 3 in this scenario. If silver settles below $4.25 at expiration, then you would lose $640. If silver does move and settles above $4.75 at expiration, then your net profit is $1,860. If silver really took off to $10 per ounce, you are still limited to the $1,860 profit.

Because this is a spread, you can leg into or out of a position. If, on the one hand, the silver market fell to, say, $3.50 first, both the 425 and the 475 calls would decline in value. If it is financially beneficial and if there is a good amount of time remaining, then you may consider buying back the short 475 call and staying long the 425 call, provided that you have enough free equity in your account to pay the difference of the 425 call. If this is possible, then you are now in an unlimited profit potential situation and are not locked into a defined profit situation. If, on the other hand, the market exploded up to $4.75 first and you sold the 425 call, that would leave you net short a 475 call with unlimited risk and you would be subject to a margin requirement. Most traders buy the spread and liquidate the spread, but the opportunity to leg out of a spread does exist.

Bear Put Spreads or Debit Spreads

The terms *bear* and *put* imply a bias toward a downward price move, so you can assume this strategy involves a spread that goes short the market by using puts. Again, *debit* spread means that you are paying for the trade and the costs are being debited from your account.

Other courses or books may refer to this as a *vertical bear put spread*. What is usually involved in this strategy is the purchase of a close-to-the-money or an in-the-money put and at the same time the sale of a further away strike price put option of the same expiration date. As mentioned previously, the close-to- or in-the-money put option may cost a great deal of money as it is near to the price of the underlying futures contract price, especially if there is substantial time remaining until the option's expiration. Traders spread this cost off by selling or writing a further out of the money put option. When you sell or write a put, you collect premium or receive a credit in your account. This credit reduces the cost of the close-to- or in-the-money put.

The profit/ loss profile for this strategy is a limited risk and a lower expense for the investor as premium costs are reduced by the sale of the higher strike price call. The profit potential is limited to the level between the two strike prices minus the premium costs, the commission, and fees. It is the exact opposite of the bull call spread in the sense of trading market direction.

Vertical Calendar Spreads

Vertical calendar spreads are very similar to the bull call and bear put spreads except that the word *calendar* means that the strategy has to do with different calendar months. The parameters involved in this strategy require that an investor be accurate not only for the direction of the price move, but also for the magnitude of the move and the time frame for which that move occurs. Because it involves similar but not the exact same months, there is a higher degree of risk associated with this strategy. As a result of this increased risk factor, there may be—and usually is—a margin deposit required in addition to the premium, commission, and fees involved if it is a debit spread.

Many combinations can be used for calendar spreads. Buying a further out contract month and selling an option with less time until expiration is generally how you initiate this spread. Some reasons for using this spread are that there could be disparities between the call options and futures prices of the respected contract months, volatility levels may vary between calendar months, or a trader may simply think he or she can time the market. In any one of these situations, a trader could take advantage of these disparities by selling the close-to-the-money and close-to-expiration call options and at the same time buying further out-of-the-money call options with more time value.

Let's say you expect silver to move higher between November 28 and the time March options expire in February. You believe the market could rally up to the $4.50 level by then, but could go as high as $5.00 by maybe March or April. A good example of a calendar spread would be to sell the March 450 calls and to buy the May 475 calls. If prices do not move, then the rapid time decay of the close-to-expiration March calls will offset the cost of the longer-term May calls. Another feature is you can leg out of the short 450 call option if it becomes profitable to do so. This strategy requires that you monitor the underlying futures contract regularly.

Bull Credit Spreads

You could utilize bull credit spreads if you have a neutral or bullish bias on the underlying futures market. In this strategy you sell a close-to-the-money put and buy a further out-of-the-money put. The idea is to collect premium in a steady or rising market as time decay decreases the option's value. The purpose for doing a spread is to limit your risk in case an extremely unpredictable adverse market move occurs. By selling the closer-to-the-money put, you will be collecting more premium than you pay for the out-of-the-money put you are buying.

Your risk is limited to the difference between the two strike prices minus the premiums that you collected. The profit potential is also limited to the net premium that you collect minus the commissions and related fees. Again, it is important to know these fees so that you can work them into your profit/loss calculations.

For those who believe in income-generating trades, a good example is to use this strategy with stock index futures where options expire nearly every month. Stock index futures attract these option strategists because it is necessary to sell premium in an option market that has expensive values to make the risk worth the reward. The higher the volatility, the higher the premium is, especially for close-to-the-money puts. Stock index options meet that criteria. In a slowly uptrending market, a trader can put on these positions and collect premium, knowing what the risk and rewards are. There is no need for precise timing to execute this trade strategy, only a conviction that the futures market will remain at or above the same level by the options expiration day. A margin requirement or good-faith deposit may be required for this strategy.

Bear Credit Spreads

If you have a neutral or bearish bias on the underlying futures market, you could use bear credit spreads. In this strategy you sell a close-to-the-money call and buy a further out-of-the-money call. The idea is to collect premium in a steady or declining market as time decay decreases the value of the option. The purpose for doing a spread like this is to capture some premium and to limit your risk in case of an extremely unpredictable adverse market move. Your risk is limited and so is your profit. This is the exact opposite strategy of the bull credit spread. A margin requirement or good-faith deposit may be required for this trade as well.

Ratio Spreads

The term *ratio* implies that there is a weighted difference for the ratio spread strategy. This is usually a *credit* spread or an *even cost* spread, meaning traders receive money or pay no premium for entering this trade. For this illustration, I use a *bull call ratio spread*. Traders would use this strategy if they were slightly bullish on the market, buying a close-to-the-money or in-the-money call option, and then selling or writing two or more out-of-the-money higher strike price call options. Generally, because of the exposure from the upside risks, the common strategy is a one to two ratio, buying one call and selling or writing two call options.

This is usually a strategy that gives you a little premium or credit, which is one of the motivating factors for deciding to do this particular trade. It uses the market's money to help finance your trade or even pays you to have a position in the market. If you think the price of a particular futures contract may rise in a certain period of time but may not exceed a certain level, then this is a good strategy to implement. If the market remains flat or reverses lower at expiration, then the out-of-the-money call options will offset the loss of the close-to-the-money or in-the-money calls and possibly provide a profit after commission and fees.

Because this particular strategy involves writing or selling calls on a ratio basis, one or more calls are usually uncovered, and a margin requirement or good-faith deposit would be required for this trade. Remember, because you have at least three positions in this strategy, there are three or more separate commissions and related fees involved.

As with other spreads, you have the flexibility to leg in or out of one or any combination of the call options. This is a practice known as *adjusting* your position. Anytime you adjust your position, you may be increasing or reducing your risk. When your exposure to risk increases, usually so does your margin requirement. The probabilities that an explosive upward price change will not happen in the market are on your side. However, if an unexpected event does occur, then this position will expose the trader to an unlimited loss potential.

A *bear ratio put spread* would be the exact opposite of this trade. In this strategy, you would buy a close-to-the-money or in-the-money put and sell two or more further out-of-the-money puts. You would use this strategy if you are slightly bearish on the market. Again, due to the exposure of the downside risks, the common strategy is a 1-to-2 ratio where you buy one put and sell or write two put options. Because this particular strategy involves writing or selling puts on a ratio basis, one or more puts are usually uncovered and a margin requirement or good-faith deposit would be required for this trade.

Ratio Back Spreads

The term *ratio* implies that there is a weighted difference for a ratio back spread trade. There is one major twist to this strategy versus a ratio spread, and that is the term *back*, which refers to a backward ratio. This spread is usually a debit spread or an even cost spread, meaning traders may have to pay a little money or have no premium costs for entering this trade.

A call ratio back spread is an example of this kind of strategy. First, you would sell or write one close-to- or at-the-money call. You would collect premium for that call and then use that money to buy or help finance two or more of the next or higher strike price call options. You would use this strategy if you were very bullish on the market. As a result of writing the call options, there may be, and usually is, a margin or cash deposit associated with this strategy in addition to the premium if it is a debit spread, plus commission and related fees.

In times of extreme volatility when a market is rising, call options may be inflated or overvalued. These circumstances would be an ideal time to use this strategy. It would allow you to enter the market using little, if any, out-of-pocket money to pay for the option premiums and still participate in a market move. Again, with at least three positions, you have three or more commissions and fees to account for in your profit/loss calculations.

As with the other spreads, you have the flexibility to leg in or out of one or any combination of the call options to adjust your position. You need to monitor the underlying futures market and the time value constantly with this strategy. Generally, this particular strategy is initiated with more than 90 days and not less than 30 days until expiration. You need to evaluate carefully the out-of-the-money long call option values when the time gets to within 30 days of expiration as the time decay will erode the value of the out-of-the-money long calls quickly, leaving exposure to the short close-to-the-money option.

This strategy allows you to participate in a market move with defined risk and unlimited profit potential. Although the maximum loss is limited with this strategy, there are two different loss parameters. One level of your risk is if the market at expiration is above the strike price of the call option you sold or wrote and below the two or more calls you bought (plus the premium, if any, that you paid and commissions and related fees). You need to calculate the price difference between the two strike price levels to establish a loss scenario here. The second level of risk is if the market at expiration settles below the call you wrote or sold. Then your risk is limited to the premium you paid plus the commissions and related fees. The payoff for the risks involved in this strategy is again the potential for unlimited profits that may occur in a runaway bull market.

Ratio Put Back Spread

A ratio put back spread is the exact opposite of the previous strategy and involves selling a close-to-the-money or in-the-money put and buying two or more further out-of-the-money puts. You would use this strategy if you were extremely bearish on the market. Again, because of the costs associated with buying options, the common strategy is a one-to-two ratio. Because this particular strategy involves writing or selling a put and exposes a trader to a slightly larger risk between the two strike prices, a margin requirement or good-faith deposit would be required for this type of strategy.

Covered Calls or Puts

The covered calls or puts method is used when you are long the underlying futures contract and may want to sell or write a call option to collect the premium from that option. The term *covered* refers to the fact that if the market does move higher and if the short call option is assigned a short futures contract, then there are no inherent risks as the option writer holds the underlying futures contract that would, in effect, offset the position at a profit.

The purpose for this type of strategy is to earn money if the market price remains stable or lower than the strike price of the option at expiration. There are no additional margin requirements involved for this strategy other than the initial margin requirement for the underlying futures contract, but there are additional commission and transaction fees involved. The drawback to this strategy is that if the market does take off to the upside, the covered call option strategist profit potential is limited. Because they are long a futures contract, the risk parameter is still unlimited.

The exact opposite is true for a covered put option writer. You would be short a futures contract and would sell or write an out-of-the-money put to collect the premium.

Synthetic Futures Positions

The term *synthetic futures positions* refers to the effect of using a combination of option strategies that will, in essence, give you more or less similar results and consequences that are much like an underlying futures position. A synthetic long futures contract is a long call and a short put. In this case you are basically financing part or all of the call purchase with the premium that was collected from the put option. This is another example of using the market's money to buy the premium rather than debiting your account.

Because this strategy also requires writing options, you should be aware that the risks are unlimited. However, the profit potential is unlimited as well. As a result of the risks involved, there is a margin deposit required in addition to the commission and related transaction fees. A synthetic short futures contract would be the exact opposite, a long put and a short call.

Delta Neutral Option Spread

The term *delta* refers to the calculation of the percent change you can expect in an option's value based on a price move in the underlying futures contract. A delta neutral option spread usually is a strategy that involves simultaneously selling an equal amount of out-of-the-money calls and out-of-the-money puts. Looking at the delta figures, you want to write both the put and the call with the same delta numbers or balance a futures position with the number and type of options that keep delta for the total position near zero.

This strategy is used when you believe the market may remain in a trading range or in a sideways channel. The theory behind the delta neutral option spread strategy is simple. If the underlying futures market moves higher, then call options should appreciate and put options should depreciate. Under ideal circumstances, the value of your net position may not change much, if at all, keeping the monetary difference of the equity in your trading account neutral. Remember, with every change in the underlying futures contract, there will be a change in the delta. If the market trades lower again, then the values of the put options should increase and the values of the calls should depreciate.

You profit from this type of strategy when the futures market remains in the trading range at expiration or the time decay erodes the premium values to a point that the trader can cover both sides of the trade with a profit after commission and fees. Generally, it is possible to cover the position at any time prior to options expiration. The concept is to be as equal or neutral in regards to the delta number as you can at all times.

Many variables can be applied to the delta neutral option spread. For instance, you could sell one put and then sell a combination of calls. If the delta on an out-of-the-money put is, say, 39 and you think the underlying market is too close to the strike price of a call with a delta of 39, then you could sell three calls of a higher strike price that may only have a delta of 13. So $3 \times 13 = 39$. You are short one put with a delta of 39 and short three calls with a combined delta of 39, keeping your total position neutral or equal on either side. This strategy can be adjusted if the market breaks out of its trading range by adding more short calls or puts.

Because this strategy requires writing options, you should know that the risks are unlimited while the profit potential is limited. As a result of the risks involved, there is a margin deposit required in addition to the commission and related transaction fees.

Long Straddles

I was once told to think about riding a horse when thinking about the concept of long straddles. When you ride a horse, your legs are straddled on both sides of the animal's back. The same is true with this trading strategy. When you initiate this strategy, you are on both sides of the market by purchasing a call and a put option, usually at the same time. Generally speaking, you buy at-the-money or close-to-the-money calls and puts within the same expiration month.

You might initiate this strategy when you have no opinion on market direction other than that you believe a breakout of the current trend or trading range is imminent. The risks involved are limited to the premium you pay for both of the options if the market price of the underlying futures contract does not move by the options expiration date plus the commissions and related transaction fees. The parameter for profit potential is unlimited once the costs of the option's premiums, commissions, and fees are covered. As a spread, you do have the flexibility to leg out of one side of the straddle if your market opinion changes and market conditions permit.

Short Strangles

To help me understand short strangles, I was told to think about what strangling someone is like. When implementing this strategy, you are writing or selling both puts and calls and you want to choke or suck the premium values out of the market. Short strangles are very similar to the delta neutral option spreads except that you are not so concerned about keeping the delta equal.

Generally, you sell both at-the-money or close-to-the-money puts and calls because you have an opinion that the market does not have any definite trend direction and prices may stagnate for a while. Time decay will usually erode the premium values, and that is what you want. This is really an unlimited risk spread, which involves two commissions and related fees. Again, because this strategy requires writing or selling options, you should know that the risks are unlimited while the profit potential is limited. As a result of the risks involved, a margin deposit is required.

This is a short version of some of the more popular options strategies. There are many other variables to trading options. If you are not familiar with how options work, my suggestion is that you read up on the various strategies. Many books have been written on the subject. If you want to get a little deeper into options, anything written by Larry McMillan will give you a solid education.

CHAPTER 14

Closing Bell

My Top 10 List

*Whatever the mind of man can conceive and be-
lieve, it can achieve.*
    —Napoleon Hill (*Think and Grow Rich*, 1937)

To sum up this book, I wanted to deliver trading methods, techniques, and terms in a logical and simple approach. I certainly gained a lot from writing this book as the mental cobwebs were cleaned out, and I was able to get an exciting and comprehensive refresher course from all the old techniques and the new developments and products that have been introduced throughout the years. I sincerely hope that this information was enlightening for the novice as well as for the advanced trader.

This is my first book. It combines two of the most exciting and volatile trading decades in the history of speculating in futures and the relatively new world of options trading. No matter how much I study and no matter how much research I do, there is still not a perfect trading plan that will generate profits every time I trade.

The goal that every trader wants to attain is to just make sure that the profits exceed the losses in the end. There are two ways to achieve this goal. One is to reduce losers and let winners ride so the capital amount that is taken in exceeds the losses. The other method is to have more winning trades than losers. I am a firm believer that the markets act randomly. Not every pattern develops as expected, not all support levels hold, and there certainly are plenty of instances of head fakes, false breakouts, and just plain old bad trading days.

You can take many different approaches to trading. Each individual trader must try to find what works best for him or her. You need to discover whether you can emotionally handle extreme stress from holding large positions overnight or finding a niche in day-trading techniques or simply developing the patience needed for long-term trend trades.

The purpose of this book is just to show you what works for me and to describe some of the techniques that I have used and picked up over the years. One casual observation is that I have noticed a common denominator among the more successful traders: They exhibit a genuine sense of confidence and are hard-working and well-organized in their thoughts and actions. Some are a little cocky but, for the most part, the more successful traders are more reserved or quiet individuals. Maybe that comes from the concept of "walking quietly but carrying a big wallet."

In this business you need to start with a desire to make money and, of course, the old saying applies, "It takes money to make money." You do need trading risk capital. Again, my definition of risk capital is money you can afford to lose, money that you are not afraid of losing, and money that, if you do lose it, will not make you hold a grudge against the markets. That statement was made as a reminder that education is expensive, bad trades do happen and that if you lose, then you need to reevaluate and reeducate, and then understand what went wrong.

A very successful trader once told me that fundamental, technical, or any other analysis "won't do me a damn bit of good if I don't have the money to trade or the courage to pull the trigger." You also need confidence, you need to rely on your own trading skills, and you absolutely need to be honest with yourself and admit when you are wrong, then act accordingly.

For those who do experience trading success, take money out of your trading account! Diversify your trading profits. One great analyst and trader, Fibonacci expert Joe Dinapoli, told me before going on the radio show that he likes to buy selected properties in real estate, whether it is in Bangkok, Massachusetts, or Florida.

I have heard many a trader start out with $5,000 or $10,000, make a large sum trading a particular market move, and decide to just build their account. Quite frankly, I really do not remember any of those people achieving that goal. I have seen traders give most, if not all and more, back to the markets. One reason is they become overconfident. They think, "If I can take $5,000 to $30,000, maybe I can take $30,000 to $1 million!" Greed sets in, they trade larger positions, take on more risk, and forget what got them their initial profits. If you are a one-lot or two-lot size trader, then take money out of the market on a consistent basis and reinvest elsewhere. Wealth creation is the goal, and diversification is the key to success in life.

There are no guarantees that you will become a more successful trader as a result of reading this book. However, I do believe it will help you achieve a better understanding of this business and excite your interest to continue your technical and fundamental analysis of the markets. Every individual has a desire to improve his or her life: Wishing, dreaming and goal-setting are all fine traits to have. The biggest obstacles to success are the inner demons or character defects we have as human beings. I am not the first and will certainly not be the last to say this, but understanding human psychology is a vital part of trading.

The importance of gaining control of some of the negative personality traits, which we all have as human beings, cannot be overemphasized if you want to be a successful trader. These traits, if not overcome quickly in the early stages of trading, can lead to destructive trading habits and eventually the demoralizing agony of defeat. Although this book was intended mainly to illustrate the importance of integrating pivot point analysis with candlestick charting signals and other indicators, I really can't stress enough the importance of human psychology.

THOUGHTS FROM OTHER EXPERTS

Not only do I believe that psychology is important for trading, but so do some of my peers and those who I consider to be master traders and technicians. Here are comments from some of the top experts in their field, highly respected traders who were kind enough to appear as guests on my radio program. (The recordings are archived and can be heard on my web site www.nationalfutures.com.)

- When I asked Larry Pesavento, president of Trading Tutor, which book (out of the seven or so that he wrote) he would recommend to a new trader, I thought he would say something about pattern recognition combined with Fibonacci analysis. His answer surprised me. His choice was Mark Douglas's book, *The Disciplined Trader.*
- I also asked Alan Farley, author of *The Master Swing Trader*, writer for the street.com, and founder of the hard right edge.com, what book he would recommend, giving him an opportunity to plug his very successful and highly acclaimed book. Instead, he admitted that his favorite trading book was also Mark Douglas's *The Disciplined Trader.* Farley revealed that he reads three to five pages of that book every night before he goes to bed.
- I had the opportunity to have John Bollinger, Chartered Market Technician and creator of the famed Bollinger bands, as my radio guest twice in 2003. (As an aside here, just to show you the interesting backgrounds that some traders and analysts have, Bollinger was a professional gripper and a cameraman in Hollywood where he says he "tinkered" with computers. He had a strong passion for the markets and began to trade his own money. Much to most people's surprise, he was never a broker.)

Bollinger's work with computers dates back nearly 30 years. Not only does his expertise on Bollinger bands benefit all kinds of traders from individuals to institutions and from stocks to commodities, but his studies on group sectors and the equity markets also are immense. (His latest achievement is found at www.powergroup.com.)

The first time he appeared on my program, he offered fabulous advice on the market and instructed listeners with a real-time example on using Bollinger bands on the mini-sized Dow futures contract. With the Dow at 8500 at the time and at the top band of resistance, he explained how the market could "walk the band" and continue higher. The Dow, in fact, managed to rally another 800 points.

As you can imagine, this seemed like a good time to ask, "John, what do you think folks should do? Buy your book?" His surprising answer: Go to your local community college and take a course in human behavioral psychology. (For the record, we also did discuss his book, and he offered to send an autographed copy if purchased directly from his web site at www.bollingerbands.com. I believe that is a standing order. If not for the education, you might want it as a collector's item from one of the great market technicians.)

I also asked Bollinger what was the first book he read on technical analysis, and he said it was one of Martin Pring's books. Interestingly enough, I had had Pring on the radio show earlier in the year and asked him what was the first book he read on technical analysis. He said Edwards and Magee's *Technical Analysis of Stock Trends*. That also was one of the first books I had ever read on technical analysis in the early 1980s. It is still a classic to this day, and many principles I use have come from those teachings.

MY FAVORITE TOP 10 TRADING THOUGHTS

Based on my own experiences as a trader and on conversations with many top analysts and traders on my radio program and elsewhere, here is a top-10 list of observations I would like to pass along to you after 23 years in the trading business. You may recognize some of these thoughts as market clichés, but they have stood the test of time and should be helpful for you as well.

1. You only have three choices when you are in a bad position, and it is not hard to figure out what to do: (1) Get out, (2) double up, or (3) spread it off. I have always found getting out to be the best of all three choices.

2. No opinion on the market or you are doubtful about market direction? Then stay out. Remember, when in doubt, stay out.

3. Don't ever let anyone know how big your wallet is, and don't ever let anyone know how small it is either.

4. If you snooze, you lose. Know your markets, when they trade, and what reports will affect the market price.

5. The markets will always let you in on the losers; the market's job is to keep you out of winners. Dump the dogs and ride the winning tide.

6. Stops are *not* for sissies.

7. Plan your trade, then trade your plan. He who fails to plan, plans to fail.

8. Buy the rumor and sell the fact. Watch for volatility in these situations; it usually marks tops or bottoms in the markets.

9. Buy low, sell high. Or buy it when nobody wants it, and sell it when everybody has to have it!

10. It's okay to lose your shirt, just don't lose your pants; that is where your wallet is.

One last thought I want to leave with you. It applies not only to everyday life but to trading the markets as well: Success is measured not so much by the wealth or position you have gained, but rather by the obstacles you have overcome to succeed!

Good luck in all of your investing and trading endeavors. And, remember, you are trading to take money out of the market, not to build a big account to satisfy your ego or to invest in your grandchildren's retirement fund. Be sure to take money out of the market for yourself and immediate needs so you can enjoy the fruits of your labors.

Glossary

abandoned baby   Candlestick pattern that resembles a bar chart version of an island top or bottom formation. Generally, the gap island candle is a doji.

all or none   A specific order that instructs the floor broker to fill all contracts in an order or none at all.

American-style option   An option that trades on U.S. exchanges and can be exercised at any time during the life of the option prior to expiration.

arbitrage   The action of a simultaneous buy and sell of a similar or like commodity or futures product that may be made in different contract months, on different exchanges, or in different countries to profit from a discrepancy in price.

assignment   The notification to a holder of a short option position that his or her position has been exercised by the opposite party (buyer), and he or she has been issued a position in the underlying derivative market. The holder of a short call would be assigned a short position at the strike price level, and the holder of a short put option would be assigned a long position at the strike price level.

associated person   An individual who solicits orders, customers, or customer funds on behalf of a futures commission merchant, an introducing broker, a Commodity Trading Advisor, or a Commodity Pool Operator.

at the money   When the strike price of an option is equal or very close to the price of the underlying derivative market price.

automatic exercise   A procedure whereby options that are in the money at expiration are exercised without instruction from the option holder. Buyers of options may abandon such options if they did not offset the position, but need to notify their FCMs and or instruct their brokers to do so.

backwardation   A condition in which futures prices are lower in each succeeding contract month rather than higher in a normal carry charge market due to a supply or demand imbalance.

bar charting   A method of charting a period's price action as a vertical line that represents the high and low with a small horizontal line marking the open and closing prices.

basis   The price difference between a futures contract and the underlying cash market. The basis can be affected by supply/demand functions and carrying costs.

bearish   A downtrending market or a period in which prices are declining.

belt-hold candle   A candle that can be a bearish or bullish candle. The bullish candle opens on the low, forming a flat bottom or shaved-bottom appearance. The bearish candle opens at the high, forming a flat top or shaved-top look.

beta   An option term that measures the percentage of price move of the option in relation to the underlying futures contract.

bid   A reference to buy at a certain price.

Black–Scholes   The standard formula for pricing the value of options. Fischer Black and Myron Scholes developed the calculation.

breakaway gap   A chartist term that applies when prices move substantially away from a congestion or consolidation area. The gap area leaves a space or hole on the charts.

broker   A registered representative of a brokerage firm who is paid commissions for accepting and placing orders for customers.

bullish   An uptrending market or a period in which prices appreciate in value.

bull spread   In most commodities and financial instruments, the term refers to buying the nearby month and selling the deferred month to profit from the change in the price relationship.

butterfly spread   Buying and selling two spreads in opposite directions with the center delivery month common to both spreads.

calendar spread   An options trade where one buys and sells options in different expiration months in the same underlying contract.

call option   A derivative product that gives a buyer the right, but not the obligation, to be long or to be a buyer of an underlying derivative product at the strike price level.

candlestick charting   Charting method that provides a visual presentation of the relationship between the open, high, low, and close. Color schemes are used to illustrate a candle's real body, which is the difference between the close and the open. If the close is lower than the open, the body is usually shown as black; if the close is higher than the open, the body is usually shown as clear or white.

carrying charges   The cost associated with holding or storing cash or physical commodities and financial instruments. Three variables are involved: storage, insurance, and finance charges or interest payments on borrowed money.

cash settlement   A means to settle a contract on the last trading day. Instead of physical delivery, the product is settled by the contract's cash value. Stock indexes, the U.S. Dollar Index, and a number of other futures contracts are cash settled.

clearinghouse A company or separate corporation of an exchange that is responsible for reconciling trading accounts, clearing trades, collecting and maintaining margin monies, regulating delivery, and reporting trading data. Clearinghouses act as third parties to all futures and options contracts, acting as a buyer to every clearing member seller and a seller to every clearing member buyer.

clearing member A firm that holds seats on an exchange and has the right to clear and reconcile trades of individual floor traders on that exchange.

close The settlement or last price at the end of a trading session established by the exchange.

commodity A physical product that is used in commerce and is traded mainly on a regulated commodity exchange. The types of products range from agricultural, such as meats and grains, to metals to petroleum. The term is also often applied to financial instruments such as foreign currencies, stock index futures, single stock futures, and various interest rate vehicles such as T-notes and T-bonds.

Commodity Futures Trading Commission (CFTC) The federal regulatory agency overseeing the U.S. futures industry, established under the Commodity Futures Trading Commission Act, as amended in 1974 and renewed periodically. The commission consists of five commissioners, one of whom is designated as chairman, all appointed by the president subject to Senate confirmation, and is independent of all cabinet departments. This agency regulates all nonbank Forex dealings as well as the futures industry.

commodity pool An enterprise in which funds contributed by a number of persons are combined for the purpose of trading futures contracts or commodity options.

Commodity Trading Advisor (CTA) A specific registration that requires an associated person to be registered with the National Futures Association for two years. A registered individual or entity can then advise others, for compensation or profit, about buying or selling futures contracts or commodity options. A CTA can exercise trading authority over a customer's account as well as provide research and analysis through newsletters or other media.

coupon The interest rate on a debt instrument expressed in terms of a percent on an annualized basis that the issuer guarantees to pay the holder until maturity.

crop reports Reports compiled and released by private forecasting agencies and the U.S. Department of Agriculture providing pertinent information regarding estimates on planted acreage, yield, and expected production as well as the growing conditions and progress of the crops.

crush spread The purchase of soybean futures and the simultaneous sale of soybean oil and soybean meal futures contracts.

daily trading limit The maximum price range set by the exchange each day for a contract.

day traders   Speculators who trade positions during the day in the derivative markets and liquidate them prior to the close to avoid exposure to adverse risk overnight.

dead cross   A chart pattern whereby a sell signal is generated when one or more shorter-term moving averages cross below a longer-term moving average.

deferred month   The more distant month in which futures trading is taking place, as opposed to the active nearby or front contract delivery month.

delivery   The transfer of a cash commodity from the seller of a futures contract to the buyer of a futures contract. Exchanges are responsible for establishing the specific quantity, quality, and procedures for physical delivery.

delta   A calculation percentage measure for how much an option premium changes based on the change in the underlying derivative product, interpreted as the probability that the option will be in the money by expiration.

discount rate   The interest rate charged on loans by the Federal Reserve to member banks.

doji   A candlestick term used to describe a time period when the open and close are nearly identical. It is a strong sell signal at a top, but a cautionary warning at bottoms.

Elliott wave   Analysis theory that was developed by Ralph N. Elliott based on the premise that prices move in two basic types of waves. Five impulse waves move with the main trend and three corrective waves move against the main trend.

Eurodollars   U.S. dollars on deposit with banks outside of the United States.

exchange for physicals (EFP)   A transaction generally used by two hedgers who want to exchange futures for cash positions.

exercise   The process by which options traders implement their right to convert an options position into the underlying futures or derivative market. For example, buyers of call options would convert their calls for a long position, and buyers of put options would convert their puts to a short futures contract.

expiration date   The established time when options expire.

face value   The amount of money printed on the face of the certificate of a security; the original dollar amount of indebtedness incurred.

falling three methods   A bearish continuation pattern similar to the Western version of a bear flag. It can be a four-candle pattern, but usually has five candles.

Federal funds   The interest rate charged to member banks on money loaned by other member banks.

Federal Reserve System   The central banking system in the United States, created by the Federal Reserve Act in 1913, designed to assist the nation in attaining its economic and financial goals. The structure of the Federal Reserve System includes a Board of Governors, the Federal Open Market Committee, and 12 Federal Reserve banks.

Fibonacci numbers and ratios   The sequence of numbers that adds a number to the preceding number to produce a series that continues to infinity. The ratios are the math calculations derived from dividing the series numbers or in some cases the square root of the numbers. The important ratio numbers are 0.38 percent, 0.618 percent, 50 percent and 100 percent.

fill-or-kill   A customer order that is a price limit order that must be filled immediately or canceled.

financial instrument   A document having monetary value or recording a monetary transaction. There are two basic types. One is a debt instrument, which is a loan with an agreement to pay back funds with interest. The other is an equity security, which is a share or stock in a company.

first notice day   According to Chicago Board of Trade rules, the first day on which a notice of intent to deliver a commodity in fulfillment of a given month's futures contract can be made by the clearinghouse to a buyer. The clearinghouse also informs the sellers with whom they have been matched. Each exchange sets its own guidelines and rules for this process.

floor broker   An individual who executes orders for the purchase or sale of any commodity futures or options contract on any contract market for any other person.

floor trader   An individual who executes trades for the purchase or sale of any commodity futures or options contract on any contract market for such individual's own account.

forex market   Usually refers to the over-the-counter market where buyers and sellers conduct foreign currency exchange business.

forward contract   A cash contract in which a seller agrees to deliver a specific cash commodity to a buyer sometime in the future. Forward contracts, in contrast to futures contracts, are privately negotiated and are not standardized.

full carrying charge market   A futures market where the price difference between delivery months reflects the total costs of interest, insurance, and storage.

fundamental analysis   A method of anticipating future price movement using supply and demand information.

futures commission merchant (FCM)   An individual or organization that solicits or accepts orders to buy or sell futures contracts or options on futures and accepts money or other assets from customers to support such orders. Also referred to as *commission house* or *wire house*.

futures contract   A legally binding agreement, made on an exchange trading floor or via computer, to buy or sell a commodity or financial instrument at a specified time in the future. Futures contracts are standardized as to the quality, quantity, and delivery time and location for each market. These guidelines are established by the exchange and overseen by the CFTC.

futures exchange   A central marketplace with established rules and regulations where buyers and sellers meet to trade futures and options on futures contracts.

gamma   An option valuation term used to measure how fast delta changes, given a unit change in the underlying futures price.

Gann, William D.   An early pioneer in technical analysis. He is credited with developing mathematical systems based on Fibonacci numbers, cycles of various lengths, and the Gann square.

GLOBEX   A global electronic trading system used on the Chicago Mercantile Exchange (CME).

golden cross   A bullish term used to describe a chart pattern when one or more shorter-term moving averages cross above a longer-term moving average. It generally generates a buy signal.

grain terminal   Large grain elevator facility with the capacity to ship grain by rail or barge to domestic or foreign markets.

gravestone doji   A candlestick pattern that represents a wide-range period where the open and close are near the low of the period's range.

gross domestic product (GDP)   The value of all final goods and services produced by an economy over a particular time period, normally a year.

gross national product (GNP)   Gross domestic product plus the income accruing to domestic residents as a result of investments abroad less income earned in domestic markets accruing to foreigners abroad.

hammer   A candlestick pattern that forms at bottoms. At market tops the same construction is called a *hanging man*. The shadow is generally twice the length of the real body.

harami   A two-candle pattern that marks tops and bottoms. The second candle of this formation is contained within the real body of the prior session's candle.

hedger   An individual or company owning or planning to own the underlying product and concerned that the cost of the market may change before either buying or selling it in the cash market. A hedger achieves protection against changing cash prices by purchasing (selling) futures contracts of the same or similar commodity and later offsetting that position by selling (purchasing) futures contracts of the same quantity and type as the initial transaction.

hedging   The practice of offsetting the price risk inherent in any cash market position by taking an equal but opposite position in the futures market. Hedgers use the futures markets to protect their businesses from adverse price changes.

high wave   A candle that has a wide range with a small real body that develops in the middle of that range. It has significance as a reversal formation, especially if several of these form in succession.

horizontal spread   The purchase of either a call or put option and the simultaneous sale of the same type of option with typically the same strike price but with a different expiration month. Also referred to as a *calendar spread*.

implied volatility   The term used to measure an expected price move based on the underlying futures market for an option.

index option   Options on a stock index, either cash or futures.

initial margin   The good-faith deposit that must be posted initially to enter into a futures position. Margins are subject to change without notice. It is the responsibility of the exchanges to set these price amounts.

intercommodity spread   The purchase of a given delivery month of one futures market and the simultaneous sale of the same delivery month of a different, but related, futures market.

interdelivery spread   The purchase of one delivery month of a given futures contract and simultaneous sale of another delivery month of the same commodity on the same exchange. Also referred to as an *intramarket* or *calendar spread*.

intermarket spread   The sale of a given delivery month of a futures contract on one exchange and the simultaneous purchase of the same delivery month and futures contract on another exchange.

in-the-money option   An option having intrinsic value. A call option is in-the-money if its strike price is below the current price of the underlying futures contract. A put option is in-the-money if its strike price is above the current price of the underlying futures contract.

intrinsic value   The amount by which an option is in-the-money.

introducing broker (IB)   A person or organization that solicits or accepts orders to buy or sell futures contracts or commodity options but does not accept money or other assets from customers to support such orders.

inverted market   A futures market in which the relationship between two delivery months of the same commodity is abnormal.

island chart pattern   A pattern formed when the market gaps in one direction and then in the next session, gaps open in the opposite direction leaving the prior period's bar or range isolated on the chart like an island. At tops this is extremely bearish; at bottoms it is considered extremely bullish. This is a rare chart pattern and is similar in nature to the Japanese candlestick pattern called the *abandon baby*.

J-Trader   An independent electronic trading order-entry platform provider by Pats Systems that routes orders to exchange electronic trading systems.

lagging indicators   Market indicators showing the general direction of the economy and confirming or denying the trend implied by the leading indicators.

last trading day (LTD)   The final day when trading may occur in a given futures or options contract month.

leading indicators   Market indicators that signal the state of the economy for the coming months. Some of the leading indicators include average manufacturing workweek, initial claims for unemployment insurance, orders for consumer goods and material, percentage of companies reporting slower deliveries, change in manufacturers' unfilled orders for durable goods, plant and equipment orders, new building permits, index of consumer expectations, change in material prices, prices of stocks, and change in money supply.

LEAPS   Long-term Equity Anticipation Securities. These are options that have an extended life as long as five years. Generally used for options on stocks.

leverage   The ability to control large dollar amounts of a commodity with a comparatively small amount of capital.

limit order   An order in which the customer sets a limit on the price or time of execution.

liquid   A characteristic of a security or commodity market with enough units outstanding to allow large transactions without a substantial change in price. Institutional investors are inclined to seek out liquid investments so that their trading activity will not influence the market price.

liquidate   Closing a position with an offsetting transaction in the futures markets. A long holder would sell and a short holder would buy to make their market position flat.

long   The position in a market when one buys contracts or owns a cash commodity.

long-legged doji   A specific doji that forms when the open and close occurs near the middle of a wide-range trading session.

maintenance margin   A set minimum margin that a customer must maintain in his or her margin account. If the cash amount in the trading account drops below this level and a margin call is generated, the trader must either send additional funds to get the account back to the initial margin level or liquidate positions to satisfy the call.

managed futures   Client assets are held in an account that is traded by professional money managers known as Commodity Trading Advisors on a discretionary basis, using global futures markets as an investment medium.

margin call   A call from a clearinghouse to a clearing member or from a brokerage firm to a customer to bring margin deposits up to a required minimum level.

marked-to-market   The act of debiting or crediting a margin account based on the close of that day's trading session.

market order   An order to buy or sell a futures contract of a given delivery month to be filled at the best possible price and as soon as possible.

market profile   A method of charting that analyzes price and volume in specific time brackets.

momentum   A measurement of the rate of change in prices.

morning doji star   A bullish three-candle formation where the middle candle is formed by a doji.

moving average   A technical price analysis method calculated by adding the prices for a predetermined set number of periods and then dividing by that number of periods.

naked option position   Going short premium, either a put or call, without having the underlying derivative product to cover the option position.

National Futures Association (NFA)   The self-regulatory agency for futures and options on futures markets. The primary responsibilities of the NFA are to enforce ethical standards and customer protection rules, screen futures professionals for membership, audit and monitor professionals for financial and general compliance rules, and provide for arbitration of futures-related disputes.

nearby month   The futures contract month closest to expiration. Also called the *spot month*.

offer   A price at which one will sell a commodity. Buyers must accept the *ask price* or offer price to execute a trade.

offset   Taking a second futures or options position opposite to the initial or opening position.

one cancels other   A contingency order instructing a broker to cancel one side of a two-sided entry order.

opening range   A range of prices at which buy and sell transactions take place during the first minute at the opening of trading for most markets.

open interest   The total number of futures or options contracts of a given commodity that have not yet been offset by an opposite futures or option transaction nor fulfilled by delivery of the commodity or option exercise. Each open transaction has a buyer and a seller, but for calculation of open interest, only one side of the contract is counted.

open outcry   Method of public auction for making verbal bids and offers in the trading pits or rings of futures exchanges.

option   A contract that conveys the right, but not the obligation, to buy or sell a particular item at a certain price for a limited time.

out-of-the-money option   An option with no intrinsic value. A call whose strike price is above the current futures price or a put whose strike price is below the current futures price.

overbought   A technical situation when the price of a specific move has risen too far too fast and is set up for a corrective pullback or a period of consolidation.

oversold   The opposite of overbought, when the market price has fallen too far too fast and is in a position for a corrective rally or a period of consolidation.

par   The face value of a security. For example, a bond selling at par is worth the same dollar amount as it was issued for or at which it will be redeemed at maturity.

piercing pattern   A candlestick formation involving two candles formed at bottoms of market moves. The first candle is a long dark candle; the second candle opens lower than the dark candle's low and closes more than halfway above the first candle's real body.

pit   The area on the trading floor where futures and options on futures contracts are bought and sold. It is customary for Chicago markets to refer to the individual commodity trading areas as *pits*. New York markets refer to these areas as *rings*.

pivot points   The mathematical calculation formula used to determined the support or resistance ranges in a given time period. These formulas can be used to calculate intraday, daily, weekly, monthly, or quarterly ranges.

point-and-figure   A charting style that tracks the market's price action by representing increases by plotting a column of Xs on a chart and downside corrections with columns of Os. Time is not an issue with this method, which uses only pure price movement.

position   Either a long or short trade that puts a trader into the market, it can also refer to how many contracts a trader is holding.

premium   The dollar value amount placed on an option.

prime rate   Interest rate charged by major banks to their most creditworthy customers.

producer price index   An index that shows the cost of goods and services to producers and wholesalers.

purchase and sale   A round-turn trade transaction in the futures market.

put option   An option that gives the option buyer the right, but not the obligation, to sell the underlying instrument at the strike price on or before the expiration date.

range   The price established by the high and low of a given time period.

real body   The section of a candlestick defined as the area established between the opening and closing of a particular time period.

relative strength index (RSI)   A technical indicator used to determine if a market is in an overbought or oversold condition. This indicator was developed by Welles Wilder Jr. to help determine market reversals.

resistance   A level above the current market price that attracts sellers, thus creating a ceiling for prices.

rickshaw doji   A doji that has an unusually large trading range.

scalper   A trader who trades for small, short-term profits.

settlement price   The last price paid for a commodity on any trading day. The exchange clearinghouse determines a firm's net gains or losses, margin requirements, and the next day's price limits on each contract's established settlement price. Also referred to as the *daily settlement price* or *daily closing price*.

shadow   The area on a candlestick that depicts trading that occurs at prices outside the range of the real body for a period. The upper shadow is between the high and the open or close, the lower shadow is the difference between the low and the open or close.

shooting star   The candle that forms at tops of markets where the shadow is at least twice the length of the real body and the real body forms near the low for the session with little or no shadow at the bottom. This candle resembles an inverted hammer.

short   The position in a market when one sells a contract with the intention of buying back at a lower price for a profit or at a loss if the price is higher. Option traders would be considered short if they were a writer of that option.

speculator   An investor who is looking to profit from buying or selling derivative products with the anticipation of profiting from price moves by trading in and out of his or her positions.

spinning tops   A candle where the real body is small and has a large range with shadows at both ends.

spot   Usually refers to the cash market or front contract of a physical commodity that is available for immediate delivery.

spread   The price difference between two related markets or futures contracts.

spreading   The simultaneous buying and selling of two related markets with the expectation that a profit will be made when the position is offset.

stochastics   A technical indicator created by George C. Lane that gives an indication when a market is overbought or oversold.

stock index   An indicator used to measure and report value changes in a selected group of stocks.

stop-limit order   A variation of a stop order in which a trade must be executed at the exact price or no worse than a specific price. The limit side of the order limits the slippage. It does not ensure a trade will be executed if the next best price is beyond the limit side of the stop order until the limit or stop price is reached again.

stop order   An order to buy or sell when the market reaches a specified point. A stop order to buy becomes a market order when the futures contract trades at or above the stop price. A stop order to sell becomes a market order when the futures contract trades at or below the stop price.

strike price   The price at which the futures contract underlying a call or put option can be purchased or sold.

support   A price level that attracts buyers.

technical analysis   The study of price and or volume to anticipate future price moves. Studies can include price patterns, mathematical calculations, and data regarding the open, high, low, and close of a market.

theta   The calculation associated with determining the value of an option on a theoretical basis in a given time period.

three crows   A candlestick pattern consisting of three dark candles that close on or at their lows. After an extended advance, this formation can be a strong reversal pattern.

three white soldiers   The opposite of the three crow's formation, this is the pattern consisting of three candles that close at their highs and can indicate a continued advance. This pattern is a reliable indication that prices are moving higher, especially if they develop after a longer period of consolidation at a bottom.

variable limit   According to the Chicago Board of Trade rules, an expanded allowable price range set during volatile markets.

vega   The calculation that measures an options value to the change in the volatility.

vertical spread   Buying and selling puts or calls of the same expiration month but different strike prices.

VIX   The Volatility Index provided by the Chicago Board Options Exchange. It is dubbed the *fear index* as it gauges the implied volatility on the stock index contract. The index is now calibrated from a sample of out-of-the-money puts and calls on the S&P 500 index instead of the original contract that was based on the S&P 100 index (OEX) contract.

volatility   The measurement of the change in price over a given time period. It is often expressed as a percentage and computed as the annualized standard deviation of percentage change in daily price.

volume   The number of purchases or sales of a contract during a specified period of time, often the total transactions for one trading day.

windows   A Japanese candlestick term referred to as a gap in Western analysis.

X-Trader   An online electronic trading platform provided by Trading Technologies.

yield   A measure of the annual return on an investment. Also referred to as the *amount of interest on a debt instrument.*

Bibliography

Bollinger, John, *Bollinger on Bollinger Bands* (McGraw-Hill, 2001).

Dorsey, Thomas J., *Point & Figure Charting*, Second Edition (John Wiley & Sons, 2001).

Douglas, Mark, *The Disciplined Trader* (Prentice Hall Press, 1990).

Douglas, Mark, *Trading in the Zone* (Prentice Hall Press, 2001).

Edwards, Robert D., and John Magee, *Technical Analysis of Stock Trends* (John Magee, 1997; first edition, 1948).

Farley, Alan, *The Master Swing Trader* (McGraw-Hill, 2000).

Frost, A. J., and Robert Prechter, *Elliott Wave Principles* (New Classics Library, 1978, first printing).

Gann, William D., *How to Make Profits in Commodities* (Lambert Gann Publishing, 1949).

Hadaday, Earl, *Contrary Opinion* (Key Books, 1983).

Lefèvre, Edwin, *Reminiscences of a Stock Operator* (John Wiley & Sons, 1993; originally published by George H. Doran and Company, 1923).

McMillan, Larry, *McMillan on Options* (John Wiley & Sons, 1996) and *Options as a Strategic Investment* (Prentice-Hall Press, 1993).

Murphy, John J., *Technical Analysis of the Futures Markets* (New York Institute of Finance, 1986).

Nison, Steve, *Beyond Candlesticks* (John Wiley & Sons, 1994).

Nison, Steve, *Japanese Candlestick Charting Techniques* (New York Institute of Finance, Simon & Schuster, 1991).

Pesavento, Larry, *Fibonacci Ratios with Pattern Recognition* (Traders Press, 1997).

Pesavento, Larry, *Opening Price Principle: Best Kept Secret on Wall Street* (Traders Press, 2000).

Sklarew, Arthur, *Techniques of a Professional Commodity Chart Analyst* (Commodity Research Bureau, 1980).

Williams, Larry, *How I Made $1 Million Last Year Trading Commodities* (Windsor Books, 1973).

Williams, Larry, *The Right Stock at the Right Time* (John Wiley & Sons, 2003).

Index

Abandon baby pattern, 47–48
Absolute value, 7
Adjusting position, 229
Advancing soldiers pattern, 51
After-hours trading, 14, 178
Agricultural products/markets, 6,
   14–15, 19, 82
American Petroleum Institute,
   29
American style options, 220
Anderson, Mark, 17
Ascending triangles, 81
Asian financial crisis, 62
At the market, 178–179
At-the-money option, 223, 229,
   232–233

Bar charts, 34–48, 160. *See also
   specific types of bar charts*
Barron's, 21, 167
Bear credit spreads, 228
Bear flag formation, 52, 83
Bearish analysts, 162, 167
Bearish divergence, 146–148
Bearish engulfing pattern, 48–49,
   52–53, 60–61, 102, 122
Bearish falling three method, 52
Bearish harami pattern, 50–51,
   57–60, 102, 106–107, 110, 116,
   126, 128–129
Bearish investors, 174
Bearish key reversal, 35

Bearish market, indicators of, 69,
   167
Bearish traders, 167
Bear put spreads, 226
Bear ratio put spread, 229
Beige Book, 23
Benchmark candle, 54–56, 140–151
Beta, 221
Beyond Candlesticks (Nison), 66
Bid/ask spread, 61
Black-Scholes option pricing, 168,
   221
Blue-chip stocks, 15
Bollinger, John, 68, 237–238
Bollinger bands, 68, 237
Bond market, 6, 21, 94. *See also*
   U.S. Treasury bonds
*Bottom Line Financial and
   Futures Newsletter*, 56, 109,
   118
Bottoms
   candlestick charts, 46–47, 49,
      51, 53–54
   double, 71, 128, 156, 158
   formation of, 132
   head-and-shoulders, 71–73,
      114–115
   identification of, 146
   inverted head-and-shoulders,
      71–73
   pinpointing, 93
   rounding, 86–88

Bottoms (*continued*)
　rumors and, 23
　W, 71, 158
Breakaway gap, 74–75, 89, 100
Breakeven point, 142
Breakout patterns, 90–92
Breakout point, 82–84, 96, 101
Breakout signals, 37, 40
Broker(s)
　full-service, 186
　as information resource, 181,
　　185
　order execution, 182, 185
　selection factors, 186–187
Brokerage firms, functions of,
　11–12, 174–175
Bull call ratio spread, 228
Bull call spreads, 225–226
Bull credit spreads, 227–228
Bull flag formation, 65
Bullish analysts, 162, 167
Bullish Consensus, 63
Bullish convergence, 146
Bullish engulfing pattern, 48–49,
　55–56, 125
Bullish harami pattern, 51, 117, 124
Bullish investors/traders, 167, 174
Bullish key reversal, 35
Bullish market, 166–167
Bullish rising three method, 52, 65
Bull market, 16–17, 157, 230
Bull trends, 84
Bureau of the Public Debt, 22
Business cycles, 31
Business inventories, 25
Bust trade policy, 173
Buy-and-hold strategy, 4, 164, 214
Buyer's remorse syndrome,
　192–193
Buy signals
　call options, 63–64
　candlestick charts, 46, 54,
　　58–59, 65

　chart patterns, 71
　moving averages, 137, 139
　oops, 89
　pivot point analysis, 119
　stochastics, 146–147
Buy stop order, 180–182

CAC, 95
Calendar month, significance of,
　226–227
Call options, *see specific types of
　call options*
　buy signals, 63–64
　characteristics of, 219–220,
　　223–225, 227–229, 231
　put-to-call ratio, 167
Call ratio back spread, 229
Cancel orders, 182
Cancel replace order, 182–183
Candle/candlestick charts
　analysis of, 44, 65
　benefits of, 34, 133, 160
　body, 44–45
　candle, defined, 44
　candle patterns, 45–52
　defined, 34
　historical development, 43–44
　information resources, 66
　reading, 52–61
　time frames, 61–65
Capacity utilization rate, 25
Capital preservation, 209
Cardinal Square, 150
Cattle futures, Fibonacci price
　retracement, 154–155
Channel lines, 44
Chart analysis
　data integration, 69–70
　open interest, 68, 158
　significance of, 34, 213
　volume, 67–68, 158
Charting techniques
　bar charts, 34–38

candle charts, 34, 43–66
point-and-figure charts, 34,
38–40
types of, 34
Chart pattern recognition
candle charts, 44
components of, 34, 70–71, 148
diamond formations, 82–83
flag formations, 52, 83–84
funnel formations, 85–86
gap analysis, 73–76
head-and-shoulders tops and
bottoms, 70–73, 114–115,
157–158
importance of, 132–133
M tops, 71, 158
1-2-3 patterns, 71, 157–158
opening patterns, 88–92
pennants, 84–85
rounding bottoms and tops,
86–88
trend channels, 79–80
trend line analysis, 76–79
triangle chart patterns, 80–82
W bottom, 71, 158
wedge patterns, 82
W reversal, 72
Chicago Board of Trade (CBOT),
10, 14–15, 40, 42–43, 94, 125,
173, 179
Chicago Board Options Exchange
(CBOE), 167–169
Chicago Mercantile Exchange
(CME), 10–11, 14–15, 42, 62,
125, 172–173, 179
Close-to-the-money options,
225–230, 232–233
Closing prices, 44–45, 48, 51–52,
57–58, 89
Coffee futures
options trading example,
222–224
scale trading example, 210–211

Coiling formation, 80–81
COMEX, 179
Commercials, 7, 163–164
Commissions, 13, 207, 224, 229,
232
Commitments of Traders (COT),
Commodity Futures Trading
Commision (CFTC), 10, 61,
63, 162–163
Commodities, characteristics of, 2,
6–7
Commodity funds, 7
Commodity Futures Trading
Commission, 10, 16
Common gaps, 73–74
Construction spending, 28
Consumer confidence, 25–26
Consumer credit, 28
Consumer Price Index (CPI), 20,
24
Contract months, 14. *See also*
Calendar month
Contrarian opinion, 161–162
Contrary Opinion (Hadady), 162
Cornerstone candle, 55
Cornerstone Investors Group, 17
Corn futures, options trading, 220
Corrective waves, 157–158
Cotton futures, P3T signals,
109–111
Coupon, 23
Covered calls, 230–231
Covered puts, 230–231
CQG, 42
Crane, George, 217
Credit spread, 228
Crossover signals, moving aver-
ages, 137–139
Crude oil futures
moving average crossover sig-
nals, 137–138, 142
P3T signals, 108–109
scale trading example, 210–212

Currencies, 6
Cycle analysis/studies, 152, 214

%D, 145–147
Daily charts, 63–64, 82, 84, 104
Dark cloud cover pattern, 49–50
DAX, 95
Day session, 178
Day traders, guidelines for, 12, 41,
    93, 101, 124–125, 146–147
Day trading
    characteristics of, 1, 113, 104,
      204
    market selection, 125–131
    multiple time frames, 121–123
    pivot point analysis, applica-
      tions of, 113–121
    target resistance, 123–125
    trading tips summary, 131–133
Dead cross, 137–138, 141
Debit spreads, 225–226
Delta, 221
Delta neutral option spread,
    231–232
Demand and supply, defined, 19.
    See also Supply and demand
Depreciation, 231–232
Derivatives, types of, 2
Descending triangles, 81
Diamond formulations, 82–83
DiNapoli, Joe, 155
Disciplined Trader, The (Douglas),
    190, 237
Divergence
    moving average conver-
      gence/divergence pattern,
      143–145
    stochastics, 146–147
Dividends, 13
Doji pattern, 46–47, 56–58, 60, 106,
    119, 122, 127, 129
Double bottoms, 71, 128, 156
Double tops, 58, 106–108, 110

Doubt, dealing with, 196
Douglas, Mark, 237
Dow Jones Industrial Average, 6,
    60, 115, 125–126
Downtrends, characteristics of,
    35–36, 45, 49, 51, 59, 145–146,
    167
Downward price movement, 38
Dragonfly pattern, 46–47, 128
Durable goods orders, 25

Earnings reports, 30
Eight to ten new records pattern,
    58–59
Electronic trading, 14–16
Elevator analogy, 3
Elliott, Ralph N., 157
Elliott Wave Principles
    (Frost/Prechter), 158
Elliott Wave theory
    components of, 157–158
    development of, 157–158
    example of, 158–159
    information resources, 158
e-mini S&P 500, 15, 67, 96, 122,
    125, 173, 178
Emotional trading/traders, implica-
    tions of, 191, 196–197
Employment Cost Index (ECI), 26
Entry dates, 214–215
Equilibrium point, pivot point
    analysis, 101–102
Equities market, 152
Equity trading, 13–14
eSignal, 42
Euro currency futures contract,
    bearish divergence, 147–148
Eurodollar, 10, 82–83
European Central Bank, 21
European style options, 220
Even cost spread, 228
Evening star pattern, 46–47,
    115–116

Exchange(s), *see specific exchanges*
  functions of, 10, 14
  web sites, as information resource, 70
Exchange-traded funds, 2
Exhaustion gap, 74–75, 98, 100
Existing home sales, 28
Exit strategy, 238
Expiration date, 232
Exponential moving averages (EMA), 105–106, 108, 110, 136, 142–143, 159–160

Face value, 23
Factory orders, 25
Fair market value, 20
Fair value, 7
Farley, Alan, 237
Fast MACD line, 143
Fast market conditions, 177, 181
Fearful traders, implications of, 191, 193, 196–197
Federal Open Market Committee (FOMC), meetings and policy announcements, 22–23, 128
Federal regulation, 10
Federal Reserve, 11, 20, 212
Fibonacci, Leonardo, 150, 154
Fibonacci corrections, 153
Fibonacci indicators, 34
Fibonacci numbers, 97, 150–157, 160
Fibonacci price retracement, 154–155
Fibonacci series, 150, 152–153
Fill or kill (FOK) order, 183
First notice day, 214–215
Fixed-income investments, 23
Flag formations, 52, 65, 83–84
Flat the market, 174
Floor traders, 100–101
Foghorns, 85

Forex trading, 61
Fundamental analysis, 19
Fund management, 7
Funnel formations, 85–86
Futures commission merchant (FCM), 173
Futures trading, generally
  bull market for, 16–17
  contract specifications, 8–9, 13–14
  electronic trading, 14–15
  getting into, 6
  holding penalty, 4–5
  instruments of, 6–10
  margin, 7, 10–12
  popularity of, 1
  security deposit, 10–11
  single stock futures (SSFs), 7, 16

Gamma, 221
Gann, William D., 149
Gann theory, 149–150
Gap analysis, 73–76, 98
Gap trading, 88–89
Gecko Software, 160
Global economy, 6, 95
Globex, 172–173
Goal-setting, 198–199, 237
Going long, 63–64, 79, 174
Gold, 6, 86–87
Golden cross, 137
Good 'til canceled (GTC) order, 183–184, 199
Good-faith deposit, 7, 219, 222, 228–230
Gossip-for-the-game syndrome, 165
Government reports, *see specific types of government reports*
  economic impact of, 21–22
  as information resource, 23–29
Gramza, Dan, 42, 66

Gravestone pattern, 46–47
Greed, 191–193, 196–197, 209, 236
Greeks, 221
Greenspan, Alan, 20, 25, 175
Gross domestic product (GDP), 23

Hadady, Earl, 162
Hammer pattern, 45, 54, 56, 58, 110
Hanging man pattern, 45, 57
Harami pattern, 50
Harmonic timing event, 153
Head-and-shoulders tops and bottoms, 71–73, 114–115, 157
Hedgers, 7, 163–164
Hedging, 10
Histograms, 143
Historical data, implications of, 7, 34, 151
Historical volatility, 220
Housing starts, 27
How to Make Profits in Commodities (Gann), 150

Implied volatility, 168, 220
Impulse waves, 157
Index of Leading Economic Indicators (LEI), 24
Industrial production, 25
Inflation, 6, 24
Initial margin, 7, 11–12, 16, 139, 142
Inside bar, 37
Institute of Supply Management (ISM) Index, 25
Institutional desk traders, 41
Interest rate, impact of, 11, 20–21, 23, 28
Intermarket spreads, 185
International trade, 24
In-the-money options, 220, 225, 229–230
Intraday charts/charting, 40–42, 82, 84

Intraday rallies, 69
Intramarket spreads, 185
Intrinsic value, options, 219–220
Introducing brokers (IBs), 173–174
Inverted hammer pattern, 46
Inverted head-and-shoulders bottom, 71–72
Investment clubs, 17
Investors Business Daily, 21
Island pattern, gap analysis, 75–76
ISM Index, 30

Japanese candle charting, 34, 43, 58
Japanese Candlestick Charting Techniques (Nison), 66
Japanese Central Bank, 62–63
Japanese yen, candlestick chart patterns, 61–64

%K, 145–147
Kansas City Board of Trade (KCBT), 14, 179
Key reversal bar, 35
Kraft Foods, 10

Lagging indicators, 93
Lane, George C., 144
Large speculators, 163–165
Legging into a spread, 184
Let-it-ride mentality, 208
Leverage, 11–12
Limit buy orders, 207
Limit down, 177, 181
Limit orders, 180
Limit up, 177
Linearly weighted moving averages, 136
Liquidity/liquidation, 6, 12–13, 142
Liquidity Data BankTM, 40
Live cattle, pivot point analysis, 99–100

Livermore, Jesse, 192
Locked limit down, 177–178
Locked limit up, 177
Long position, 48, 125, 148
Long straddles, 232–233
Long-Term Capital Management
    (LTCM), 62
Long-term traders, 146
Lopsided market, 164
Losses, dealing with, 192,
    200–201, 239

McMillan, Larry, 233
Maintenance margin, 11
Mallers, Bill, Sr., 95
Margin account, 7, 10–12, 204,
    228
Margin call, 12, 211
Margin rate changes, 166–167
Marked to market, 12
Market analysis, 41, 214
Market conditions
    implications of, 233
    indicators of, 69
    order placement, impact on,
        176–178, 181
Market consensus, 161–165
Market correction, 56, 104, 144
Market drivers
    business cycles and, 31
    government reports, as informa-
        tion resource, 21–30
    interest rates, 20–21
Market events, timing of, 150
Market if touched (MIT) orders,
    179
Market mix, 63
Market on close (MOC) orders,
    180
Market on open (MOO) orders,
    180
Market orders, 172, 178–179
marketprofile^SM, 40–41

Market profiling
    applications, generally, 41–42
    defined, 34
    education sources, 42
    marketprofile^SM software,
        40–41
Market psychology, 43, 63, 114. *See
    also* Market sentiment; Trader
    mindset
Market rallies, 64, 69, 85, 106, 119,
    123–124, 131, 153
Market reversals, 5, 12, 43, 57–58,
    118
Market selection, 125
Market sentiment, implications of
    Commitments of Traders
        (COT), 162–165
    contrarian opinion, 161–162
    margin rate changes, 166–167
    market consensus, 161–165
    Market Vane, 162, 169
    media attention, 165–166
    put-to-call ratio, 167, 169
    VIX (volatility index), 167–169
*Market Vane Bullish Consensus,
    The*, 162, 169
Master Swing Trader, The
    (Farley), 237
MATIF, 95
Maturity date, 23
Measuring gap, 74–75, 100
Media, impact on market,
    165–166
Midpoint gap, 74–75, 100
Momentum traders, 138, 140
M-1/M-2, 30
Monetary policy, 23
Monthly charts, 82
Morning star pattern, 47, 49, 114,
    124
Mortgage Bankers Association Pur-
    chase Applications Index, 28
Mortgage rates, 20

Moving average conver-
gence/divergence (MACD),
61, 101, 133, 142–144, 160
Moving averages, 61, 97, 105–106,
108, 133, 135–142, 159–160
M tops, 71, 158
Multiple candle patterns, 64–65
Multiple contracts, 214
Multiple-leg spread strategy, 221
Multiple one-bar signals, 38
Multiple position traders,
139–140
Murphy, John J., 38, 119, 204

Nasdaq 100 futures, 1, 15, 115
National Association of Purchasing
Managers (NAPM) survey, 25
National Futures Association, 61,
108, 186–187
National Oilseed Processors
Association, 29
Neckline, chart patterns, 72–73,
114
New home sales, 27–28
New York Stock Exchange, 88, 122
Niederhoffer, Victor, 142
Nison, Steve, 43–44, 66
Normal market conditions, 176,
181
NYBOT, 179
NYMEX, 179

One-bar signals, 37–38
One-contract traders, 139
1-2-3 patterns, 71, 157–158
1-2-3 swing top formation, 71
Oops signal, 88–90
Opening patterns, 88–92
Opening prices, 44–45, 48, 52,
57–58
Opening range breakout, 90–92
Open interest, 68–70, 133, 158
Open order, 183

Options, *see specific types of
options*
abuse of, 218
benefits of, generally, 12–13
exercising, 219
Greeks, 221
information resources, 233
pricing, 221
risk management, 221–222, 224
terminology, 218–219
trading steps, 222–224
trading strategies, generally,
221–222, 224–223
types of, 220–221
valuation, 219–220
writing, 218
Options for Beginners (Caplan),
233
Order cancels order/one cancels
other (OCO), 183
Order entry selections, 171–176
Order placement, *see specific
types of orders*
accuracy of, 175
errors, dealing with, 175
futures contracts, 14
online, 172, 174–176, 185–187
order entry selections, 171–176
overview of, 171–176, 186–187
telephone orders, 174
Oscillators, 105, 158–159
Out-of-the-money options,
219–220, 225, 227, 230–231
Outside bar, 36
Overbought market, 144, 158, 162
Oversold market, 116, 123, 144,
158, 162

Paper profit, 12, 191
Paper trading, 160, 192
Pattern recognition, importance of,
160. *See also* Chart pattern
recognition

Pennants, 80, 84–85

Performance bond requirements, 11, 111, 219

Personal income and spending, 27, 29

Pesavento, Larry, 91, 237

Piercing pattern, 49–50, 129

Pillar of strength candle, 54–56

Pillar of weakness candle, 55

Pivot point analysis
  daily numbers, 97
  day trading tips, 133
  equilibrium, 101–102
  examples of, 94–95, 102–103
  Fibonacci numbers, applications of, 155–156
  implications of, 34, 43, 50, 57, 66, 75, 93, 133
  moving average crossover signals, 141–142
  pivot point formula, 95–96
  P3T signals, 103–112, 120, 127–128
  support/resistance, 93, 96–97, 101–111, 115–116, 125–130
  verification, importance of, 97–101, 148

Pivot point number, defined, 95

Point-and-figure charts, 34, 38–40

Positive affirmations, significance of, 199

Precious metals, 6

Premium, options, 13, 218–220, 224, 228–230

Price breakouts, moving averages, 137

Price corrections, 149–150

Price/earnings ratio (P/E), 30

Price range forecasting, 93

Price reversals, 38–39, 86, 89, 129

Pring, Martin, 238

Producer Price Index (PPI), 20, 24

Productivity, 26

Proedgefx.com, 61

Profit generation, 133

Profit-taking, 5

P3T signals (Person's Pivot Point Trade signal), 103–112, 127–128

Put options, *see specific types of put options*
  characteristics of, 219–220, 226–231
  put-to-call ratio, 167, 169

Pyramiding, 205–210

QQQ, 2

Range, defined, 132

Ratio back spreads, 229–230

Ratio put back spread, 230

Ratio spreads, 228–229

Reagonomics, 94

Relative strength index, 97, 158–159

Reports, as information resource, 28–30. *See also* Government reports

Resistance level
  implications of, generally, 44
  moving average crossover signals, 137–138, 140–141
  pivot point analysis, 93, 95–97, 101–111, 115–116, 123–130
  trend channels, 79–80
  trend line analysis, 78

Retail sales, 27

Retail traders, 41

Retesting, trend line analysis, 78–79

Retracement, 154–155, 158

Reversal amount, 39–40

Reversal patterns, candlestick charts, 49–50

Reverse pyramid, 209

Reverse splits, 13

Rickshaw pattern, 46–47, 129
Rising wedge pattern, 82
Risk capital, 196
Risk exposure, reduction strategies, 185
Risk management guidelines, 60, 100, 221–222, 224, 236–239
Rolling over, 185
Rounding bottoms and tops, 86–88
Rumors, 239

S&P 100 index (OEX), 2, 167–168
S&P 500,1, 6–7, 102, 118–119 35, 114, 116–117, 143, 146–147, 150–153
Santa Claus rally, 153
Saucer bottom, 87
Scale trading, 210–212
Screen "watchers," 193
Securities and Exchange Commission (SEC),16
Security deposit, 7, 10–11. *See also* Good-faith deposit; Margin
Self-confidence, importance of, 189–190, 197, 199
Self-evaluation guidelines, 190–192
Sell-off, sources of, 165
Sell signals
 chart pattern analysis, 50, 53, 61, 115
 day trading, 129–130
 indicators of, generally, 69
 moving average convergence/divergence (MACD) pattern, 143
 moving averages, 137, 139
 oops, 88–89
 pivot point analysis, 101–102
 P3T, 107–108
 stochastics, 146–148
Sell stop order, 181
Settlement price reversal bar, 37
Settlement prices, 144–145

Shooting star pattern, 48–49, 54, 56–57, 105–106, 126–128
Short call option, 225, 227, 230–231
Short strangles, 233
Short trading strategy, 53, 59–60, 64, 79, 100, 127, 180–181
Silver futures, 56–57, 77, 104–105, 140–142, 225–226
Single stock futures (SSFs), 7, 16
Size of contract, significance of, 7
Sklarew, Arthur, 97–98
Slippage, 181, 207
Slow MACD line, 143
Small speculators, 163–165
Soybean futures, 85–86, 206–208
SPAN margining, 11
Speculators, 7, 163–165. *See specific types of speculators*
Spinning tops pattern, 46, 56, 115
Spread off, 185
Spread orders, 184–186
Spread trader, 185
Standard Portfolio Analysis of Risk System, 11
Star pattern, 46
Stochastics, implications of, 61, 97, 101, 104–105, 110, 116, 119–120, 133, 144–149, 155, 158–160
Stock indexes, 6–7, 10
Stock splits, 13
Stock symbols, 13
Stop close only orders, 106, 111–112, 181–182
Stop limit (SL) orders, 182
Stop-loss orders, 126–127, 180–181, 183, 199, 207–208
Stop orders, 89, 180–181, 214
Stop placement, candle chart analysis, 53, 58–59
Stop reversal, 214
Straddle order, 184
Stress, dealing with, 197, 199–200

Strike price, 13, 219–221, 228–230, 232

Successful traders, characteristics of, 192, 198–200

Sugar futures, 98–99

Supply and demand, 6, 34, 166

Supply complacency, 210

Support and resistance, *see* Resistance level; Support level

Support extension, Fibonacci ratio, 156–157

Support level
  implications of, generally, 44
  moving average crossover signals, 137, 139–141
  pivot point analysis, 93, 95–97, 101–105, 109, 111, 124–126, 130

Support lines
  broken, 77–78, 80, 86
  trend channels, 79–80

Swing traders/swing trading, 113, 119, 147

Switch order, 184

Symbols, in futures contracts, 13–14

Symmetrical triangle pattern, 80, 82, 88

Synthetic futures positions, 231

Tactical trading
  defined, 205
  miscellaneous techniques, 213–215
  pyramiding, 205–210
  S&P 500 Friday 10:30 a.m. rule, 212–213
  scale trading, 210–212

Target trading, 93

Technical analysis
  defined, 33
  implications of, generally, 5–6

techniques. *See* Chart analysis; Charting techniques; Chart pattern recognition; Market profiling

Technical Analysis of Stock Trends (Edwards/Magee), 238

Technical Analysis of the Futures Markets (Murphy), 204

Technical indicators
  characteristics of, 34, 159–160
  Elliott Wave theory, 157–159
  Fibonacci numbers, 150–157, 160
  Gann theory, 149–150
  moving average convergence/divergence (MACD), 142–144, 160
  moving averages, 135–142, 159–160
  stochastics, 144–149, 155

Techniques of a Professional Commodity Chart Analyst (Sklarew), 97–98

Theta, 221

Three crows pattern, 51

Three white soldiers pattern, 51

Time frames, multiple, 121–123

Time value, options, 219

Timing cycles, Fibonacci numbers, 151–153

Tips, acting on, 165–166

To-do list, 198–200

Tops
  candlestick charts, 46–47, 50–51, 53
  double, 58, 158
  expanding pattern, 85–86
  formation of, 132
  head-and-shoulders, 70–73, 114–115
  identification of, 146
  M, 71
  pinpointing, 93

Tops (*continued*)
 rounding, 86–88
 rumors and, 239
 spinning, 46, 56, 115
Tower of weakness, 61
Trader mindset
 buyer's remorse syndrome,
  192–193
 emotions, 196–197
 realistic approaches, 192–194, 196
 self-evaluation, 190–192
 significance of, 88, 189–190,
  197–198, 236–237
Trading hours, 14
Trading in the Zone (Douglas), 190
Trading log, 176, 187
Trading mentality, 3–4. *See also*
 Trader mindset
Trading plan, importance of, 206,
 239
Trading worksheet, 194–197
Trailing stops, 112, 181, 207–209
Transaction fees, 13, 224, 229, 232
Trend channels, 79–80, 159
Trend confirmation, 158
Trend line analysis, 40, 44, 76–79,
 160
Trend reversal, 69
Triangle chart patterns, 80–82

Undercapitalization, 211
Unemployment rate, 26
U.S. dollar, 24
U.S. Dollar Index futures chart, 57,
 59–60, 105–108
U.S. Treasury bills, 16, 22–23
U.S. Treasury bonds, 22–23,
 126–129
U.S. Treasury notes, 6, 22–23
Unit labor costs, 26
Uptrends
 candlestick charts, 45–46, 48,
  51, 60

Elliott wave theory, 158
 gap analysis, 75
 moving average conver-
  gence/divergence (MACD)
  pattern, 143
 oops signal, 89
 options strategies, 228
 put-to-call ratio, 167
 trend channels, 80
 trendline analysis, 76–77
 triangle chart patterns, 82

Vega, 221
Verification, importance of,
 97–101, 148–149
Vertical bear put spread, 226
Vertical bull call spread, 225
Vertical calendar spreads, 226–227
Visualization, 199–200
VIX (volatility index), 167–169
Volatility
 in chart analysis, 86
 impact of, 3–4, 11, 239
 options strategies and, 227,
  229–230
Volatility rate, options, 220
Volume, in chart analysis, 67–68,
 133, 158
VXO, 169

Wall Street Journal, 21
Wasting asset, 219
W bottom, 71, 158
Weather forecasts, implications of,
 29
Wedge patterns, 82
Weekly charts, 82
Whipsaw, 86
Wholesale Price Index, 24
Williams, Larry, 68, 88
W reversal, 71–72
Writing options, 228–232